THE UNIVERSITY COLLEGE OF RIPON AND YORK ST. JOHN YORK

New Readings

CRPYK.

New Readings

Contributions to an understanding of literacy

Edited by
Keith Kimberley, Margaret Meek
and Jane Miller

A & C BLACK· LONDON

First published 1992
A & C Black (Publishers) Limited
35 Bedford Row, London WC1R 4JH

ISBN 0–7136–3569–X

© 1992 A & C Black (Publishers) Limited

A CIP catalogue record for this book
is available from the British Library.

Typeset in Lasercomp Ehrhardt by
August Filmsetting, Haydock, St Helens
Printed and bound in Great Britain by
Page Bros, Norwich

CONTENTS

Preface

This is a book about reading, written by teachers and parents, by writers for children and by other specialists in the field. The work it contains represents years of experience and expertise and some of the most powerful recent research. It is not offered as a contender within the recent and acrimonious debate about reading, because the terms of that debate are, for the most part, hostile to what is at issue. Instead, we have worked for continuities and breadth. The idea for the book was Keith Kimberley's. With entirely characteristic generosity and sense, he proposed that some of Margaret Spencer's students and colleagues should collaborate on a book to mark her retirement from the Department of English, Media and Drama in the University of London Institute of Education. The book he had in mind would register our gratitude to Margaret and our dismay at losing her by gathering the best current work in the areas where she has been inspirational as a teacher and a writer.

Keith Kimberley died at the end of January 1991. His death was a shocking interruption of his life, his work and our work with him. So that this book has now become his as well as Margaret's. My hope is that it will ring with his wishes for it and with his beneficent sanity about what matters most for all those who are committed to improving state education in this country. It was always clear that a book about reading which would celebrate the work of Margaret Spencer could hardly do without her presence in it. Our hope was that she would be as involved in the book as she wanted to be. Typically, she has provided its introduction, its final essay and most of the linking and explanatory material; so that this will be no sort of *festschrift* or surprise for her, but the product of her own hard work.

I had known Margaret some time, though as her student rather than her colleague, when – somewhat boldly, I suppose – I recommended that she read an article in *The Times Educational Supplement* by a writer who was unknown to me, Margaret Meek. I thought she might find the piece sympathetic. I should have guessed, of course, that Margaret Meek and Margaret Spencer were the same person: neither divided nor two-faced, but abundant, blessed with the energies and talents of two, and the achievements. Margaret Meek Spencer is known internationally and for many things: for the books she has written and edited, for the work she continues to do with teachers as their teacher, but also as collaborator and co-researcher. Wherever literature for children matters – in libraries, classrooms, for the writers themselves, in publishers' offices, on review pages – Margaret's work is known and admired. She has always been a remarkable teacher. This book testifies to her unique contribution to research in the broad terrain of literacy, her own research, her students' and the work she has done with groups of teachers who are reflecting on their own practice and on the development of the children in their care. I began from the gratitude which inspired this book. These essays are offered to her with the gratitude of all who have taken part in producing them.

There are several people who deserve our thanks. Colin Mills was prodigal with ideas in the early stages. Sharon Grattan and Patricia Kelly have given invaluable support. I would also like to thank the Editors of *English in Education* for permission to publish the essay by Tony Burgess, and the Editors of *The English Magazine* for permission to publish those by Peter Traves, Keith Kimberley and Gemma Moss.

Jane Miller
University of London Institute of Education, 1991

INTRODUCTION · MARGARET MEEK

Known Voices in a New Key

In dreams begin responsibilities – Yeats

The voices of those who have written this book are familiar wherever there are discussions and debates about language, literacy, reading, literature, culture and children learning. Their turns of phrase, their utterances and emphases, are woven into the roles they have played in teacher education in general and, more particularly, in the teaching of English as an organised body of considered thought. They are my colleagues and my friends. Here they generously offer me and other readers something important to read at a critical time. But instead of what we might have anticipated, a colloquial wisdom drawn from a shared intellectual past, we have a series of dialogues with the future, considerations of change, to be read differently.

At some point in this most recent year in a decade of dilemmas each writer has had to confront, in actual situated practices, the consequences of changes in the education system. And these are changes which are, as always, symptoms of deeper shifts in society as a whole. Teachers often have to do this in practical ways earlier than other people, because children come to school with the imme-diate social effects of change written into their lives. There were Asian children learning to speak, read and write English in school long before there was a government report about 'multicultural' education. The present changes are, however, sharper, for they are promulgated as educational laws. The need to reconceptualise what counts as evidence in analyses of teaching and learning in school lies behind these essays. Their topics are immediate and urgent.

What emerges is a challenge to the 'common-sense' view of education and the notion that everyone's experience of school is a reasonable basis for judging the teaching and learning of modern children. Despite the fact that reading and writing nowadays are not what they were twenty-five years ago, that 'facts' and 'information' are historically constructed, that teaching is more than telling, learning more than repeating, and access to effective training and higher educa-tion no more 'equal' than it ever was, the notion prevails that teachers are lacking in responsibility if they prefer to look forwards rather than backwards.

As Clifford Geertz has shown, common sense is a cultural system, 'histori-cally constructed...and subjected to historically defined standards of judgement'. He adds,

> 'We know very little what it is, these days, to live a life
> centred round, or realized through, a particular sort of
> scholarly or pedagogical, or creative activity. And until we
> know a great deal more, any attempt to pose, much less to
> answer, larger questions about the role of this or that sort of
> study in contemporary society – and contemporary
> education – is bound to break down into passionate
> generalities inherited from the past.'

In this book, 'passionate generalities' about the past are replaced by detailed analytic protocols and exemplars of responsible and creative thinking and teaching. Their origins lie in careful research, which has been widely acknowledged.

Evidence of scholarly, pedagogical and creative activity runs through each of these essays, with different emphases derived from each writer's special focus. The first part of the book is mainly about reading. It shows the exemplary forms of observation now expected of those who are expert in this field, observations which will, in the near future, become the essential evidence of children's progress. More generally theoretical studies are in Part Two, where the writers examine ideas of education and society within which schooled literacy is expected to sit and to be assessed. Literature, the play and dialogue of the imagination and the activities that authors of books for the young engage in, are brought together in Part Three. This section shows how the intensely-felt early experiences of children and young adults become engagements with literary texts. When writers transform these experiences into narrative the young become powerful, as writers are powerful. So, as they read, the hopes their teachers have for them become part of children's desires.

The views of reading in these pages are embedded in the conviction that literacy allows those who can read and write to respond critically to a range of social practices that are typical of a literate society. Reading is also a metaphor for diverse perceptions of signs and other semiotic productions. Because it is about making and receiving meanings reading is essentially dialogic and dialectical. As societies change, so texts and reading change. Whether we realise it or not we are all learning to read all the time, yet we still find old texts written into new ones. Barthes said we are always 'rewriting the text of the work within the text of our lives'.

Children in school are just beginning to do that. But as Josh, in Carol Fox's essay, clearly shows, the intertextual competences of even the youngest readers, the ways they log the words of stories read to them in their own narratives, are a distinctive kind of memory-in-make-believe. Before and after they meet the world's practical texts children are saying things that let us know how the 'play of the imagination' includes the texts of artists and writers who, revisiting their own childhoods, create for those who are more newly in the world a dialogue with their futures. These pages contain both the words of the children and of those who are serious about what they create for them to read.

If these understandings, elaborated and refined in these essays, are part of the understanding of teachers who help young children to learn to read, then the interpretation of meanings will be a part of what counts as a reading lesson. If reading is dialectical, then pupils learn the skills of reading both with and against a text. If literacy, in terms of the National Curriculum, is an entitlement, then we cannot confine the learners to a closed set of coded instructions and then expect them to think for themselves about literature.

What all teachers implicitly know, and what classroom observations make plain, is that children initiate the learning that their teachers are most concerned they should do. They have purposes for reading and writing. Yet the 'common-sense' notion of pedagogy is that they should always do as they are told until 'a private individual creativity' struggles out. Here the stance is different. Teaching is located where 'social use and responsibility towards the real world' are seen, in

Tony Burgess's words, 'as two indispensable features of a contemporary view of knowledge... As social human beings, we have at our disposal not language as such but uses of language made possible by cultural resources and by forms of cultural action developed within human societies.' Children's learning depends on the social recognition of their moves to belong to a society which, eventually, they will change.

Teaching and learning come together here as one form of cultural action. Although not all the writers represented here take the same stance to their work – and they are not all teachers – there is a common tension in these essays between obligations which they would designate as 'responsibility' and those which they recognise as 'creativity'. It is this tension, in all its manifestations, which gives this book its promissory hold on the next stage of revisions to our education system.

During the year of the preparation of this book public discussion of how reading should be taught has reached new depths. The results of patient enquiries by the APU and the NFER have been overlaid by irresponsible attacks on teachers' professional skills. Those who are interested in the development of a critical pedagogy in schools have found it difficult to be heard above the din of distracting factions. Despite this, teachers of English have taken care to find ways to react responsibly to the exigencies of the National Curriculum and to place in the foreground the capabilities of all pupils as writers and readers in the context of new and changing literacies. No one did this with more courage and devotion than Keith Kimberley. He analysed the proposed system of examinations, patiently and thoroughly, convinced that 'the most powerful strategy which appears to be available to all teachers concerned with language is to demonstrate, to all who will pay attention, the strength and reliability of teacher assessment and record keeping'. To recognise creative potential in apparent restraint is an exemplary pedagogical feat, far-sighted and hopeful. His words grasp the essence of the book he wanted to bring into being. 'The positive work of teachers with students in maintaining high expectations of what all students can achieve has to be at the heart of a national system for the assessment of students if it is to have any chance of success.'

Geertz, Clifford (1983), *Local Knowledge. Further Essays in Interpretive Anthropology*, Basic Books

PART ONE

Reading and Learning

Most of what we know about the language learning of young children is the result of acute listening to what they say and punctilious analysis and evaluation of everyday language events. Here we see and hear Josh and Sundari, powerful, inventive storytellers, weaving the super-text of their social life into their enactments and narrations. Myra Barrs' essay extends Carol Fox's rich analysis by concentrating on 'the tune on the page'. She asks how 'the rhythms of written language might be internally represented and stored to appear in early writing'. Henrietta Dombey's Anna takes significant initiatives in bed-time story episodes. Gillian, in Eve Gregory's account, lacks this experience and so feels excluded from lessons that bilingual children seem to learn more confidently. All these children know, in a variety of ways, that stories and books are important. David Lewis demonstrates the kinds of reading encounter that modern picture books make possible.

When we admit important evidence of this kind into considerations of children learning to read, we are apt to marvel at the difference between the apparent ease with which most children accomplish this feat and the complicated explanations which expert listeners and watchers give of this process. What emerges is the obligation of all those responsible for children's success in early reading to understand their intention to move towards successful, inventive mastery, and the variety of the ways in which they engage with the task of what Halliday calls 'learning how to mean'. No assessment of children's progress can ignore what they powerfully know.

CAROL FOX

'You Sing So Merry Those Tunes'. Oral Storytelling as a Window on Young Children's Language Learning

Children learn to use language in the company they keep. But their everyday turn-taking with adults does not fully display their knowledge of the language they attend to in the world. In their play, especially when they initiate extended formal monologues and other adult sequences (the tv weather man is the example in this piece), we hear them 'doing the voices' in ways that show how varied and *aware* is their linguistic scope. This is particularly the case when they stretch their utterances to the boundaries of sense and nonsense. From her extensive collection of oral narratives which children have told for fun, Carol Fox has chosen some which show us just how subtle our analysis of children's language must be if it is to match the complexity, richness and skill of their performance.

> The Prime Minister says –er–Mr Michael Foot has
> presented Mrs Thatcher-er-er-to go to Ireland for her
> produce* and–and here we go back to Carol Fox
> *pronounced as in 'producer'   *Josh 5:5*

Although the data which I began to collect from five pre- school children in 1980 were intended to furnish material for a study of narrative competences, sometimes, when I invited five-year-old Josh to tell me a story, we would switch on the tape-recorder and he would utter not the usual fantasy tale but some other genre altogether. That genre would be signalled by clear characteristics which he obviously associated with the new form. Several 'poems' (his term) appeared. These were usually in the present tense, descriptive but non-narrative, often about the sea, and commonly uttered in dirge-like tones quite unlike his breathless style of storytelling. Five-year-old Sundari would also tell poems or sing songs during her stories usually inventing a back-up first-person narrator, with the exotic name of 'Angeli', to announce the song and do the singing. These poetic interludes from both children interested me because sense-making did not seem to be what they were all about. Here's an example of what I mean from one of Angeli's songs:

> Oh I weared on the step, how I weary went
> and I weared on the step so-o weary...
>   *Sundari 5:6*

Sundari may or may not have known what 'weary' meant, but it is clear that she enjoys the word enough to use it as often as possible even if she has to turn it into a verb. Jimmy, in a descriptive story at 4:9, does something similar:

It was a icicle car for icicled snowball person

Jimmy 4:9

The quotation which heads this piece is taken from the first imitation news-reading produced by Josh at 5:5. News-reading is certainly narrative a lot of the time (we even refer to news *stories*), but Josh is not just telling what happened; he is role-playing the news-reader, just as Sundari role-plays the singer Angeli, and Josh role-plays the poetry reader using flat, rather mournful tones he must have heard at some time. In such role-play making sense does not always take priority. Rather, the form of a particular discourse, or genre, has attracted the children into playing with it, often with bizarre results. When I first heard Josh make the news announcement above it sounded so true to the language of the news that I had to scan the sentence during transcription to check that it really was meaningless. At this stage Josh's news-readings are marked by a collocation of topical names, 'The Prime Minister', 'Mr Michael Foot', 'Mrs Thatcher', 'Ireland'. The only explanation I can offer for 'for her produce' is that Josh must have thought news-readings were characterised by rather heavy words one did not necessarily understand! By the time he was six Josh had 'told' several more news-readings and weather forecasts, and now showed a much firmer grasp of the discourse rules belonging to these utterances. I shall return to them later.

I had better attempt at this point to define the term *discourse*, because I shall make frequent use of it, and it is easily confused with 'register' or even 'genre'. Following Halliday (1975) I am using discourse as communicative, interactive language in which specific social roles and relationships are implicit. The discourse of the tutor and student in a seminar will imply roles and linguistic conventions which are distinct from the discourse of two boys playing a game of cowboys and Indians or a news-reader presenting the 9 o'clock news on BBC1. I include story as a form of discourse, with specific roles, relationships and structures, even when I am referring here to oral narrative monologues spoken by young children into a tape-recorder, for there is still an addressee, albeit one who is internalised by the children as remote and silent.

Valerie Walkerdine (1982) has claimed that children probably know a large number of discourses they have never actually participated in in real life by the time they come to school at five. She suggests that in school children are required to learn new discourses, those of mathematics, for instance, and that they can become confused if teachers signal inappropriate discourses to them by using misleading 'opening metaphors': embedding a mathematical operation in a story or a game might be an example. I am not at all sure that children do not *need* familiar discourses like story and narrative for longer in the Junior school than many of us like to think, and I have written elsewhere about the ways in which the seeds of distinct 'subject' discourses get embedded in stories at quite a young age (Fox 1989). But here my concern is with Walkerdine's claim that children know about many discourses they have heard by a process of metaphorical association, an 'opening metaphor', which brings the roles and practices of a specific discourse into instant, spontaneous play. 'Play' is the operative word, for unless we take children's play with language – their role-play, story-telling, poem-making – seriously, and observe the knowledge of discourse structure they have the opportunity to explore in such play, we may underestimate their linguistic competences. Indeed, we may be greatly at risk of doing that already in the assessment of oral language in the National Curriculum.

Before I develop this theme by returning to my story material, it is worth adding the point that Walkerdine's reflections on learning the language of mathematics echo one of Margaret Spencer's major educational insights – that you learn to read by behaving like a reader (Meek 1988). Walkerdine seems to be saying, if I understand her, that children need to learn to behave like mathematicians by taking up roles in mathematical discourses, rather than being side-tracked by inappropriate discourses. Similarly, by behaving like storytellers, news-readers, weather persons, poets and singers, Josh and Sundari learn the discourse structures of each.

The Cool Web (Meek et al 1974) takes its starting point from Barbara Hardy's 'Narrative as a primary act of mind' (Hardy 1968). Recently, Andrew Wilkinson (1990) has suggested that argumentative discourse may be just as fundamental as narrative as a means of mental and linguistic organisation. While not denying that argument is fundamental, it seems to me that it cannot compete with narrative in its *scope* as a structuring device. The children I have studied use and explore many other discourses (including argument) *within* the stories that they tell. Perhaps this is because narrative is so intimately bound up with the way we experience *memory*, as Bartlett (1932) and Langer (1953) have pointed out. Real-life interactions, even properly conducted arguments involving very young children, do not give the opportunities for linguistic exploration of every kind afforded to children by what I have come to regard as fairly serious play.

If we have not paid enough attention to the role of metaphorical association in children's entry into the discourse roles surrounding them in infancy, it is true also that we have not attended sufficiently to the power relationships implicit in all linguistic interactions. Urwin, in a book to which Walkerdine also contributes, suggests that we may understand early language behaviour better if we consider that children do not acquire the linguistic system so much as their positions in certain sets of discourses which make up the social world of the child (Henriques et al 1984). In the discourses of infancy, adults, as in most things, have most of the power. In play, however, children can make that power their own, taking on any roles they like and exploring the appropriate language. I found in my study that if I regarded the children as acquiring roles in discourses in which they were more or less powerful I could make a connection between the extraordinarily complex syntactic structures they produced on the one hand, and narrative as a form which generates such language on the other. The powerful roles of both narrator (as storyteller) and narrated (as characters in the story) are brought into being by words alone. Mastery of the language, what they can make the words do, is what impels the children to discover, and re-invent, the linguistic system. Yet so far in linguistic study, we have too little knowledge of the discourses children have practised in the course of their play.

When I asked my B.Ed students which 'languages' or discourses they had heard nursery and infant children playing with during teaching practice, they offered the following as typical relationships: parents and children; doctors, nurses and patients; teachers and pupils; shopkeepers and customers. The students observed that there was often an authority figure (a mother or teacher most frequently), and we reflected that young children, who are not powerful members of the community, enjoy practising the language of power, very exaggeratedly sometimes, in their play. The teachers, mothers and doctors in these games often speak with fiercer authority than any the children will have encountered in life. Children learn early that power is exercised by those who know the right words.

The first identifiable discourse I observed in my five pre-school children's stories was that of written language, often written language with a literary flavour. This was not surprising, since the children were selected for the study on the basis of their extensive book experience, and my aim was to show how written structures influence oral language. Literary language was apparent in one of the first, very simple, stories told by Josh at 5:0:

> One sunny morning little Joshua was awake he found in his
> bedroom marvellous presents he put them by his side and
> showed them to his mother 'Oh' he cried 'It's Christmas...'
>
> *Josh 5:0*

Here the distinctive discourse features are reversals of word order, rhythm, and the form of the direct speech. These are not features of ordinary conversation and there are no complex sentences here. Yet the sound of book language is very clear. Even when Josh told stories about tv superheroes they were resonant with the rather quaint forms of children's stories in books.

The literary flavour of much of this story material is probably most simply illustrated at the level of the word and the phrase. The children sometimes used words mistakenly, even meaninglessly, at least in adult terms, because, I believe, getting the 'tune' of the narrative discourse to sound right occasionally took priority over making literal sense. I regard these usages as analogous to the miscues children make in their reading. Miscues are a valuable 'window on the reading process' (Goodman 1982) and, far from revealing mindless stabbing at print, 'good' miscues show readers actively constructing meaning from text. The children in my study re-invented language. They coined words and phrases, often by converting them from one grammatical function to another, in their effort to use terminology appropriate for telling stories:

> he had to hobble over the *walking bridges* like this
>
> *Sundari 5:6*

> and then a monster came to that road a huge monster it was
> called a *hooligan* and that is a dragon
>
> *Justine 5:0*

> once upon a time in the middle of the night the Incredible
> Hulk was walking *down by midnight* punching houses down
>
> *Josh 5:2*

Sometimes the usage is more bizarre:

> it was *humble* in the sea   *Sundari 5:6*

> and then the witch said 'Poppies will make them *grant*'
>
> *Josh 5:5*

Such inventions and malapropisms show a concern to explore language, to invent it and push it beyond its conventional boundaries. This is what creative writers do. They say things in new ways, thereby extending our interpretative faculties and enlarging the possibilities of language itself. As writing teachers we are concerned to develop this awareness of the possibilities of language in our pupils too. If I were a classroom teacher of young children now, I would want to watch for such usages, even the misusages, for I would value them as evidence of children's active interest and involvement in learning language.

Word order and phrase structure is often as strange in the stories as vocabulary:

> they were really truly of their home and going to it
>
> *Josh 5:3*

> a little-Bo-Peep story was a long time ago told by a little
> girl   *Sundari 5:6*

> and that was naughty of his kind
>
> *Robert 3:7*

While these constructions do not lack meaning in the way that some of the children's lexical choices do, nevertheless they would be very unusual in the context of an everyday conversation. These strange phrase structures are creative in the Chomskyan sense. The children may well have heard constructions *like* them before, but they are not quoting something which has actually been uttered, even in a book. Direct quotations from books do occur, and do sound appropriately literary and archaic, but they are not quite as strange as the examples I have given from the children's invented stories:

> as morning approached the little dewer man spread his
> dewdrops to meet the day
>
> *Josh 5:1*

This comes from a fairly close retelling of 'Hansel and Gretel'. It is not an exact rendering of the original, however, which had 'sandman' for 'dewer man' and 'greet' for 'meet'. Though the major analyses of my data were investigations of the children's literary competences, using adaptations of systems derived from Genette (1972) and Barthes (1970), I also looked at the material at the sentence level, for I was struck by the complexity of syntactic structures such as:

> she liked doing things playing about at the beach on sunny
> days when cool wind was blowing making sandcastles
> playing with her little necklace with people on it and some
> little raindrops falling from the people and bags on it what
> the teddybears were in what the people were holding.
>
> *Sundari 5:6*

After a laborious T-Unit analysis of the entire story data (49,000 + words) I discovered that the five children showed a greater length of grammatical span in their sentences than comparative data showed was usual at their ages. The technicalities of T-Units need not concern us here. Suffice it to say that what you do is divide the story into its main clauses together with any dependent or co-ordinating clauses. This avoids counting whole stories, whose clauses are strung together with a series of 'ands', as one sentence. Hesitation phenomena like 'er' and unintentional repetitions of words are bracketed out of the analysis. You then divide the total number of words in the story by the total number of T-Units, giving a mean T-Unit length for each story. This procedure is borrowed from Hunt (1964, 1965).

The results of this analysis were initially quite startling, apparently placing pre-school children, who had not been regarded as linguistically precocious, several years ahead of their age in development. Indeed, all the children, even $3\frac{1}{2}$ year-old Robert, told some stories which other studies implied would place them at the level of children in their teens. The explanation was that the other studies (Loban 1963–76) had elicited the talk from their subjects *in conversation with an adult*, whereas I was looking at largely uninterrupted story monologues. A further analysis of the T-Unit means of my children's conversations with their parents, which often appeared on the tapes before and after the story monologues, showed that in this context, or discourse, the children's scores were exactly comparable to those given for children of equivalent age in other studies.

T-Unit (Sentence) Length in Narrative monologues compared to conversation with adults in 4* children

Child	Conv. + Adult	Narr. Mon	Age
Robert	4.0	6.7	3:7–4:1
Justine	5.0	8.5	4:1–5.2
Jimmy	6.1	8.2	4:9
Josh	5.2	8.3	5:0–6:1

*It was not possible to include the fifth child, Sundari, in this comparison as there was no conversation with her mother on any of her story tapes.

Long sentence lengths in themselves prove nothing. A sentence can be long because it is formed like this:

> he ate all the houses up too the concrete and all the books
> and all the curtains and all the glass and all the tinsel and all
> the teachers and all the schoolchildren...   *Justine 5:0*

or because it is formed like this:

> and she gave her some egg sandwiches which were really the
> stones and which the bread sandwiches were really little flat
> round stones made like a little biscuit which she put colours
> in brown as well.   *Sundari 5:4*

The first example is a colourful list of noun phrases, a frequent sentence-type in the oral tradition of children's stories. It has an important function in the story and is no less worthwhile than the second, which is not a list but a complex sentence containing several embedded sub-clauses dependent on the main clause. Over the entire study I found that complex sentences like this example from Sundari accounted for well over half of all the T-Units of 12 + words produced by four of the five children. The exception was Robert, who was only $3\frac{1}{2}$ at the time of his storytelling. In addition to complex subordination as an explanation for long T-Units, I identified 9 other types of long sentence. Four of these further 9 categories involved the speaker in grammatical transformations: passives (very rare), narratised speech, reported speech, and co-ordinating clauses. The remaining categories cover devices such as repetition, oral formulae, and lists, all common in stories for children. When all the grammatical categories are added together, then grammatical complexity can be seen to account for 60.7% of Robert's long sentences, rising to almost 90% of Josh's, the youngest and oldest child respectively.

In their conversations with their parents, by contrast, there were too few sentences of 12 + words to make such an analysis feasible. I do not want to make enormous claims here. The particular kind of conversations which occur on the tapes are rather brief (though the samples of language collected are large), and the children are talking to the person they are most familiar with, usually their mother. I am not saying that children do not produce sentences which are every bit as complex in their everyday talk, but that it is much harder to 'catch' them doing it. It appears from my study, though, that story-telling privileges the production of extended and complex sentences by its very nature. Children must furnish details, be explicit (especially if the 'audience' is the tape-recorder), and generally create a story context relying solely on words and intonation. There are implications for school. It ought to be added that one of these children was observed by a nursery teacher to have very 'immature' language, while another was suspected during his reception year at school of having very little at all!

Josh's stories were recorded over a period of 13 months, amounting to 29,000 words in all. Among them were conversations with me, stories retold from books, invented stories (by far the largest category), news-readings and weather forecasts, one pre-sleep monologue (without the child's knowledge that the tape-recorder was on) and poems. For each discourse/genre category I performed the analysis described above. The results look like this:

T-Unit means for different discourse categories

Type of discourse	Mean T-Unit length	Total words	Number of monologues
News/Weather	9.8	834	5
Poems	9.0	738	13
Retellings from books	8.4	3789	12
Invented stories	8.2	19541	57
All dialogue in stories	7.4	4506	
Pre-sleep monologue	6.5	328	1
Conversation with adult	5.2	1276	

Josh age 5:0–6:1

It was in news-readings and weather forecasts that Josh's language sounded furthest away from ordinary conversational discourse, and since this category produced the highest mean T-Unit length I looked closely at the language. I found that of the T-Units in news-readings of 12 + words, 25% involved passive constructions. Here are some examples:

> Mr Whitelaw said that all the rates of Thatcher's money
> must be taken to Carol Fox

> Somewhere in Australia a hundred bargains has been cut off
> by Thatcher

> (It should be said that Josh's news-readings were meant to
> be comic and were accompanied by a great deal of laughter.)

In the other discourse/genre categories given for Josh, and in the stories of all the other children, passives are *very rare indeed*. In fact, on reading the story transcripts, one could be forgiven for concluding that this construction is generally beyond children of this age. The passive has always, in fact, been considered a late addition to the grammatical repertoire by linguists. I too would quite happily have made such an assumption had I not, quite by chance, received these imitation news-readings during Josh's storying. Now I believe that probably a very large number of five-year-olds are familiar with news-reading discourse.

Weather forecasts also include distinct grammatical features strongly associated with the language weather persons use. Every single T-Unit of 12 + words in the weather forecasts is long (and long T-Units are in the majority) because of syntactic complexity. The grammatical categories which predominate are adverbial and noun phrases. For example:

> and there will be some more rain and cloud in the west of
> Greenland   *Josh 5:5*

Additionally, weather forecasts are the only discourse category in the study which consistently employs the future tense.

Within narratives themselves the children show the beginnings of language and concepts they will later develop in the curriculum areas of school. I have written about these elsewhere (Fox 1989). They know that stories need knowledge to make them authoritative and convincing. I suppose the equivalent for an adult is the background research for a novel. The difference is that in these oral productions the knowledge slips into the stories spontaneously, reflecting an unconscious awareness of the ways stories persuade us of the reality of their invented worlds. The children, though, do not tell the stories to display their knowledge, but to have fun by playing with what they know. Josh's news broadcasts and weather forecasts are never serious. On the contrary, he uses the form of the discourse to be subversive and rude. Taking the human body as a metaphor for the geography of Newcastle he clothes that body in weather language, falling about with laughter as he does it:

> and it will be very nice and smudgy and soft and warm in
> the west bum   *Josh 6:1*

Re-inventing the weather forecast gives Josh power. Do not many of us ask our children to be quiet while we listen hard to those brief slots at the end of the news? But Josh seizes the chance to use that power to explore something of much deeper interest to him than weather maps, his own body, part by part.

Let us return to the power relationships in human discourses. When children play with language, acting out adult roles, making up poems and songs, and particularly telling stories – some of which exceed 800 words in my study – they are engaging in speech acts which reverse the usual power relations in their lives. They must speak, often at length, without interruption, and they have the freedom to include and explore anything they like. This includes areas of experience which are often suppressed in their interactions with adults, in the interests of politeness and learning 'appropriate' forms of address for various addressees and appropriate registers for conducting what are largely the discourses of the adult language and of adults. Yet, with all its subversion, lampooning, gusto and fun, children who are allowed to tell stories show that it is in the practice of discourses which are not 'for real' that conventional and appropriate forms of language are developed, even when the child has to push against the limits of her competences to produce them. Josh, for example, knows that weather persons get chatty sometimes, so, with quite a struggle, he adds to one of his forecasts:

> at Newcastle incidentally the trem-the temp-tremp-temp-
> temperature has gone up to sixty, sixty – degrees
>
> *Josh 6:1*

'Temperature' and 'degrees' are difficult but appropriate words, but it is the word 'incidentally' which gives this utterance a flavour of authenticity.

When I began this study more than ten years ago, enormously aided and inspired by Margaret Spencer's supervision of my work, I thought I would be exploring a fairly straightforward relationship between written and spoken language. There were only two very large and generalised discourses before my eyes, those of spoken language, and those of written literature. After many years of transcribing and looking, other discourses appeared, both within narratives, and in contrast to them. At every level of analysis – word, phrase, sentence, story structure and literary discourse structure – I found that the competences revealed in storytelling material far exceeded both my and others' expectations of young children. Before teachers begin to assess what children have learned they will need to discover what they already know. In my view, asking them to tell stories, to the teacher, or at home, or to groups of their peers, or to their best friend, or solely into the tape-recorder, probably gives the best chance we have to get a comprehensive reflection of what they are capable of, not only in speaking, but in listening too. For all the discourse features I have been describing here surely reflect the most attentive listening to the language going on around them. All the children in my study were fluent readers and writers at the age of seven, according to their teachers in different parts of the country. And for three of them I have examples of writing which show their competences to be well above average there, too. The implications of my story study for literacy were present at the start. Those for oral language emerged in the course of the study.

I would like to finish with a relevant story. A few years ago I found myself witness to an unusual verbal exchange, as things go in our house. Josh, aged nine then, had been the victim of a mugging and was required to make a statement to two policemen. As one of the policemen took out his notebook and pencil and asked Josh to tell him what had happened, I heard something which went like this:

> Well...at about two o'clock this afternoon I was walking
> along Davigdor Road in the direction of Seven Dials when I
> noticed two big boys behind me one of them was tall with a
> red sweatshirt with the words...etc. etc.

While this statement proceeded, the three adults present tried not to smile. The moral of the story is that you do not have to wait until your child (or pupil) gets mugged in order to find out whether she knows how statements to the police are made. Narrative discourse could well have thrown up such a competence years before.

This essay, which draws on the author's doctoral research, was written in 1990.

*The title of this article is a quotation from one of Sundari's stories.

Barthes, R. (1970), *S/Z An Essay*, Hill & Wang
Bartlett, F.C. (1932), *Remembering*, Cambridge University Press
Fox, C. (1989), 'Children thinking through story' in *English in Education*, vol. 23, no. 2, NATE
Genette, G. (1972), *Narrative Discourse*, Basil Blackwell
Goodman, K. (1982), *Language and Literacy*, 2 vols. (ed. F.V. Gollasch), Routledge & Kegan Paul
Halliday, M.A.K. (1975), *Learning How to Mean*, Edward Arnold
Hardy, B. (1968), 'Towards a poetics of fiction' in *Novel: a forum on fiction*, Brown University
Henriques, J., Holloway, W., Urwin, C., Venn C. and Walkerdine V. (1984), *Changing the Subject*, Methuen
Hunt, K. (1964), *Differences in Grammatical Structures Written at Three Grade Levels*, report of the US Office of Education, Tallahassee, Florida (Research Project no. 1998)
Langer, S. (1953), *Feeling and Form*, Routledge & Kegan Paul
Loban, W. (1976), *Language Development: kindergarten through grade 12*, NCTE Research Report no. 18
Meek, M., Barton, G. and Wardlow, A. (1977), *The Cool Web*, The Bodley Head
Meek, M. (1988), *How Texts Teach What Readers Learn*, Signal Press
Walkerdine, V. (1982), 'A psychosemiotic approach to abstract thought' in M. Beveridge (ed.), *Children Thinking Through Language*, Edward Arnold
Wilkinson, A. (1990), 'Argument as a Primary Act of Mind' in *English in Education*, vol. 24, no. 1, Spring, NATE

MYRA BARRS

The Tune on the Page

We now realise that there are more aspects of learning to read than are usually included in the common practices devised to teach reading as sets of classroom procedures. Having watched Josh adopt and adapt to tones of adult discourses, we know that how a text sounds has a great deal to do with what it means.

Here Myra Barrs examines the rhythmic and tonal patterns of language as a means of linking the totality of the story or the poem to the words that compose it. This investigation has implications for further descriptions of how children distinguish different kinds of discourse. The themes of this essay have links with James Britton's exposition of inner speech on page 151.

Though discussions of the differences between spoken and written language generally emphasise the absence of extralinguistic features in written language and the lack of any markers, such as intonation, which, in speech, carry much of the meaning, it nevertheless seems reasonable and uncontroversial to assert that behind every written text there is a voice. It is true that most texts written today are not written to be read aloud but all have the potential to be read in this way, and written language never entirely loses its connection with spoken language, despite the differences between them. Often the understanding of a written text depends on a reader's awareness of its 'tone'. The understanding of irony and some kinds of humour obviously rests centrally on this sense of how the text might *sound*. But an appreciative understanding of a literary text often involves a sense of its rhythms and tunes, and these can be experienced internally without necessarily being enacted or read out loud.

Yet discussions of children's learning of written language often suggest that what they have to learn is a completely new use of language, one which is structured very differently from spoken language and which is an 'autonomous representation of meaning' – a self-contained, self-consistent text that is created through language alone. In Olson's words:

> The relations between utterances and text become acute
> when children are first presented with printed books. As I
> have pointed out, children are familiar with using the
> spoken utterance as one cue among others. Children come
> to school with a level of oral competence in their mother
> tongue only to be confronted with an exemplar of written
> text, the reader, which is an autonomous representation of
> meaning. Ideally the printed reader depends on no other
> cues than those represented in the text; it is addressed to no
> one in particular; its author is essentially anonymous; and its
> meaning is precisely that represented by sentence meaning.

As a result, when children are taught to read, they are
learning both to read and to treat language as text.

(Olson 1977)

Often this new learning is seen as hard because these new language uses and
structures are different in kind from those that children have met before.

It is important to note that the process of understanding
written speech differs radically from the process of
understanding oral speech...Written speech emerges as a
result of special learning

(Luria 1981)

It is rare for children to be seen as drawing, in such learning, on an established
competence and one which serves all language learners well, a sense of the tune.

Intonation, the ability to tune language, is a key factor in all language learning, both the learning of the mother tongue and all subsequent language and
literacy learning. It was Halliday who, in *Learning How to Mean* (1975), showed
that Nigel was already able to convey meanings through intonation alone, before
lexis or syntax came into the picture at all. The sound 'eh' (with a steady tone) meant
'give me' or 'do this'. When pronounced with a high tone it meant 'do this imme-
diately', but pronounced in a falling tone it could mean 'that's nice' or 'I'm sleepy'.
Halliday's work has done a great deal to reveal the function that intonation has in the
structuring of spoken language.

Another much earlier study by a parent of his own child also stressed the role of
intonation, particularly in the early stages of language development. Charles Darwin
kept notes on the development of one of his sons in the early 1840s. Thirty-seven
years later he published an article based on them in the July 1877 issue of *Mind*,
under the title 'A biographical sketch of an infant'. At one year old Darwin's son
invented the word 'mum' to mean 'food': 'And now instead of beginning to cry when
he was hungry he used this word in a demonstrative manner or as a verb, implying
"Give me food"'.

Darwin noted the characteristic intonation that the baby gave to this word:

I was particularly struck with the fact that when asking for
food by the word *mum* he gave to it (I will copy the words
written down at the time) 'a most strongly marked
interrogatory sound at the end'. He also gave to 'Ah', which he
chiefly used at first when recognising any person or his own
image in a mirror, an exclamatory sound, such as we employ
when surprised. I remark in my notes that these intonations
seem to have arisen instinctively and I regret that more
observations were not made on this subject...M. Taine also
insists strongly on the highly expressive tones of the sounds
made by his infant before she had learnt to speak. The
interrogatory sound which my child gave to the word *mum* is
especially curious; for if anyone will use a single word or a
short sentence in this manner he will find that the musical
pitch of his voice rises considerably at the close.

Darwin drew from these observations evidence for his theory that human speech began as song – 'before man used articulate language he uttered notes in a true musical scale as does the anthropoid ape Hylobates'. Some later writers have also arrived at Darwin's hypothesis.

Ulric Neisser in a chapter on 'Auditory Cognition' from his book *Cognitive Psychology* (1967), explores the internal representations that speakers and listeners have of the structures of spoken language and decides that these representations 'must be auditory, making use of whatever resources are available to the sense of hearing'. He concludes:

> Most linguists would probably agree that pronunciation
> ranks with 'function words' and endings as an indication of
> structure. In my view it has a more fundamental status than
> the others. They are merely cues to structure, and it is to be
> expected that different languages will emphasise different
> cues. *The rhythm of speech, however, is very nearly the structure
> itself, corresponding intimately to the listener's internal
> representations* (my italics).

This enormously suggestive passage leads one to speculate about the ways in which the rhythms of written language, too, reflect its structures, and how these rhythms might be internally represented and stored.

Marian Whitehead, in her paper 'Proto-Narrative Moves in Early Conversations' (1983) notes that mothers' and caregivers' 'baby talk' is characterised by strong, essentially narrative, tunes:

> There are indications that a special voice pitch, exaggerated
> intonation patterns and repetitive or highly redundant
> language usually associated with oral narrative occur in the
> earliest social and linguistic experiences of infants.
> Collections of samples of maternal speech with infants in
> reasonably naturalistic situations have highlighted a baby-
> talk register (Bruner, 1975 and 1978; Snow and Ferguson,
> 1977; Messer, 1980). This maternal speech style...is high in
> repetition and interrogatives and also distinguished by a
> higher voice pitch and a lexicon of baby-talk words.

Whitehead follows Roger Brown in seeing these features as reflecting the caregivers' purpose of teaching their infants to communicate, and facilitating this by 'linguistically marking salient features of the environment'. But these exaggerated intonation patterns also have the function of teaching the patterns themselves; as well as marking features of the environment, mothers and caregivers are also marking particular conversational tunes for babies.

Whitehead draws an important parallel between these early learning experiences and early experiences of being read to. 'As the books are mediated by the adult teller he (the baby) will hear again the same higher pitched voice, slower speech and exaggerated intonation which first launched him into human dialogue.'. Again, these features must be seen *both* as marking elements which need to be attended to – this time in the story world rather than the real world – *and* as an introduction to the complex tunes and structures of written language.

Though for many years discussions of the learning and teaching of reading assumed that decoding lay at the centre of the process, observation of parents and young children show them attending to very different aspects of the experience. What parents and children seem above all concerned to do is to make the text *mean*. Shirley Payton's study of a pre-school child's encounters with written language gives insights into the way in which both Cecilia and her parents strive to make links between the story world and story language and Cecilia's real-life knowledge. In the following extract the father is reading to Cecilia. The story is *Hansel and Gretel*, and at one point Cecilia, who is three and a half years old at the time, interrupts the reading with a question:

F. (reads) '...burnt to a cinder.'
C. A nice little doll, cinder?
F. Cinder? Cinderella?
C. Cinder doll
F. Sindy doll, no it's not a Sindy doll. A cinder is a little
  piece of burnt up wood or something.
          (Payton, *Developing Awareness of Print* 1984)

The work that is going on, on both sides, is apparent; the whole extract provides an illuminating example of an active learner attempting to make this new language fit the world as she knows it.

Henrietta Dombey's analysis of one extract from a bedtime story reading (not the one included here, *eds.*) similarly shows Anna, who is five, and her mother talking round the text so as to relate it to known experiences:

Mother: The Little Red Hen took the wheat to the mill
          and the miller ground it into flour
Anna: Whu, whu, why you got a hole in there?
Mother: Well, in a mill they're upstairs and it's like going
          into an attic and you climb up.
      You know when you go in the attic and you climb up
    and up the ladder and go through a hole
      It's like that in a mill.

But Dombey also remarks on the way in which both mother and child make 'perhaps slightly exaggerated use of stress and intonation to convey the information structure of (their) utterances', and notes that Anna's mother uses the ways of marking meaning that are normal in conversation, 'pauses, stress and intonation contours' to introduce the new patterns of written language. 'What she does is to supply Anna with two sources of thematic information, introducing the patterns associated with written language by the familiar vocal means'.

Reading aloud thus becomes a bridge between orality and literacy, the way of demonstrating the tunes on the page. Most adults who read aloud to young children find themselves guilty sometimes of over-marking the tunes of the text in a 'Joyce Grenfell' fashion; but some exaggeration of intonational patterning seems an inescapable part of this kind of demonstration of the workings of written language.

Similarly, young children re-enacting familiar texts, or engaging in story monologues, can be observed to make considerable use of intonation to recreate or mark the meanings and also to signify that 'this is a story'. Alice, at nearly three, engaging in a solo performance of an improvised story, appeared most concerned to sustain the tune. Though she often lost the thread of the story itself, she never lost control of the tune, which often continued regardless (apparently) of content and of her occasional asides.

> Alice: Once upon a time there was a very old woman.
> She said to one another, she said to one another...
> (Mother! Howarth! that's the very old
> woman...That's
> on page...forty three)...is a very long way to go.

As children learn to read independently they also learn how to mark the tune for themselves or 'tune the text' in Margaret Spencer's words. The way they come to do this is through imitation. Mothers and teachers are often struck to hear their own intonational pattern being reproduced in children's independent reading. In reading with an adult, children can sometimes be observed to be 'shadowing' the adult's voice. In one passage from her study of Karen, a five-year-old reader, Anne Thomas describes her surprise at discovering how much Karen was making use of this technique.

> The third element, echo-reading, was the most surprising of
> my findings. It was not something I was listening for so it
> slipped by me until I listened to the early tapes. There it
> was – echoes of my voice. This feature of her behaviour was
> not apparent in all readings; the prerequisites seemed to be
> rhythmical texts, repetitive/recurring passages, or short
> memorable simple texts. As I started to read (*Funnybones*)...I
> became aware that she was reading the text – every word – half
> a pace behind me.

It is interesting to compare this use of imitation with other examples of children learning an adult art by echoing or shadowing the adult performance. For instance, Balinese children learning traditional dancing are encouraged to dance just in front of the adult, moving their arms and bodies with the movements of the adults' bodies, and learning the basic steps through this 'shadowing' of the finished adult performance.

Anne Thomas observes that memorable rhythmical texts seem to have had a particular function in Karen's learning of the 'tunes' of written language, and other examples demonstrate this kind of spontaneous use of rhythm as a support to learning written language. A video made by the Centre for Language in Primary Education, of children at Horn Park Infants School, London, shows one boy whose preferred route into reading is evidently through texts that offer strongly rhythmical supportive patterns. The video first shows him reading to the teacher a rhyme that he knows well ('Daddy fell into the pond'). Then he chooses another poem, 'The Moon', that he does not know. The teacher takes over the reading, with the child echo-reading in just the way that Anne Thomas describes it, 'half a pace behind' the teacher's voice. Finally he is seen reading to himself and with a friend, always choosing strongly patterned rhymed texts ('Brown Bear, Brown Bear') and finally losing interest when his friend chooses to 'read' a text which is not structured in this way. He seems to be completely absorbed in learning the strongly marked tunes that characterise his favourite texts.

Reading researchers have often remarked on the importance of rhyme and song in beginning reading (Wade, 1982; Bradley and Bryant, 1985). Jane Torrey's study of a self-taught five-year-old black working-class child showed that his main source of instruction was television commercials, with their repetition, use of word play, tunes and jingles (Torrey, 1969). It is also observable that many books which appeal most strongly to beginning readers feature rhyme, or a strongly marked rhythmical text (for example, *Each Peach Pear Plum*, *Green Eggs and Ham*, *Rosie's Walk*). Such texts may have a special role to play in the beginnings of reading because of the clearly marked supportive tunes that they go to. As Neisser puts it in his discussion of auditory memory, 'A rhythmic pattern is a structure which serves as a support, an integrator, and a series of cues for the words to be remembered.' This is the function that rhythmical texts serve for children needing such support in their early attempts at independent reading.

Bussis, Chittenden et al., in their major reading research project described in *Inquiry into Meaning* (1987), found that several of the children they studied showed a particular responsiveness to literary structures and the grammatical structures that carry them, and that they relied on them in their reading:

> Carrie's record...provides an example of a child who displayed sensitivity to literary structures from the time she was in kindergarten throughout the period covered by the research (Grades 1 and 2). Her first oral reading (*In the Village*) was taped in January of kindergarten and reflects some combination of sight vocabulary and memory aided by picture cues. What is noteworthy about this rendition is Carrie's faithfulness in representing adverbial and prepositional phrases. She doesn't always read them accurately and she sometimes inserts them gratuitously, but the structures, as such, seem clearly to exist in her mind. When she reads 'now' instead of 'another day', for instance, she obviously misreads the words, but she doesn't misread the grammatical intent. Her entire rendition suggests that phrase structures act as place-holders for words.

The researchers' account suggests the way in which children, by becoming sensitive to the movements and patterns of written language, are also coming to internalise its grammatical structures and make them part of their own cognitive system ('the structures...seem clearly to exist in her mind'). They comment that, on the whole, children in their study began to encounter writing with literary tunes and more careful patterning only as they became more proficient readers.

> There is an irony in such progress because artful writing entails the creation of truly rhythmic structures, and rhythmic structures are easier to anticipate than the choppy and stilted prose typical of so many books for beginners. Moreover, rhythm is inherently pleasing.

The intrinsic pleasures of rhyme and rhythm are universal properties of language and have their equivalents in all languages, including the sign language of the deaf. Bellugi and Klima, in studying American Sign, looked for the counterparts of poetry and song in that language. The examples they found help to illuminate the nature of the satisfactions that patterned language provides:

> A deaf woman signed us a lullaby that her mother used to
> sign to her every night; she said she thought it was the best
> song in the world when she was a child. We may translate it
> as follows, including periods to indicate pauses:
>
> > Sleep...sleep...sleep.
> > Wake-up
> > Eat...cake
> > Ride...beautiful...white...horse
> > Sleep...sleep...sleep.
>
> In this little song, the signs are somnolent, slow, deliberate
> and rhythmical, with long pauses between. The song has a
> hypnotic quality for deaf and hearing alike.
>
> (Bellugi and Klima 1972)

All languages, then, have heard or unheard melodies, and Bellugi and Klima's examples are particularly fascinating in their evocation of the bodily pleasure and physical satisfaction that rhythmical language offers.

Some of the children in the Bussis and Chittenden study were 'quasi readers', who were capable of re-enacting quite long texts from memory. In these cases, the researchers hypothesised that the more stylised structures of formal writing were serving as an integrative support for their remembering of the text and that the children had memorised not individual words but the big shapes – the overall structures – as well as the sentence and phrase structures which facilitated the recall of the words themselves. But all the children in the study recognised and anticipated literary structures in texts that had such qualities, and seemed to draw from rhythmical language a momentum and flow which helped them with their negotiation of the text and with their orchestration of the different aspects of the reading process.

Children's ability to find the 'tune on the page' is, then, a significant element in their beginning reading and their reading aloud. It seems likely that it is also an important factor in their silent reading. Anne Thomas' study of the role of intonation in the learning to read process suggests that children who are effective silent readers are able to create with ease the appropriate tune for the text they are tackling independently:

> Anna read a story called *One Eye, Two Eyes, Three Eyes*. She
> read at a very fast rate and fluently, pausing only momentarily
> at expected juncture points, taking but two and a half minutes
> to read the first two pages. In spite of the speed she managed
> to read with a great deal of feeling, particularly in the dialogue
> sections...Intonational patterning has not been marked on the
> script in any detail; suffice it to say she created the tune and
> was totally at ease with this particular genre.
>
> (Thomas 1981)

Children learn to identify the characteristic tunes of different genres, and these serve as a further support for their reading. Information texts go to different tunes from those of fictional texts. Christine Pappas, in the course of her research on 'The Ontogenesis of the Registers of Written Language' has observed that when five-year-old readers are invited to 'read' two texts, a story and an information text, it is possible to tell what kind of text they think they are reading from their intonational patterning. But information texts, which have less formal narrative patterning in their language, may provide less support for the reader than fictional texts with their more stylised structures.

All of this supports the likelihood that 'texts that teach' will be *tuneable* texts, with tunes and structures that support the reader. Some texts, as Margaret Spencer has demonstrated, have a special role to play in learning to read because they mark such tunes particularly clearly and thus teach the reader the appropriate way to read them. Books like *Not Now, Bernard, Peace at Last* and *Mr Gumpy's Outing* delight children with their recurrent tunes, which help to structure the whole narrative experience. ('Oh no!' said Mr Bear, 'I can't stand *this!*')

Some of the texts which are offered to beginning readers, however, are texts in which it is impossible to find a tune. Barrie Wade's demonstration of the fact that it is impossible to tell whether the sentences in his extract from a Ladybird book are sequenced correctly – they can be read just as well backwards as forwards – is convincing evidence of the lack of this most important kind of structure in such texts, despite the emphasis that they generally place on structure (Wade 1982).

If we are not already experienced readers of a certain kind of text we may initially need someone else to tune the text for us. Susannah Steele tells how, after she had read a new story to her class, she invited some of them to prepare a reading of the text themselves. They found some initial difficulty in reading this unfamiliar text aloud and came back to her for help with 'Remind us of the tune, please Miss!'.

However experienced we are as readers, it is always possible that we may encounter texts that are completely unfamiliar to us and that we need help in negotiating; often such help can take the form of a demonstration of how the text should be read aloud. The value of reading aloud, and of continuing to read aloud to children, from an ever widening range of texts, is obviously implicit in all this.

Even when texts are read silently it seems likely that their tunes continue to be experienced internally in some way. The writer, Eudora Welty, describes her own experience of the inner voice that mediates for her the tunes of written language in this way:

> ...the feeling that resides in the printed word reaches me
> through the inner voice. I have supposed, but never found
> out, that this is the case with all readers – to read as listeners
> – and with all writers, to write as listeners...
>
> (Welty, 1983)

We shall need to investigate the way in which the tune on the page becomes the tune in the head, and how far any kind of vocalisation, including sub-vocalisation and inner vocalisation (if this is not a contradiction in terms) is an integral part of effective reading.

On the one hand there have been suggestions that sub-vocalisation (which often precedes the move to entirely silent reading) is *not* an indication of what goes on when children begin to read silently. Carol Chomsky suggests that skilled readers bypass phonology and that reading aloud, or vocalisation, employs phonological processing rules that are merely an impediment to silent reading (Chomsky 1970). Vygotsky's observation that written language, although it may begin as second order symbolism, eventually becomes direct symbolism ('Understanding written language is first effected through spoken language, but gradually the path is curtailed and spoken language disappears as the intermediate link') appears to support this point (Vygotsky 1978).

Yet a sense persists that, even in silent reading, we are attending in some way to an inner voice and to the text's tunes. The answer is likely to lie in Vygotsky's work on inner speech. Just as Vygotsky traced the line of development from social speech, through egocentric speech or speech-for-oneself (becoming gradually more fragmented and abbreviated) to inner speech and, ultimately, verbal thought, so it may be possible to track a similar development from reading together and aloud, through sub-vocalisation, to 'inner reading', in which the reader continues to experience, albeit in a far more condensed form, the outlines of the rhythms and tunes that, in reading aloud, act as such important integrative structures for the meaning.

Vygotsky did briefly discuss the relationship between written language and inner speech. In one isolated passage in *Thought and Language* he speculated that the act of writing must imply a translation from inner speech to written language – from the 'maximally compact' form of language to its 'maximally detailed' form. It is clear that reading might, similarly, be seen as an act of translation into inner speech – a matching of the 'tune on the page' with the 'tune in the head'. Vygotsky makes a significant assumption in this passage. He assumes a developmental relationship between inner speech and the development of written language when he writes:

> Written language demands conscious work because its
> relation to inner speech is different from that of oral speech:
> the latter precedes inner speech in the course of
> development, while written speech follows inner speech and
> presupposes its existence.

All of this opens up a remarkable field for investigation and suggests that it may be important to observe the relation between egocentric monologue, speech-for-oneself and the beginnings of silent reading. It will be hard to follow this invisible process far since, as Neisser suggests: 'Reading is externally guided thinking...we may not understand it until we understand thought itself' (Neisser 1967).

Some of James Britton's introspective experiments on the recall of certain 'powerful remembered cadences', in which particular fragments of text, like tips of a drowned landscape appearing above the surface of the water, enable him to recreate the whole, suggest how close is the link between grammatical structures, the characteristic tunes of texts and our inner representations of such tunes. Britton describes how, in composing a few lines of a poem, he becomes aware that one phrase he wants to use is part of a known tune:

> I struggled with the second line that should approach that
> idea: one attempt began 'Here were...' – but as I worked on
> that construction (which above all involved *listening to it*) I
> became aware that it already carried *somebody else's meaning*,

that is to say, it was another of those powerful remembered
cadences that I have discussed on previous occasions...
    What is interesting is that so semantically neutral a phrase
– so simply structural a signal – as 'Here were' should have
that evocative power...what I must conclude is that the
structural framework – the grammatical forms that enter such
expressions – are a more powerful part of the total literary
experience than we usually reckon (see p 154).

Britton's description of the 'skeletal fragments' of half-remembered tunes may
hold some indication of the compressed fashion in which we continue to experience the intonational and structural patterning of texts as we read silently. It is
interesting that, like the authors of *Inquiry into Meaning*, he finds a close relationship between the characteristic cadence of a text and its grammatical form, and
considers these elements to be basic to the way in which written language is internally experienced and stored.

    For written language is stored in the ear. We experience the characteristic
rhythmic structure of texts or genres through their intonational patterning, and
when we write we draw on the store of tunes we know and on our sense of how such
tunes are made. Part of learning to write is therefore a question of learning how to
write the tune, and of learning what resources there are at our disposal to enable us to
create tunes for our readers.

Some examples. The writer of the story from which the next passage is taken, a
six-year-old girl, creates a basic narrative situation with great economy in the first
two sentences of the story. Thereafter, the tune of the writing mirrors the would-be
mother's hopeful quest, her disappointment ('But no, she could not find one') and
the sudden surprising shift in the narrative when a baby unexpectedly appears.

> The circus was coming, and the animals had babies. But one
> animal did not have a baby. She looked high and low for a
> baby to suit her. But no, she could not find one.

This extract shows a writer learning how to mark the tune for her readers and
drawing, of course, on her experience of listening to stories, for the storytelling
voice is clearly heard.

    In the next extract, the beginning of another story, one of the seven-year-old
writer's main concerns appears to be to construct a tale in a traditional style,
which conforms to the rules of fairytale. The 'rule of three' which this story
follows is strictly observed, and this structure is reflected in the movement of the
prose and the story's 'tune':

> Once upon a time there lived three brothers. There was big
> brother, middle-size brother and small brother. One day big
> brother decided to go and seek his fortune.
>   He walked a long way away from the house. Soon he
> met an old woman. She showed him three bags on the
> ground. She told him he could choose one of them.
>   'Which one do you prefer?' she asked him. There was a
> big bag, a middle-sized bag and a small bag.

In this strongly marked structure, the rhythmical pattern of the prose corresponds to the formal shape of the traditional narrative. The writer's concern to emphasise this shape is obvious from the page, but when she herself reads these opening sentences it becomes even clearer. She almost sings the story, marking particularly strongly the tune of those sentences in which the 'rule of three' structure of the story is apparent.

Finally, an extract from an adventure story shows the nine-year-old author achieving a perfect pastiche of Enid Blyton (naturally without intending a pastiche). It is not easy to imitate a particular author's style so exactly; adults with whom I have worked have attempted to parody Blyton without comparable success. It is above all the characteristic tune that enables us to describe this passage as Blytonish, and the writer has internalised, from her extensive reading of this author, the features of the writing which contribute to this tune. Like many young writers at this point in her development she is an unconscious impersonator, taking on the voices and tunes of different texts:

> *Adventure by the Sea*
> 'This is going to be fun!' shouted Carol. 'I shall go swimming every day,' yelled Pete. 'So will I,' said Jenny. 'I'll think about it,' said Len slowly as if in a dream, which made everybody laugh. The reason was that Carol and her brother Pete and their mother and father Mr and Mrs Norman together with their friends Jenny and Len were going on holiday to the sea. 'I can smell the sea,' said Mr Norman. 'So can I,' said Mrs Norman. Soon they could see the sea. 'That must be the cottage we're staying in,' said Mr Norman. 'It's got a lovely view of the sea.' They parked the car near the house and Mr Norman opened the door. The children explored the house. 'Us boys can have this room and you girls the room next door,' said Pete. 'Good idea,' Carol said.
>
> When they finally settled in it was tea-time. After tea the children talked about what they would do the next day. 'I'm going to read,' said Pete when they had finished. 'I've got a thrilling story about adventure at sea... 'I wish we could have one' butted in Len. What he didn't know was that they were going to have one!
>
> Len yawned. He sat up. Where am I?, he thought. Oh yes, I'm on holiday. Better be quiet or else I'll wake Pete up. Len got up and tiptoed to the window. Some way away he could see an island...

When teachers respond to children's writing, they often begin by reading the writing aloud. This simple technique enables both child and teacher to focus on the way the writing sounds and to hear its emergent tunes. Learning how to hear the tunes one is creating is fundamental to learning to write, because such tunes are holistic structures, overarching shapes, which carry the broad meanings. When teachers read children's early texts 'as if they made sense' they give expression and emphasis to these meanings and demonstrate the latent structures in the writing. They also enable children, by this means, to hear what it is about the writing that may need work. As Britton emphasises, working on written language 'above all involves *listening to it*'.

The reader or writer who is learning to attend to the tune of the text is therefore learning to focus on its overall organisation and the 'big shapes' that carry its meaning. Such a focus will prove more valuable to a learner than a pre-occupation with local detail, because detail needs a structure to slot into. Writers without a sense of the overall direction of their texts often find themselves in trouble. Readers and writers with a well-developed sense of the tunes of texts, on the other hand, are generally able to spot where their own performance is faltering and make the necessary changes.

For writers, especially inexperienced writers who are not yet writing fluently, it will be particularly important to learn to focus on the big shapes they are making and to appreciate the value of reading a text aloud so as to hear what it is doing. Essentially, this simple technique enables writers to change gear and experience the text at a different reader's pace, a pace at which the tune becomes more apparent. This provides a reminder of the global context in which they are operating; it is also a kind of enactment of their future readers' experience, a way of actually *becoming* the 'reader in the writer'. Experienced writers may be able to dispense with this kind of voicing of a text and become largely silent listeners to the silent tunes that they are making, except when they meet problems that need to be heard.

What this suggests is that 'learning listening' (Pradl 1988) is as much a part of acquiring written language as it is of acquiring spoken language. And in becoming attuned to the tunes of texts readers and writers can be seen as simply adding to the repertoire of tunes which, as experienced users of spoken language, they already possess.

Bellugi, Ursula and Klima, Edward S. (1972), 'The roots of language in the sign talk of the deaf' in *Psychology Today*, June

Bryant, Peter and Bradley, Lynette (1985), *Children's Reading Problems*, Basil Blackwell

Bussis, Anne *et al.* (1985), *Inquiry into Meaning: an investigation of learning to read*, Lawrence Erlbaum

Chomsky, Carol (1970), 'Reading, writing and phonology' in *Harvard Educational Review*, vol. 40, no. 2, May

Darwin, Charles (1877), 'A biological sketch of an infant' in *Mind*, July

Dombey, Henrietta (1983), 'Learning the language of books' in Margaret Meek (ed.), *Opening Moves*, Bedford Way Papers, no. 17, University of London Institute of Education

Halliday, M.A.K. (1975), *Learning How to Mean*, Edward Arnold

Luria, A.R. (1981), *Language and Cognition*, J. Wiley & Sons

Neisser, Ulric (1967), *Cognitive Psychology*, Appleton-Century-Crofts

Olson, David R. (1977), 'From utterance to text: the bias of language in speech and writing' in *Harvard Educational Review*, vol. 47, no. 3, August

Pappas, Christine C. (1989), 'Ontogenesis of the registers of written language: young children's sense of the story and information book genres', paper given at the NCTE Annual Convention, Baltimore

Payton, Shirley (1984), 'Developing awareness of print: a young child's first step towards literacy', *Educational Review*, University of Birmingham

Pradl, Gordon (1988), 'Learning listening' in Martin Lightfoot and Nancy Martin (eds.), *The Word for Teaching is Learning*, essays for James Britton, Heinemann Educational/Boynton Cook

Snow, Catherine E. and Ferguson, Charles A. (eds.) (1977), *Talking to Children: language input and acquisition*, Cambridge University Press

Steele, Susanna, informal communication with the author

Thomas, Anne (1981), 'Intonation and learning to read: what does a teacher understand about the reading process from an investigation of intonational patterning?', unpublished paper written for Diploma: *Role of Language in Education*, University of London Institute of Education

Thomas, Anne (1987), 'Snapshots of a young reader and her books' in *Texts That Teach*, *Language Matters*, no. 1

Torrey, Jane (1969), 'Learning to read without a teacher: a case study' in *Elementary English*, vol. 46

Vygotsky, L.S. (1962), *Thought and Language*, M.I.T. Press

Vygotsky, L.S. (1978), *Mind in Society: the development of higher psychological processes*, Harvard University Press

Wade, Barrie (1982), 'Rhyming with reason' in *Children's Literature in Education*, vol. 13, no. 4, Winter

Welty, Eudora (1983), *One Writer's Beginnings*, Harvard University Press

Whitehead, Marian (1985), 'Proto-narrative moves in early conversations' in Margaret Meek (ed.), *Opening Moves*, Bedford Way Papers, no. 17, University of London Institute of Education

Children's books referred to in the text

Ahlberg, Janet and Allan (1978), *Each Peach Pear Plum*, Kestrel Books

Ahlberg, Janet and Allan (1980), *Funny-bones*, Heinemann

Burningham, John (1970), *Mr Gumpy's Outing*, Cape

Hutchins, Pat (1968), *Rosie's Walk*, Bodley Head

McKee, David (1980), *Not Now Bernard*, Andersen Press

Martin, Bill Jnr., illustrated by Eric Carle (1984), *Brown Bear, Brown Bear What Do You See?*, Hamish Hamilton

Murphy, Jill (1980), *Peace at Last*, Macmillan

Dr Seuss (1962), *Green Eggs and Ham*, Collins

HENRIETTA DOMBEY

Lessons Learnt at Bed-time

Since Shirley Brice Heath told us that, 'A close look at the way bed-time story routines in Maintown taught children how to take meaning from books raises a heavy sense of the familiar in all of us who have acquired mainstream habits and values', we may have felt uneasy about privileging this cultural practice. Henrietta Dombey lifts the 'heavy sense of the familiar' by showing that when adults and children read a book together (not necessarily at bed-time) the event is wholly unlike any other childhood language interaction. As Anna and her mother read the story of *Rosie's Walk* they both weave a complex pattern of events and understandings from the narrative. Contrary to Heath's assertion, this is not 'schooled' behaviour. See how Anna takes the initiative while her mother's concern is not to question her understanding but to let her enjoy the book as a complete whole.

Few professionals who have given the matter much thought maintain that children begin to learn to read only when they start school. Instead, we all see that learning to read has a long pre-history. In the industrialised world pre-school children spend their lives in print-saturated surroundings and learn much of the form and function of written language before they start school. Some children learn even more. The experience of hearing stories read aloud is widely recognised as one which gives uniquely powerful lessons about literacy (Holdaway 1975, Scollon and Scollon 1979, Meek 1982).

In psycholinguistic terms, the listening child is developing a familiarity with the meanings and linguistic forms of printed texts which will materially assist her in later attempts to read, that is to make sense of written texts on her own. Through her experience of stories read aloud, she is developing a store of useful 'information in the head', to use Smith's term, that will enable her to be less dependent on the 'information on the page' (Smith 1971). In sociolinguistic terms she is learning something of the functions that written language can perform, something of what Halliday calls the 'functional extension' that written language can provide (Halliday 1978). And, of course, she is learning the powerful literary satisfactions that books can give. But exactly what happens in such 'listening' sessions has not been thoroughly explored.

It is true that Heath in her celebrated documentation of the literacy events involving young children of a white middle-class community with college-educated parents, and those of black and white working-class communities, has written of the importance of story-reading in the middle-class 'Maintown' homes (Heath 1982). In particular she has drawn attention to the 'life to text' and 'text to life' moves whereby these 'Maintown' children are helped to establish connections between their own first-hand experience and the second-hand experience of the book. But her emphasis is on cultural differences rather than on a detailed articulation of the means by which cultural practices are achieved.

Through the revealing prisms of discourse analysis and narrative structure I would like to examine what is happening in one such event: a story reading between a parent and child in a home similar to those of 'Maintown' in terms of its social class, educational background and expectations of literacy.

It is hard to see significance in the comfortable and familiar. Certainly, most readers of this chapter will have experienced similar bed-time story sessions, as children, baby-sitters or parents. But the commonplace merits examination: through such commonplace practices as these, children develop significant cultural competences and understandings. To look closely and systematically at the complex patterning of the verbal to and fro between mother and child reveals how this enables the child to come into possession of the language and meanings of this particular written genre. I want to suggest that such a story reading is a complex social interaction through which the child is learning how to make 'readings' of a narrative text.

Anna is three and a half, and her mother is reading her Pat Hutchins' *Rosie's Walk*, which Anna has heard four times before. There are only two sentences in the printed text, but the reading of these is surrounded and interspersed by thirty-nine conversational utterances. These merit examination. They are not an irrelevant distraction, but the means through which Anna takes on the narrative they surround. This conversation has clear boundaries. The announcement of the title at the beginning and the reference to bed-time at the end function as a frame, setting limits on what is said. And although this may not be apparent initially, within these limits the conversation has a coherence quite untypical of conversations with young children in other situations.

The transcript extract that follows shows the first half of this story reading. The printed text is shown on the right side of the page, and asterisks indicate indecipherable speech. Omitting the narrative utterances, I have grouped the conversational utterances into exchanges, numbered on the extreme left of the page.

Rosie's Walk   Pat Hutchins   (Puffin, 1970)
(Third of three stories that session)

E1	1	M	C'mon 'cos I want to go and have my supper.
	2		Hurry up.
	3		Rosie's Walk
	4		Rosie the hen went for a walk
E2	5	A	A fox is following her.
	6	M	Oh!

ROSIE'S WALK
    By PAT HUTCHINS
Picture of carefree hen walking through cluttered rural scene, followed by watchful fox
Cover

Picture of hen setting out across picturesque farmyard with fox eyeing her greedily from under hen-house
2
Rosie the hen went for a walk
1–2

7		Across the yard	*Picture of hen walking past fruit trees, unaware of fox jumping after her* across the yard *3–4*
8		Boum *****	*Picture of hen walking on unaware while fox bumps his nose on rake he has landed on* *5–6*
9 10	 A	Around the pond, **** fish in the pond	*Picture of hen walking beside pond, unaware of fox jumping after her. No fish in picture.* around the pond *7–8*

	11	A	Splash!	*Picture of hen walking on unaware of fox landing in the pond. No fish in picture* *9–10*
E3	12		How they, how the fox just don't get out?	
	13	M	Oh I expect he'll climb out.	
E4	14	A	Why?	
	15	M	Why will he climb out?	
	16	A	Yeah.	
	17	M	Well, why d'you think he'll climb out?	
	18	A	Like when he wants, when he, the hen to eat.	
	19	M	Yes he wants to eat Rosie.	

	20	M	Over the haycock,	*Picture of hen walking over haycock unaware of fox right behind her* over the haycock *11–12*
E5	21	A	Is, is he catching her?	
	22	M	*er turns page* no	*Picture of hen walking away from haycock unaware of fox buried in it* *13–14*
E6	23	A	Wh why?	
	24	M	(Laughter) 'cos he's a silly old fox, that's why	
	25	A	'cos he's gone in the hay.	
	26	M	Gone in the hay.	
E7	27	A	Could he get out?	
	28	M	um, Yes.	
	29		Past the mill.	*Picture of hen walking past mill unaware of catching her foot in pulley rope, and of fox following her* past the mill *15–16*
	30	A	He's doing that, doing that	
	31	M	Is he?	
E8	32	M	*turns page* Aah!	*Picture of hen walking on unaware of fox submerged in flour behind her* *17–18*
	33		She doesn't even notice him, does she?	

At first sight, it looks far from orderly. Even if we exclude the indecipherable speech, many of the exchanges between mother and child lack the formal completeness of exchange structure models such as those proposed by Coulthard and Brazil (1981) or Berry (1981). Not one has the complete Initiation, Response and Feedback format identified by Sinclair and Coulthard (1975). Indeed, of the nine exchanges in this extract, only six include a verbal response as well as an initiation. The remaining three are one-part 'exchanges', but of course Anna and her mother are face to face and share the same physical context: actions, gestures and facial expressions complete many of these apparently incomplete exchanges. Her mother needs no verbal response when she asks Anna to hurry up. There is no indication that either partner has failed to respond acceptably to what the other has said. But this coherence within the exchanges comes from the intermingling of words and paralinguistic communication, not from the words alone.

To examine the structure of their conversational interaction in more detail I draw on the framework developed by Wells and Montgomery (1981). In this framework each conversational move is typified both interpersonally, that is in terms of the discourse role adopted by the speaker, and ideationally, in terms of the commodity being exchanged. So we are looking at the patterning both of the roles taken by Anna and her mother, and of what it is they are talking about.

When we look at the interpersonal patterning of the exchanges we see that it is Anna who is taking the leading role. Anna initiates seven of the nine exchanges. She may be the novice in the matter of story-reading, but she is the one who decides what shall be talked about. This is a striking repetition of the interactive patterning found by Trevarthen to typify pre-speech communication between babies and their adult caretakers, and by Wells to be characteristic of conversational interaction between rapid language learners and their parents (Trevarthen 1979, Wells 1981).

To Anna's initiatives her mother acts as supporter rather than bystander, extending six of these into verbally complete exchanges, which follow the rules of reciprocity. Anna is less generous. Neither of her mother's two initiatives is granted a verbal response. Of course, embedded as these exchanges are in a shared physical context, as I have suggested, their lack of verbal completeness does not necessarily mean a failure to communicate. On the other hand, a high proportion of verbal completion surely shows a movement towards verbal self-sufficiency. Anna's mother treats her initiatives in a way that shifts the discourse towards the explicitness and formal completeness of written language.

This movement towards written language is also evident in the ideational structuring of the discourse. The only exchange whose commodity is not information occurs before the story title has been announced. In all the rest the commodity is information rather than goods or services: and with the exception of the final exchange, the information is all story-related.

Not only is there consistency of topic, there is also a more particular continuity in many of these story-related exchanges. Out of the nine exchanges, five are grouped together in sequences of two and three exchanges, where the initiation of the second and subsequent exchange is contingent on a proposition constructed in the preceding one. This development of story-related information results in a thematic consistency that seems rare in conversations involving young children. Mother and child are not flitting from topic to topic but constructing a series of closely related propositions.

These exchanges are, of course, centred on a narrative text. As they talk, Anna and her mother are not concerned to establish connections with Anna's first-hand experience (although this often plays a part in their readings) but to realise the narrative, to actualise its potential narrative structures and to build a complex, textured and coherent whole. In this story-telling this involves close interpretation of the pictures, for the printed text of *Rosie's Walk* is deceptively uneventful. The richer story, sharp with the constant threat to the innocuous hen of being pounced on and eaten by the unmentioned fox, is to be found in the pictures alone. To use Barthes' terms, the comments of both mother and child focus on the kernel events of the fox following Rosie and his desire to eat her; they ignore the satellite events of the frog on the lily pad and the goat by the hay (Barthes 1975). Outside the story context these pictures could be read in many other ways, but mother and child are reading them for a complex purpose: to establish the story and to actualise the hermeneutic code of this verbal and visual narrative.

In doing so they are not using the stance of the narrative text. The sure voice of Genette's classical subsequent narration has been replaced by the tentative voice of the spectator, who feels an excited uncertainty about the outcome of the events she is witnessing (Genette 1980). Their comments represent the actions and characters as operating in the present, not the past. What is in the picture is happening now, whereas what is in the verbal narrative has already happened. The ever-present sense of uncertainty about what might happen next is in marked contrast to the immutable certainty of the narrative. Mother and child seem to be concerned not simply to establish an invariant story, but also to construct a fictive world containing possibilities that extend beyond the invariant story of the spoken narrative. As they look at the pictures their intention seems to be to construe them not simply in order to identify elements in the story, nor just to supply elements missing from the verbal narrative. They seem instead to construe them in order to articulate a world where many things might happen. Just after this extract, Anna's mother says with apparent conviction,

I think he's going to get her this time

despite the fact that she has read the story to Anna many times before and both know that the fox will be perpetually frustrated in his attempts to catch Rosie. Anna reveals a similar concern with the possible story future rather than the certain story past when she asks whether the fox is able to get out of the hay. At the end she announces firmly that the fox can't get Rosie in her cage.

Through their conversational talk mother and child are creating a story world and moving about inside it, making judgements on its elements and exploring its possibilities and laws. Within this world there are many things to talk about, and as other readings of this story indicate, the topics chosen vary from one reading to the next. At each reading a different 'reading' is constructed. Yet where they talk of what might happen, their speculations are bounded by the limitations of the story world of this particular genre. There is no suggestion that the fox might get bored, that Rosie might get run over by the lorry from the egg marketing board or that the farmer might eat her for supper. For in this genre the characters behave autonomously and consistently, the significant events that take place are the outcome of this behaviour, and the social and mechanical complexities of the modern world are, by and large, kept at bay.

We cannot know in detail the extent to which the potential structures of the narrative are actualised for Anna. But an examination of the conversational utterances has shown us her concern to articulate the set of kernel events, to savour the hermeneutic tension, and not to overstep the bounds of the genre.

All this has taken place in conversational exchanges principally initiated by Anna, but in which her mother plays a vital, if self-effacing, role. Anna's mother does far more than deliver to her the words of the narrative, although her manner of doing this, in particular her use of intonation, is of key importance in giving it life. But if this were all that mattered Anna would be better served by tapes of stories read by justly celebrated actors than a hurried reading by a mother who wants her own supper. However, this personal reading is providing Anna with something no tape can give. For Anna's mother prompts, supports and extends her enquiries, enabling Anna to make the narrative her own.

Paradoxically, the loose and shifting structures of conversation permit mother and child to actualise the tighter and more complex structures of narrative. The discourse structures Anna is familiar with, and in which she plays the leading role, serve to elaborate and articulate the less familiar structures of the narrative, where her mother has control of the discourse. What is new is not merely juxtaposed with what is familiar: it is through the familiar that the new is given its coherence and significance and enters Anna's possession.

Anna is being initiated into the process of reading as a process of active meaning construction in which the reader makes a personal sense of whole texts. The text, of course, is markedly different from informal conversation and demands very different kinds of meaning making. Yet her mother makes no attempt to disentangle the various levels of linguistic and literary understanding of which such meaning making is composed. At one and the same time she is enlarging Anna's sense of the kinds of propositional meanings of which stories are composed, accustoming her to the narrow formality of the interpersonal meanings conveyed from writer to reader and extending her repertoire of the distinctive lexical and syntactic forms that realise these in narrative text. There is no pre-learning of the vocabulary, no preliminary session with adverbial phrases, nor any exclusive attention to the sequence of events per se. Their conversational interaction concerns none of these. Instead, all this learning of new forms and meanings seems to take place unobtrusively, even tacitly. The new forms are certainly not the object of their conscious attention. Their talk is organised and ordered by a central purpose, which is to produce, celebrate and give personal meaning to a whole narrative that brings its own semantic reward. Anna's mother acts on the expectation that this activity will be enjoyable to Anna, and that a determination to savour each story will impel Anna to make sense of the new forms as she constructs the new meanings. Her mother does not see her job as ensuring either that Anna has 'understood' each new word or structure, or that she can give a literally faithful account of the events of the story. Indeed, there is an implicit assumption that to do any of these things would be to distract attention from the central activity.

The denotation (and connotation) of the lexis, the meaning relations realised in the syntax and the event structure of the story, matter only in terms of their contribution to the narrative Anna is constructing in her head. And there is no one correct internal narrative. What matters is that within the limits set by the text Anna should construct something pleasing to herself and that this pleasure should be shared between mother and child. That Anna sees a richer understanding as more rewarding is evinced by the questions she asks. And the explanations that her mother provides are in response to such questions: they are not items on a didactic agenda whose completion will indicate a correct reading of the text.

Re-reading will deepen Anna's understanding of narrative wholes and of their parts, of functions and of their forms, and make each narrative more firmly her own. As she comes to know a number of texts very well indeed and to apprehend (albeit intuitively) the relationship between the forms and meanings of which they are composed, she will be able to make satisfying sense of more complex texts and demand fewer re-readings. But all this learning is likely to be characterised by simultaneous and unconscious attention to a number of different linguistic and literary levels.

Her mother's mediation, through her use of intonation and her responses to Anna's initiatives, will assist Anna to conquer this new territory. As Anna's familiarity with new forms and new meanings develops, this mediation will become less necessary. It is likely already that Anna is using her familiarity with other stories to help her gloss new ones: familiar forms in new combinations help her construct new meanings, familiar meanings help her make sense of new forms. As she hears more stories she will have a richer stock to draw on and will be less in need of the mediation provided by a known and trusted adult. And with each new narrative her sense of the whole will be developed more from her own internal dialogue than from external dialogue with an experienced reader. But in all the stages of her progress towards a richer experience of narrative, she will proceed along a broad front organised by her intention to 'understand the story'. If the activity is to be intrinsically rewarding this is how she must go about it. For an adult to abstract one element from the narrative and 'teach' it to Anna would be to rob her of the pleasure of making the narrative her own. To borrow Rumelhart's description of reading, the process Anna is engaged in is simultaneous, multi-level, interactive processing (Rumelhart 1976).

The conversation with her mother provides Anna with an external model for the internal conversation with the author that is necessary to any but the most superficial reading of a narrative text. Thus, her mother helps Anna to do in partnership what she cannot yet do for herself. In her actions, she implicitly shares the view embodied in Vygotsky's much quoted observation.

> What the child can do in co-operation today, he can do
> alone tomorrow.
>
> (Vygotsky 1962)

Comfortable and familiar though they may be, bed-time story-readings such as this can teach us important lessons about the complex nature of literacy learning, and perhaps even give us a model for what we might do to advance it in school, not just in the primary years, but as long as students can be helped to read with greater power and satisfaction.

An earlier version of this essay appeared as 'Making sense of narrative through conversation' in the Canadian journal *Language Arts*, vol. 10, no. 1, 1987.

Barthes, R. (trans. S. Heath) (1975), 'Introduction to the structural analysis of narratives' in *New Literary History*, 6, pp 237–72

Berry, M. (1981), 'Systemic linguistics and discourse analysis: a multi-layered approach to exchange structure' in M. Coulthard and M. Montgomery (eds.), *Studies in Discourse Analysis*, Routledge & Kegan Paul

Coulthard, M. and Brazil, D. (1981), 'Exchange structure' in M. Coulthard and M. Montgomery (eds.), *Studies in Discourse Analysis*, Routledge & Kegan Paul

Genette, G. (trans. J. Lewin) (1980), *Narrative Discourse*, Basil Blackwell

Halliday, M.A.K. (1978), *Language as Social Semiotic*, Edward Arnold

Heath, S.B. (1982), 'Protean shapes in literacy events: ever-shifting oral and literate traditions' in D. Tannen (ed.), *Spoken and Written Language*, Ablex

Holdaway, D. (1975), *The Foundations of Literacy*, Ashton Scholastic

Meek, M. (1982), *Learning to Read*, The Bodley Head

Rumelhart, D.E. (1976), 'Toward an interactive model of reading', *Technical Report no. 56*, La Jolla, California: Center for Human Information Processing, University of California, San Diego

Scollon R. and Scollon S. (1979), 'The literate two-year-old: the fictionalization of self', *Working Papers in Sociolinguistics*, Southwest Regional Laboratory

Sinclair, J. and Coulthard, M. (1975), *Towards an Analysis of Discourse*, Oxford University Press

Smith, F. (1971), *Understanding Reading*, Holt, Rinehart & Winston

Trevarthen, C. (1979), 'Communication and co-operation in early infancy: a description of primary inter-subjectivity' in M. Bullowa (ed.), *Before Speech: the beginning of interpersonal communication*, Cambridge University Press

Vygotsky, L.S. (1962), *Thought and Language*, M.I.T. Press

Wells, C.G. (1981), 'Describing children's linguistic development at home and at school' in C. Adelman (ed.), *Uttering Muttering*, Grant McIntyre

Wells, C.G. and Montgomery, M. (1981), 'Adult-child interaction at home and at school' in P. French and M. MacLure (eds.), *Adult-Child Conversation: studies in structure and process*, Croom Helm

EVE GREGORY

Learning Codes and Contexts: a psychosemiotic approach to beginning reading in school

Not all children have stories read to them at home before they go to school. Even some who have nursery school experience don't associate story-time reading with what is expected from them when they read a text on their own. When they come to school the chief concern of young children who have little pre-school reading experience is to establish 'What counts as reading in this class?' In order to help them, some teachers try to establish for beginners what Eve Gregory calls the 'life sense' of stories and succeed only in confusing them about the nature of meaning derived from texts. Then the learners are in a less advantageous position than bilingual children whose ordinary habit is to attend to linguistic structures and words and not to expect the fit of textual meanings to life situations to be straightforward. The innovative thrust of this piece is its concern with the children's views of the task of reading, and their implicit query; 'What kind of cultural practice is reading, anyway?'

Gillian is sharing a simple picture book with her teacher. It is a story she knows well from class shared-reading sessions. Here, the children are apprenticed to the teacher as skilled practitioner, listening first, then gradually taking over the role of reader themselves:

Gillian:	I can't even read yet. You read it and I'll listen to yer.
Teacher:	We'll read it together. 'If you were a bird...'
Gillian:	I can't do it. I can't even see the words.

Why has five-year-old Gillian already decided that she cannot read? She has not yet even been asked to decode individual words. Her Bangladeshi class-mate, Tajul, responds very differently. He brings numerous stories from the book-corner to share with his teacher and he actually reads some of them word for word. Yet he is still unable to speak more than a few phrases of English. Gillian, on the other hand, speaks English fluently, is an interesting conversation partner and easily retells her own life stories. Neither child comes from a bookish or school-oriented home. Neither attended nursery school. How might the very different progress of children from non-school-oriented homes be accounted for as they begin reading in school? This essay focuses on this apparent puzzle and paradox and offers one approach to explaining it.

Children like Gillian and Tajul are often called exceptional. Yet most classes have a number of exceptions. They puzzle teachers because they defy paradigms of what beginning reading entails. These paradigms are largely informed by linguistic and psycholinguistic theories which centre on the role of language, on the story or text or book, in learning to read. Thus, children need to bring experience of language, life and culture as well as a familiarity with stories and books to enable them to predict a text. Within this frame, the Gillians and Tajuls escape our expectations and remain a paradox.

But if we were to step outside these paradigms, might the reading task look somewhat different? In this essay I shall argue that a psychosemiotic approach to beginning reading in school provides some explanation for what appears to be paradoxical. This approach shifts the emphasis from the language and text of linguistic theories to the role of the classroom as a cultural site and the children's cognitive and linguistic interpretation of it. What follows is a brief outline of the approach I propose. The rest of the essay draws on theoretical studies and classroom data to explain and illustrate what this might look like in practice.

Within a psychosemiotic framework the shared reading lesson is viewed as an ideological construct where events are played out. Thus, children need to learn to position themselves in three interlocking contexts:

1) The situational context: a positioning within a context-specific discourse in a social and cultural site and the interpersonal relationships attached to it. Here, the site is the classroom and the relationships that of teacher and pupil. The focus is on the features and the rules of the site itself.

2) The interpretational context or the context of the mind: a positioning within the appropriate mental frame of knowledge which is relevant to the situation. Here, the frame of knowledge in question is what counts as reading in the minds of the teacher and pupils. The focus is on the mental processes of individuals within the site.

3) The textual context: a positioning within the text and the actual language and words or code it is expressed in. Here, the texts are the classroom story books. The focus is on the language, story and book as a specific site within the wider frame of the shared-reading lesson in school.

These layers or contexts can be exemplified through the word 'reading' itself. Reading is the code (textual context) conjuring up a mental image or interpretation (interpretational level) within the cultural site and the corresponding relationships within the school (situational context). Thus, taking a psychosemiotic approach to learning to read looks like this: beginning reading in school involves learning to position oneself as a reader within the context of the classroom as an institutional site and the corresponding relationships within it, internalising and adopting the appropriate frame of knowledge which counts as reading within the site and learning to express this in terms of a linguistic response to the text offered. These linguistic expressions I term a 'code' to signify their exclusive nature.

The following sections show how different children are able to position themselves in these contexts and suggest why this might be. I then offer reasons why a demystification (Freire and Macedo 1987), in the sense of access to the code, might be easier for some bilingual children from non-school-oriented homes than for their monolingual peers. Examples are drawn from a corpus of data collected over two years in an urban multilingual classroom. How do each of the above contexts fit into linguistic paradigms on learning to read? It would be wrong to suppose that linguistic studies have neglected the role of context generally in children's learning. However, there is a radically different emphasis and interpretation of the role of the situational context which, in turn, decisively affects the others. I shall briefly examine how each of the above contexts is viewed in these studies, before going on to introduce the psychosemiotic approach proposed.

The situational context Within linguistic theory on beginning reading the cultural site for early acculturation into stories and books is usually assumed to be the home environment. Within this environment it is axiomatic that there is a shared cultural context between caregiver and child. Story-reading takes place as a collaborative enterprise. This often takes the form of the bed-time story, where the adult is able to link the culture of the child with events in the text and relate the story to real-life experiences and vice versa (Holdaway 1979, Scollon and Scollon 1981, Dombey 1983). Young children learning to position themselves in the situational context model themselves on the adult as skilled practitioner. They are apprenticed, but not as subservient workers to a stranger, consciously working to master the separate skills of a trade. Rather, the apprenticeship takes place unconsciously and naturally, by immersion. The social relationship between the participants is one of equal status, where the adult acts as facilitator (Holdaway 1979).

Importantly, the social site itself and the relationships within it are unproblematic. Child and adult share cultural values and expectations mediated by and through the story and the book. There are no barriers between the text and the participants' interpretation of it. The shared experience of the text is central, and everything radiates from it.

Crucially, I suggest, many studies imply that the shared interpretation of the social site, equality of relationship and collaboration between participants can be transplanted from home to school without changes necessarily taking place (Holdaway 1979, Wells 1981, 1987, Cochran-Smith 1984, Waterland 1985). Here is the crux of the difference between linguistic studies and the psychosemiotic approach proposed.

The interpretational context Through modelling themselves on the adult within a shared cultural context, children learn a specific interpretation of reading. Thus, reading is not simply the labelling of packages in a supermarket or a magazine; it belongs to stories and books, '...when my baby brother's hands are big enough to hold a book, he'll be able to read,' (Scollon and Scollon 1981).

The textual context Within the shared interpretation of reading, children learn both how to position themselves in the words of the text and to fictionalise themselves by seeing themselves as a third person in relation to the text and the characters within it (Scollon and Scollon 1981). They see how life experiences can be brought to bear on the text (Iser 1977) and how far the meaning and words of the text are not arbitrary and are unchanging. They learn how to focus on the text itself (Wells 1987) and to realise that texts can 'speak to each other' (Foucault 1977, Eco 1980). Through the repeated sharing of stories, children learn both semantic and syntactic prediction of texts as well as the formal aspects of written language, e.g. collocations, ellipsis and lexical cohesions (Dombey 1983).

Thus, a direct relationship between adult, child and text within a shared cultural framework is assumed. There are no barriers between the participants and the text, and the role of the text itself is central. Decisively, it is often implied that learning to read in school retains the same characteristics and can be learned in the same way as at home. By immersing non-school-oriented children in the cultural practice of story-reading in school and through the provision of 'good books', they become acculturated into literacy in the same way as young school-oriented children are at home. But is this necessarily so? By overlooking or rendering unproblematic the situational context and believing she is modelling a cultural practice as it exists at home, the teacher may be teaching something very different from what she intends. Later in this chapter I shall show how this takes place. The vital question is: can cultural practices be transplanted from home to school without change? If not, what changes ensue and what consequences might such changes have?

An unproblematic transfer of some cultural practices from home to school has been seen as possible within a psychosemiotic approach to the development of abstract thought (Walkerdine 1981). Starting from theories of developmental psychology, Walkerdine sees learning the situational context as part and parcel of the signification process itself. Convincingly, she rejects the notion of context as an extra grafted on to children's already developed schema, as in the Piagetian model, and argues instead that language, thought and context must be viewed as interlocking parts of the signification process. For example, Walkerdine shows how understanding the language alone is not sufficient to interpret a couple's words in reaction to their baby's cries. We need to be able to position their discourse within both a social and historical dimension of behaviour and events surrounding child care, as well as within other discourses.

Walkerdine offers a number of examples to show how, by dint of participating in everyday cultural practices as they occur in school, children are able both to position themselves in relation to others within the practice and master the appropriate discursive practices relevant to them. One example from a nursery school shows how two girls are able to call up appropriate relations and discourse patterns to suit the cultural practice of tv watching in the home corner. Crucially, she claims that it is the metaphor itself – tv watching – which triggers off a switching into the appropriate set of relations and discourse.

Walkerdine's argument for the fusion of thought, language and context as essential parts of signification itself is important here, for she places context in a central role, so that thought itself is fused with context. Context exists within the cultural practice itself, which can remain unchanged when transferred into the site of the school. Everything depends, therefore, upon children's ability successfully to participate in everyday cultural practices. Thus, Walkerdine assumes that a cultural practice and the social relationships within it can be taken over in its original form into the institution of school. This assumption means she can then go on to imply that an essential starting-point for the teaching of young children is the provision of familiar cultural practices within which they can position themselves.

This approach fits well with the theory of beginning reading discussed in the last section. Following the tv example, immersion alone in the cultural practice of story-reading in school by and alongside the already initiated should enable newcomers to learn to position themselves within it. But can vital cultural practices really enter the institutional site of the school and remain unchanged, or is the tv example rather the exception, because it is within the frame of socio-dramatic play? What might be the case if the site itself were to change the original nature of the practice and the relationships within it?

Walkerdine's argument about the importance of a knowledge of the social and historical background for understanding discourse is obviously vital. Volosinov (1976) provides a similar and poignant example of this. A group of people are sitting in the doctor's waiting-room in Moscow. Suddenly, one looks out of the window and says with a sigh, 'Well!'. Fully to understand this word, Volosinov claims, knowledge of the Russian word for 'well' is not enough. One needs to feel the culture of the situation, that it is snowing outside, and that it is May, the month when finally the long Russian winter should be over. Everyone feels disappointed. In this context, the actual inner site of the doctor's waiting-room is obviously unimportant, for the focus is outside, on the wider culture and relationships within it. However, we can imagine many situations where this is not the case. Let us take Walkerdine's own example: a knowledge of the historical and social context might not be enough to understand a baby's cries. But imagine that the couple and their baby are suddenly placed under scrutiny in the psychologist's laboratory. How might this affect the practice, relationships within it and the corresponding discourse?

Foucault (1972) provides a framework which centralises the situational context as the institutional site which determines both the body of discourse and the relationships or positions individuals are able to take up within it. Applied to shared-reading lessons in school, his model means we shall need to examine the status of the individuals, as seen within a historical perspective, the institutional site – in this case, the school from which the discourse derives its source and application – also within a historical perspective, the situation the subject occupies in the discourse, as questioner or listener, the group of relations, for instance, or how schools and teachers are viewed in a historical perspective. In other words, the school discourse will affect the relations between all the participants; who is qualified to speak, for instance. Taking this perspective implies that cultural practices cannot simply be transplanted from one site to another; that shared-reading will take an essential part of its substance from the site in which it takes place.

Is it, then, at all possible to transplant a cultural practice and its corresponding discourse into school? Some argue strongly that it is not. Willes (1983) brings longitudinal data to show that even very young children starting school quickly learn the rules of a special discourse of school which is different from any other setting. In a more formal model, Bernstein (1990) argues that pedagogic discourse distorts discourse as it exists in its original field and, in so doing, changes the nature of the practice itself. For example, physics in the classroom bears little comparison to physics in the laboratory.

I am proposing that a similar distortion may take place in reception classes as teachers introduce children to shared-reading in school. The examples given take place in an urban, multilingual reception class. The children are five years old. Most enter school unfamiliar with story books. Aware of this, the teacher regularly reads with the class, groups and individuals, and encourages the children to share reading with her. Thus, she often introduces the lesson by saying, 'Today, we're going to *read*...together'. She aims to show the children that reading is about knowing the story and enjoying and gaining meaning from good stories and books. Aiming at a role similar to that of caregiver with a young child, the teacher intends to model the fluent reader, a skilled practitioner, showing the children as apprentices what they should be doing as future readers.

What might be the effect of the site upon the teacher's initiation of the shared-reading practice and how does this affect children's ability to position themselves in it? This particular story is a simple picture-book version of *The Elves and the Shoemaker*. The following examples are typical of the exchanges between the teacher and non-school-oriented monolingual children:

> Teacher: (points to illustration of shoemaker's house)
>   Do you like that house?
> Children: Yeah.
> Teacher: He (the shoemaker) was very poor. If you're
>   very poor, what can't you do?
> Child: Can't buy bubble-gum.
> Teacher: Yes. What else?
> Child: Sweets.
> Teacher: Yes. What else?

What is being modelled here? The teacher is asking the children explicit questions about their own lives. Rather than immersing children in the story and the text, these examples show the teacher hardly allowing the children to enter the text at all. They are being confined to life. This lesson is a typical one, where almost all interactions between teacher and non-school-oriented children are outside the text. So the teacher is not actually modelling what she intends: knowing what a story is and enjoying it. At the same time, she jumps in and out of the text, reading a little, then questioning the children on their lives; but she never makes explicit what actually belongs to the text and what does not. However, her responses to different children's answers show that she implicitly assumes that the children understand they are reading a story and that life-sense answers are not required. For example, during *Rosie's Walk*:

> Child: (referring to fox) He's strong, just like Big
>   Daddy! (chants) Big Daddy! Big Daddy!
> Teacher: Shh! You must sit quietly when we're reading a
>   story together.

In fact, such life-modelling is following the explicit pattern set by the teacher.

Interestingly, the school-oriented children in the group who are familiar with home shared-reading do not allow themselves to be taken away from the story. They largely ignore life-sense questions or attempt to bring the teacher back to the text. Above all, unlike those above, their interruptions are met with support:

> Child: I know that story!
> Teacher: Well, you can help us tell the story then.

I shall return to this in more detail later. Already we begin to see how non-school-oriented children might find it difficult to position themselves in the situational context. The teacher aims to model the proficient reader and convey enjoyment and interest in the story, but her explicit teaching takes the children away from it and questions them on their lives. How might this contradiction be accounted for?

Focus on the situational context and the social relationships it determines provides one explanation. The transfer of the shared-reading practice from home to school means that the teacher is not in the role of caregiver but has a job to do, i.e. to teach. In her professional role as teacher, she wants to involve all the children in the lesson in whatever way possible. However, she is aware that some of the children are not familiar with the story. She therefore involves them in the only way she can, which is to call upon their own life experiences.

Thus, the main point of the sharing is no longer story-focused as between a young child and caregiver at home, but teaching-focused. The teacher uses the non-school-oriented children's own lives as a starting-point; but, in doing so, unconsciously excludes them from the story. At the same time, a parallel lesson takes place within the story for those who are familiar with it and refuse to be drawn outside. The site of the school, therefore, changes the cultural practice from its original site, but the social relationships are not as simple as those proposed in Foucault's model, where we might expect the teacher to praise the children who follow her explicit instruction. The teacher's actual aim is for the children to get to know and enjoy the story, and it is consequently the children who show they can do this who receive praise, even if her explicit teaching is ignored. Such is the nature of the distortion of a social practice transferred from home to the institution of school.

However, an interesting pattern emerges in individual shared-reading lessons between the teacher and some bilingual children. With these beginners in the English language the teacher does not attempt to engage in a conversation about their own lives. Instead, the reading is similar to examples given between a caregiver and a very young monolingual child (Gibson 1989). The focus is on a very simple text; no expectations or demands are made of the child's response. Positioning within the situational context as a stranger might, therefore, be easier than for some children who are assumed to share the language and culture of the school. Whether or not this is the case will, I argue, depend upon the expectations and interpretations that these children bring to reading in school. It is to these I now turn.

I now want to consider how different children are able to switch into certain areas of knowledge and discourse which are appropriate for the shared-reading lesson. The extent to which they do this depends upon the way in which they position themselves within the interpretational context or the 'context of the mind' (Cazden 1982). Walkerdine's reference to a cultural practice in terms of a metaphor which calls up a pattern of shared interpretations is valuable here. The question is, how far do different children share the school interpretation of reading? How do they position themselves in the school metaphor of reading and its corresponding areas of knowledge?

Knowing when to switch into an appropriate area of knowledge can be linguistically, cognitively and culturally complex. Ferguson (1982) gives a clear and simple example of this. He shows how Moroccan Arabs use a voiceless labial stop /p/ when using baby-talk, although this sound does not exist in their adult language. Not only this. Adults actually fail to perceive the sound or to produce it appropriately when learning a foreign language. Ferguson asks whether there might be some sort of cognitive barrier between one inventory of sounds and another, or, more generally, why different sounds are interpreted differently and a feature belonging to one context cannot simply be transferred to another. He relates these findings to school by arguing that cognitive skills cannot be identical across linguistic registers and that appropriate rule-learning is complicated and may sometimes need conscious instruction.

Positioning ourselves mentally in a cultural practice in school and switching into certain areas of knowledge and the appropriate discourse may not be as straightforward as in the tv watching example. The question is, can we learn to do it by immersion in the practice itself, through a sort of osmosis, or do we need more conscious instruction and practice? Hundeide (1985) and Freedle (1986) suggest that our own personal schema, formed through group and cultural routines, take us some way in understanding situations and determine our interpretive position within them. However, we are always going to need to respond to situations outside those of our known group routines. How do we learn to do this?

It may depend upon both the complexity of the task and our stage in mastering it. Take, for example, the practice of 'car driving in Britain'. Within this metaphor is the code or routine, 'headlight flashing = courtesy = you may pass'. In other countries, the same practice calls up a very different interpretation of the code which may be 'headlight flashing = I have right of way = stop!'. Imagination and common-sense tell us that it is more efficient and safer explicitly to be taught, consciously to analyse the differences and learn and practise the routine. Eventually, switching into the appropriate area of knowledge in appropriate situations takes place automatically. An example of more formal learning is given by Freedle in piano playing. He suggests that the early stages of learning may depend upon an analytic cognitive ability and conscious learning, whereas later stages may be unrelated to cognition. In other words, once a basic skill has been mastered, it becomes separate from conscious analytic skills, and new bits can be added to it.

How might these examples apply specifically to school and shared-reading lessons within it? The teacher uses the metaphor of reading to introduce her lessons, usually saying, 'We're going to read a story together.' She then goes on to assume that the children share her metaphor of what reading is without explicitly teaching it: that it calls up a frame of stories and books, an area of knowledge of stories generally and this story particularly, as well as calling upon 'story' rather than 'life-sense' during readings.

The children from school-oriented backgrounds are able to position themselves within her metaphor. Exactly how they do this is discussed later. However, some children from non-school- oriented backgrounds are likely to call up a very different interpretation of reading in school and consequently do not understand the task they are presented with in early reading lessons. Studies show how school reading may have little meaning for these children and how they are likely to make poor progress in class (Schieffelin and Cochran-Smith 1984). Their families may well actually 'read' just as much. Longitudinal emic data from the USA provides evidence that lower socio-economic indigenous and ethnic minority families spend just as long on reading activities as their middle-class counterparts, but these are of a non-book nature (Anderson and Stokes 1984). A study of mothers and their children with reading difficulties in London's docklands shows that reading is not interpreted as enjoyable but as hard work, not sharing stories but learning the words, not encouraged by a teacher as facilitator but consciously and explicitly taught (Gregory 1988).

Thus, a common interpretation of reading and its appropriate area of knowledge is not brought by all children to the school site. In this class of children, Tony, a Cantonese speaker from Hong Kong, quickly rejects attempts by the teacher to share reading. He seems unable to choose a book, and when one is chosen for him he tries to repeat every word the teacher says. His interest is in collecting words rather than in the story itself. Tony's grandfather refuses the books he brings home with the explanation, 'First, he must learn to read, then he may have the book.' The pain of learning to read is rewarded by the pleasure of possessing the esteemed book. To give the child a book before he is worthy of it degrades its value. Tony is just one child who is finding difficulty in 'positioning' himself within the context of the mind of reading in school. Bernier (1982) refers to these basically different interpretations as the 'ideological mapping' reflecting our socialisation within ideological groups which, as teachers or pupils, we bring to tasks in school. It is in the nature of schooling, argues Bernier, that automatic reward is given to those whose life-space is characterised by a narrow parallelism, which just happens to coincide with schooling folkways.

In what ways might being a stranger to the language and culture of the school possibly help children? We have seen that conscious learning may be advantageous or, indeed, necessary, in some situations (Freedle 1986). In his study, 'The Stranger', Schutz (1964) argues that the newcomer to a society brings precisely this conscious awareness of the host's cultural practices, thus enabling a more critical and possibly questioning stance. In addition to learning about a new culture, the young bilingual child is learning to associate a new language and discourse structures with new semantic boundaries. Walkerdine's (1981) model suggests how context, the signifier (or word) and the signified (or object) are welded together to form appropriate behaviour. Stepping into a certain context (e.g. tv watching) calls up appropriate signifiers and signifieds.

If some individual shared-reading lessons between teacher and bilingual child take on the pattern of the cultural practice as it exists between caregiver and young child, we may assume that the child is learning to associate new English words and discourse patterns with the appropriate boundaries or areas of knowledge of 'reading' as interpreted by the teacher. Put simply, by learning that the semantic boundaries for 'aunt' and 'uncle' are different in English from the first language (where in some languages different words may exist according to whether the relative is on the maternal or paternal side, etc.) a young bilingual child is developing a cognitive flexibility (Ben-Zeev 1977, Miller 1983, Hamers and Blanc 1990) which may well be useful in sorting out the boundaries between story and reading and life.

If certain 'boundary rules' do exist – and if we accept that rules can be learned – why have they bypassed children such as Gillian, who say 'I can't do it'? To say, 'I can't read' means that a child has already made the important discovery that rules do exist, that required answers are somehow within the book and the text and that printed words are not arbitrary, but part of a secret code from which the children feel excluded. What is the nature of this code within which children must position themselves?

I want to argue here that the text acts as a code to which children have greater or lesser access, and to ask how different children learn to 'position' themselves within the story, text and words of the book and how transparent the teacher makes their task.

I have demonstrated how the situational context influences the teacher to 'teach' the children and how she goes about this by questioning non-school-oriented children on their lives rather than on the unfamiliar text. I have also shown how school-oriented children largely ignored these life references and kept within the text. What is the result of this teaching on the non-school-oriented children's positioning? Gillian's reaction is one typical example. The teacher begins reading the story, and Joanna, a school-oriented child, joins in, 'Once upon a time, there was a poor shoemaker...'. Gillian interrupts and points to the shoemaker in the picture, 'That your grandad?' The teacher's answer is significant, 'Mmm....' (she then points to the shoemaker in the illustration) 'Can you see the shoemaker?' A similar pattern is often repeated with other non-school-oriented children.

Gillian's answer would be perfectly logical within life-sense knowledge. There is evidence, too, that other text-sense does not escape her and similar children. For instance, she does not confuse the name of one brand of crisps with another, neither does she think that any old name she might invent from life-sense will do. What she is doing here is copying the teacher's pattern of instruction and returning a life-sense answer. However, this is not what is required, as is clearly shown by the teacher's reaction. Children who offer knowledge on the text, on the other hand, are given both feedback and praise: 'You can help us tell the story', for example. Yet nowhere is it made explicit that this is required, nor are non-school-oriented children shown how to go about doing this. Two different reading lessons are, therefore, taking place; one on life and one on the story and text. We can conclude that children like Gillian are not being given the criterial knowledge or shown the rules of the game, which require staying within this and other stories and within the appropriate text. Baker and Freebody (1989) refer to a 'teacher-text partnership' aligned against the children. What we see here is a partnership extended to some children but remaining a secret to others.

The bilingual children, too, have as yet little access to the story or the text it is expressed in. Nor, however, do they have enough understanding of English to confuse life and story sense during group reading lessons. In their individual reading lessons, the whole event is in a new language or code. How might this help them? In the last two sections, I have suggested ways in which bilingual children might be better able to position themselves in the situational and inter-pretational contexts. One way of cracking the textual code is through a mastery of the words themselves. Two five-year-old Sylheti speakers reading together show what this might look like. They are reading *Each, Peach, Pear, Plum*, a simple rhyming picture book. The less advanced child is being helped by her peer. This child points to each word for the other to read. When the second child stumbles, the first quickly switches out of the code into Sylheti to tell her, 'Look at the picture'. We see that the code is sometimes learned in a parrot-like fashion, where one child simply repeats the text word-for-word. Sometimes, however, it is learned in a more analytic way: for example, when similarities are noticed between the code and the first language ('Gosh!' – 'That word's like "ten" in Sylheti').

These children appear consciously to be positioning themselves in the words of the text as a code, and, in so doing, attaching the words to the appropriate mental and situational contexts. They may not yet be able to point to the 'plum pudding' when asked, but they are consciously rule-making: 'Is it "D/Gosh" (Sylheti) or "Oh my gosh, my golly/Gosh" (English)'. In this, they are sorting out criterial knowledge for specific tasks. This awareness gives them a firm basis for mastering the appropriate criterial knowledge for school reading, which escapes some of their monolingual peers. They learn the non-arbitrary nature of the written word and are able to possess individual words before they even fully understand them. This is one way of positioning themselves within the text. It questions what is really meant within our paradigm of reading for meaning. Meaning may be different for each child, and possession of words may be a way forward for some.

The teaching of reading has a special role in school; for reading needs to be learned first for school success. Everything else depends upon it. Britton (1970), Heath (1983), Wells (1987), the British National Curriculum Guidelines (*English 5–11*, 1988) and many other studies stress that the school should build upon early home learning in literacy teaching. But *whose* home learning is it to be? How far can the real world of reading conform with what takes place in classrooms, when different children have different real worlds of reading? The real world of books and stories for some children is not the real world for others (Anderson Stokes 1984).

If this is the case, an obvious question is whether all children can naturally be acculturated into reading in school through participation in a practice which is only real for some. If not, we might need to widen our interpretation of the term 'apprenticeship' to include a greater consciousness of teaching and learning of the sort which is involved in an apprenticeship to a skilled trade. Brown, Collins and Duguid (1989) refer to this in the school context as a 'cognitive apprenticeship' and cite examples of a teacher who pursues very definite strategies in mathematics teaching in her aim to authenticate the activities for the children. We might also call this a 'conscious apprenticeship', where we aim to empower children as readers through heightening their awareness of how and why they learn to read, as well as building on their knowledge of what print is and the functions it may serve. Some literacy programmes in Europe and the USA aim at precisely this (Au 1980, Brügelmann 1986).

These factors may begin to explain the paradox with which I began, though they do not solve the problem. When Gillian and others say, 'I can't do it', we may deduce that they feel powerless before the task as they perceive it. Brief examples indicate that these children are confused and disempowered by the teacher, who unconsciously excludes them from reading as it is validated in school. For Gillian to feel she 'can' will involve a 'demystification' (Freire and Macedo 1987) or a 'demythologising' (Fairclough 1990) of the reading process. One way towards this may be the conscious teaching of important boundaries to children from non-school-oriented homes about how to position themselves in reading in school. In so doing, we may begin to give children access to the basic tool with which '...to interrogate and selectively appropriate those aspects of the dominant culture that will provide them with the basis for defining and transforming...the wider social order' (Giroux and McLaren 1986).

Anderson, A.B. and Stokes, S.J. (1984), 'Social and institutional influences on the development and practice of literacy' in H. Goelman, A. Oberg and F. Smith (eds), *Awakening to Literacy*, Heinemann Educational

Au, K.H. (1980), 'Participation structures in a reading lesson with Hawaiian children: analysis of a culturally appropriate instructional event', *Anthropology and Education Quarterly*, vol. XI, no. 2

Baker, C.D. and Freebody, P. (1989), 'Talk around text: construction of textual and teacher authority in classroom discourse' in S. de Castell, A. Luke and C. Luke (eds), *Language, Authority and Criticism*, The Falmer Press

Ben-Zeev, S. (1977), 'The influence of bilingualism on cognitive strategy and cognitive development', *Child Development*, vol. 48

Bereiter, C. (1986), 'The reading comprehension lesson: A commentary on Heap's ethnomethodological analysis', *Curriculum Inquiry*, vol. 16, no. 1

Bernier, N. (1982), 'Beyond instructional context-identification – some thoughts for extending the analysis of deliberate education' in D. Tannen (ed.), *Spoken and written language: exploring orality and literacy*, Advances in Discourse Processes, vol. 9, Ablex

Bernstein, B. (1990), 'The grammar of pedagogy', lecture given at University of London Institute of Education, 16/2/1990

Bloome, D. and Theodorou, E. (1987), 'Analysing teacher-student and student-student discourse' in J. Green, J. Harker and C. Wallat (eds), *Multiple Analysis of Classroom Discourse Practices*, Ablex

Britton, J. (1970). *Language and Learning*, Penguin

Brown, J.S., Collins, A. and Duguid, P. (1989), 'Situated cognition and the culture of learning', *Educational Researcher*, Jan–Feb

Brügelmann, H. (1986), 'Discovering print: a process approach to initial reading and writing in West Germany', *The Reading Teacher*, Dec.

Cazden, C. (1982), 'Contexts for literacy: in the mind and in the classroom', *Journal of Reading Behaviour*, vol. XIV, no. 4

Cochran-Smith, M. (1984), *The Making of a Reader*, Ablex

Dombey, H. (1983), 'Learning the language of books' in M. Meek (ed.), *Opening Moves*, Bedford Way Papers, no. 17, University of London Institute of Education

Eco, U. (1980), *The Name of the Rose*, Picador

English from ages 5–11, The National Curriculum, Nov. 1988, HMSO

Fairclough, N. (1989), *Language and Power*, Longman

Ferguson, C. (1982), 'Simplified registers and linguistic theory' in L. Menn and L. Obler (eds), *Exceptional Language and Linguistic Theory*, N.Y. Academic Press

Freedle, R. (1986), 'Achieving cognitive synthesis of separate language skills: implications for improving literacy' in C.N. Hedley and A.N. Baratta (eds), *Contexts of Reading*, Advances in Discourse Processes, vol. 18, Ablex

Freire, P. and Macedo, D. (1987), *Literacy: reading the word and the world*, Routledge & Kegan Paul

Foucault, M. (1972), *The Archaeology of Knowledge*, Tavistock

Foucault, M. (1977), *Language, Counter-memory, Practice*, Cornell University Press

Gibson, L. (1989), *Literacy Learning in the Early Years: through children's eyes*, Cassell

Giroux, A. and McLaren, P. (1986), 'Teacher education and the politics of engagement: the case for democratic schooling', *Harvard Educational Review*, Aug.

Gregory, E. (1988), 'Reading with mother: a dockland story' in M. Meek and C. Mills (eds), *Language and Literacy in the Primary School*, The Falmer Press

Hamers, J.F. and Blanc, M.H.A. (1990), *Bilinguality and Bilingualism*, Cambridge University Press

Heap, J. (1985), 'Discourse in the introduction of classroom knowledge: reading lessons', *Curriculum Inquiry*, vol. 16, no. 1

Heath, S.B. (1983), *Ways with Words*, Cambridge University Press

Holdaway, D. (1979), *The Foundations of Literacy*, Ashton Scholastic

Hundeide, K. (1985), 'The tacit background of children's judgments' in J.V. Wertsch (ed.), *Culture, Communication and Cognition. Vygotskian Perspectives*, Cambridge University Press

Iser, W. (1978), *The Act of Reading*, John Hopkins University Press

Miller, J. (1983), *Many Voices, Bilingualism, Culture and Education*, Routledge & Kegan Paul

Schieffelin, B.B. and Cochran-Smith, M. (1984), 'Learning to read culturally: literacy before schooling' in H. Goelman, A. Oberg and F. Smith (eds), *Awakening to Literacy*, Heinemann Educational

Schutz, A. (1964), 'The stranger' in *Collected Papers II Studies in Social Theory*, Martinus Nijhoff

Scollon, R. and Scollon, B.K. (1981), *Narrative, Literacy and Face in Interethnic Communication*, Ablex

Street, B. (1984), *Literacy in Theory and Practice*, Cambridge University Press

Volosinov, V.N. (1976), *Freudianism: a Marxist critique*, Academic Press

Walkerdine, V. (1981), 'From context to text: a psychosemiotic approach to abstract thought' in B. Beveridge (ed.), *Children Thinking through Language*, Edward Arnold

Waterland, L. (1985), *Read with Me*, The Thimble Press

Wells, C.G. (1981), *Learning through Interaction: language at home and at school*, vol. I, Cambridge University Press

Wells, C.G. (1987), *The Meaning Makers*, Hodder & Stoughton

Willes, M.J. (1983), *Children into Pupils*, Routledge & Kegal Paul

DAVID LEWIS

Looking for Julius:
two children and a picture book

Modern books for children are often, literally, *new* books in the sense that they invite different kinds of reading from both children and adults. Innovative writers and artists in this domain assert their freedom from what Kress calls 'the stability and persistence over time' of 'institutionalised genres'. The children in this essay like reading. They find John Burningham's invitation to ask, 'Where's Julius?' unproblematic, until their father asks them to re-tell what happens. Then the particularities of the book: repeated formal statements, the piled-up details of food, the wide pictures with no text, all stand in their way. But the children know that Julius is both at home and elsewhere. Their failure to be explicit shows their father how the *metafictive* nature of the book is a formal elaboration of the opposition between the conventions of realistic statement and the artist's iconic presentation of 'pictures in the head'. The significance of this reading experience for all three is that it keeps learning to read 'open', especially at this time, when some other kinds of texts foreclose on children's growing awareness of what reading is good for.

We are just beginning to learn how texts teach and just what it is that they teach. The recognition of the supreme value of the literary text for beginner readers has gained ground in many quarters, no small thanks to the work of Margaret Meek (Meek 1988). However, I believe there is some danger that we may come to assume a higher degree of uniformity across such texts than perhaps we should. This is not so much a question of quality but of the *nature* of what we might call picture book text, that fusion of words and images characteristic of the genre. Of course, there are varieties of fiction and types of text, and picture books may be characterised in myriad ways: illustrated folktales, alphabet books, animal fantasies and so on. However, I am increasingly persuaded that contemporary picture book makers are frequently concerned with matters that cut across, even subvert, the writing and illustration of a story. In their artful and playful juxtaposition of image and word they often seek to draw attention to the fabric of the text itself. Anthony Browne, John Burningham and the Ahlbergs seem to me to be as much interested in how stories are put together and how they work as they are in telling those stories to children. If we might borrow a term coined to designate a similar trend in writing for adults, we might usefully call the work of these picture book makers *metafictive* (Scholes 1979, Hutcheon 1980, Waugh 1984).

Margaret Meek insists that literacy will not stand still while we study it. The conditions of its emergence in the young are perpetually shifting, and that means we need to pay particular attention to the nature of the texts we offer children to learn to read upon. We need to be alert to the ways in which picture book texts may be changing, but our habitual ways of looking at such texts do not always help us to see what is going on. Indeed, the study of the picture book has sometimes obscured many of its most distinctive features rather than revealing them. Looking more closely at the books themselves will help, but it is unlikely to help much unless we keep in mind the primary audience for whom they were written; and we need constantly to remind ourselves of the fact that writers and illustrators work the way they do because they share understandings with their readers. Texts and readers work hand in hand, and to see children's literature whole we need to see children reading.

Accordingly, I wish to consider here an example of two children reading and retelling a popular, contemporary picture book. The two children are my own son and daughter, and the events recorded are part of a programme of reading and retelling that took place over a period of approximately one year towards the end of the 1980s. I shall mainly be concerned with how the children's attempts to retell the story gave some access to their understanding and interpretation of the book; how my own reading of the book differed markedly from those of the children and, most importantly, how their struggles with the text provided insight into its highly distinctive, metafictive character.

The following account of the book in question – *Where's Julius?* by John Burningham – is largely a reflection of my own first reading. I chose this book to read to my children because I felt it bore a strong affinity to other works by the same author; in particular, *Come Away from the Water, Shirley* and *Time to Get Out of the Bath, Shirley*. Both of these books portray the parallel worlds of parent and child, but offer no explicit connection between the two sequences of images as we might expect in a more conventional story. The domestic and mundane adult world is portrayed on the left-hand pages, the fantastic adventures of the little girl on the right. *Where's Julius?* seemed to offer similar contrasts, and I was particularly keen to see how the children coped with this curious splitting into two of what is, ostensibly, one story.

The book opens with Mr and Mrs Troutbeck preparing breakfast for themselves and their son Julius. The reader learns, through Mrs Troutbeck's announcement to the family, what it is they are about to eat. Julius is called and they all sit down. A half-page illustration depicts the family grouped round the dining-table. This initial narrative moment occupies the first recto page. Overleaf, the reader discovers preparations underway for the next meal of the day, lunch. Once more the menu is announced and Julius called for, but this time Mr Troutbeck declares, 'Julius says that he cannot have lunch with us today because he has made a little home in the other room with three chairs, the old curtains and a broom.' As a result, Mr Troutbeck takes a tray bearing lunch to where Julius is busy with his den. Mr Troutbeck is portrayed carrying the tray, whilst the printed text above reiterates what Julius is doing and lists once more the items prepared for lunch. A detailed picture of Julius at work in 'the other room' occupies the following double page spread. His lunch lies uneaten upon a stool, though the family cat is depicted stealing a sardine. There is no printed text.

The next page once more shows a meal in preparation – this time by Mr Troutbeck – and once more Julius is absent. Now, however, it is supper-time, and so we begin to discover that the narrative sequence is given almost solely by this tripartite division of the day into breakfast, lunch and supper. In fact, the pattern is repeated over three days, and to some extent the sequence is hinted at in the pictures illustrating Julius's absences, particularly at supper-time, when the time of day is clearly late afternoon or evening. Julius's activities during his periods of absence from the household are clearly intended to be the source of much of the interest of the book and of its momentum (we want to know what he will get up to next). Although he is present for the initial breakfast, at subsequent mealtimes he is always missing when it it time to eat. He is always elsewhere, preoccupied with his own projects, which develop rapidly from recognisably 'real' and unremarkable childlike activities such as making a den in the spare room, to apparently 'unreal' adventures in the manner of the Shirley books. These adventures, or journeys, place Julius in exotic locations such as half-way up a pyramid in Egypt, or throwing snowballs at wolves in Siberia. Each time a meal is prepared, one of Julius's parents takes his meal to him on a tray, but by the end of the book Julius has relinquished his wanderings and returns to have supper at home once more.

Thus the reader is offered a sequence of narrative moments, the loci of which are the Troutbeck family mealtimes. A formula is established in the first few pages and is adhered to until the resolution at the close. One of the parents announces the details of the current meal and asks the question of the title, 'Where's Julius?' The other parent replies that Julius cannot eat with them and offers the reason: for example that Julius is climbing pyramids, throwing snowballs at wolves, shooting rapids, and so on. One of them then sets off with a tray bearing Julius's meal. These moments are separated by ellipses ('events' in between mealtimes being passed over in silence) and held together in sequence through the known and repeated order of breakfast, lunch and supper.

When I read *Where's Julius?* for the first time I was intrigued and amused by the way in which the boy's activities shift from a kind of everyday realism (building dens, digging holes) to outrageous fantasy. Burningham offers no clue as to what is going on but simply leaves the puzzle in the reader's lap, just as he does in the Shirley books. Julius, like Shirley, appears to be in two stories (or two kinds of story) at the same time. Thus if *Where's Julius?* is to be considered a story at all, then it is a very strange story indeed.

Both children were just as amused and intrigued by *Where's Julius?* as I had been, but what arrested their attention most of all was not the whereabouts of the eponymous central character, but an altogether different feature of the book, one that had escaped my notice entirely. *Where's Julius?*, it turned out, was even more unconventional than I had supposed. The focus of their attention began to emerge clearly as they attempted to retell the story some time after they had first encountered it.

I had bought the book one February afternoon with the intention of introducing it to the children later on that same day. On their return from school I told them that I had a new book and that we might read it that evening. Simon, who was just short of his eighth birthday at this time, began to look through the book, reading odd passages out aloud, commenting on the pictures, relating events to his own life ('You don't let me do that.'). Appropriately, given the book's theme, this first reading was interrupted by tea-time and then completed after the meal. Half an hour or so later I asked Simon to read the book to me. This he willingly did, adopting a characteristic 'performance' voice and prefacing the story by listing author, illustrator – and reader!

He hesitated over some unfamiliar and exotic-sounding names 'Neffatuteum' and 'Novosty Krosky', which he pronounced slowly and carefully, and he commented on several of the large pictures, each time pointing out that some part of Julius's meal was being stolen by one of the creatures portrayed there, details I had missed on my first reading. He regularly employed a parodic, sing-song, up-and-down intonation for those passages and phrases that were repeated at intervals throughout the book.

Later that same evening I suggested to Claire that she might like to hear the story and look at the book, too. Claire is two and a half years younger than her brother and she very much wanted me to read it to her as a bed-time story. So once she was settled in bed I sat beside her and we began. Claire was keen to talk about the author's name (John) and how other writers and illustrators that she knew had the same name, but once I began the story she was reluctant to intrude upon the telling; even though I tried to make opportunities for her to do so, particularly when we stopped to look at the large pictures. Like her brother she quickly recognised that each picture showed some creature in the act of stealing a part of Julius's meal, but her comments and questions tended to be brief, undeveloped responses to my gentle promptings. We had a brief discussion about what was being stolen from the sleigh by the wolves and what the fish in the final picture was holding in its mouth.

On the whole, though, Claire seemed reluctant to disturb the telling of the story for too long. The only point at which she seemed to be keen to elaborate upon the text was at the very end, when she wished to go back to count all of Julius's 'journeys'. Both children clearly enjoyed the book and neither of them made any remark to suggest that they felt the book to be in any way curious or unusual. After a period of one or two weeks, during which both children returned to the book from time to time, I asked first Simon and then Claire if they would retell the story to me.

In making this request I had no wish to 'test' the children in terms of the accuracy with which they might reproduce the text as printed, though both children did at first attempt to give a verbatim account of the book. Rather, I wished to see if retelling might provide some clues as to the nature of their reading of the story. It turned out to be the first story which both of them found extremely difficult to retell, and their difficulties – along with their attempts to overcome them – seemed to be related very closely to certain specific features of the text. It is these difficulties which I now wish to focus upon, as I believe they provide insight not only into what the children took to be the 'story' of *Where's Julius?*, but also into the nature of the text itself and into the ways in which that text guided their reading.

Both children foundered in their attempts at retelling very early on. In fact, Simon made two attempts separated by about a week. They both tried to recreate the details of each meal, but time and again they lost track of the order of the meals and were unable to continue giving details much beyond the first breakfast. They were both reduced to asking directly for assistance 'What are [they] having for lunch...?'; 'What is he doing...?'; and both finally resorted to substituting conventional nonsense syllables for the content of each meal: 'So Mr Troutbeck took the tray with the blah, blah, blah, blah, blah...'

They were noticeably more confident when recounting Julius's 'journeys', even though they both eventually gave up the attempt at trying to fit the journeys into the sequence of meals and days. With the smallest amount of prompting – 'What happened? What did Julius do?' – Claire was able to list Julius's adventures, omitting only one, and Simon, at his second attempt, once he had given up the struggle to recall the meals, could also recount each adventure in the correct order, including the final suggestion that Julius might be teaching the baby owls to fly or tucking up polar bears.

Both children were greatly frustrated and a little distressed at their inability to tell me the story as well as they had wished. They had not met such problems before, having coped with deficiencies of memory by condensing or telescoping events – indeed, summarising – or by embroidering and filling in gaps with their own inventions, Claire being rather more likely to adopt the latter strategy than Simon.

As they attempted to retell *Where's Julius?* both children seemed under a compulsion to give back the story in detail as accurately as possible. They appeared to have a need to 'speak the book'. Simon seemed to be trying to conjure the story into existence by launching himself confidently into his account of the first meal. Neither of the children employed conventional framing devices such as 'once upon a time' or 'once there was a boy called Julius', or attempted to explain who the characters in the story were. There was no easing of the listener into the world of the book. Both children began very much at the beginning as they recalled that beginning from the first page.

Where's Julius? begins *in medias res* with Mrs Troutbeck's announcement of the first meal of the day. The only concession to the reader is to identify the speaker as Mrs Troutbeck, since the picture above the written text gives no clue as to who is speaking. On subsequent pages the illustrations cue the reader into who the speaker is, and Burningham dispenses with the verbal attribution. With such a distinctive opening it is perhaps no surprise that the children should wish to fit their own retellings on to its clear contours.

I believe, however, that there are reasons over and above the singularity of the book's opening that may account for why both Simon and Claire insistently grope for the details of the story right up to the point where, as far as the mealtimes are concerned, the task defeats them and they either give up altogether or substitute repetitive nonsense for the elusive detail, thus undercutting their efforts as storytellers. The reasons lie in the way *Where's Julius?'* has been put together, and we must return to an examination of its form to clarify just why Simon and Claire had such a hard time.

If we temporarily put to one side a consideration of the visual imagery of the book and focus our attention upon the way in which the narrative is verbally carried we find that it is both episodic and repetitive in form, being constructed from events which are largely similar in structure. Gerard Genette's analysis of narrative frequency in *Narrative Discourse* (Genette 1980) is of great help in understanding this particular characteristic of *Where's Julius?*. In brief, he states that,

> a narrative, whatever it is, may tell once what happened
> once, *n* times what happened *n* times, *n* times what happened
> once, once what happened *n* times.

Narrating once what happened once Genette calls the *singulative*, as he does the narrating *n* times of what happened *n* times; the latter being a special case of the former. Narrating once what happened *n* times Genette refers to as the *iterative*: thus several occurrences of the same event might be gathered up by a narrator in a phrase such as 'once a week...' or, 'everyday...'. Genette stresses that the similarity invoked by such a phrase as '*the same event*' can only be the sameness of analogy and not of identity, since events grouped together in this way are only *construed* as 'the same' at some appropriate level of abstraction.

> The repetition is in fact a mental construction which
> eliminates from each occurrence everything belonging to it
> that is peculiar to itself, in order to preserve only what it
> shares with all the others of the same class.

The episodic character of *Where's Julius?* indicates clearly that it belongs as a whole to the singulative mode. Each mealtime, and each of Julius's adventures, is presented in some detail, both visually and verbally, and there are no instances of the formulae characteristic of the iterative, events and occurrences being specific in terms of both time and place. However, if *Where's Julius?* is singulative narrative the *repetitiveness* would seem to indicate that it is at the limit point of its singularity, at least as far as the verbal delineation of events is concerned. Although the menus for each meal are reported in great detail (a fact we shall return to shortly), as are the precise whereabouts of Julius each time he goes missing, the overall outline of these narrative moments is virtually identical. There is also a good deal of formulaic repetition: 'Julius says he cannot have breakfast/lunch/supper...'; 'So Mr/Mrs Troutbeck took the tray...' and so on. If the tale were embedded in a longer narrative then it would be very easy for its singulative form to be collapsed into the iterative. The words come readily to mind: 'Every mealtime...'; 'Julius *was always* missing...'; 'Julius *always* says he cannot have lunch...' etc. Genette states that,

> In the classical narrative...iterative sections are almost
> always functionally subordinate to singulative scenes, for
> which the iterative sections provide a sort of informative
> frame or background.

In *Where's Julius?* Burningham rejects the 'classical narrative', playfully and knowingly levering open the iterative and returning it to the singulative.

It is this curious formal twist which, at least in part, is responsible for the children's difficulties with retelling, as they are asked to base the story upon a sequence of events and occurrences which are scarcely distinguishable and differ only at the level of surface detail. The effect is one of difference within overall sameness, and it is the effort to capture and hold that difference which so preoccupies the children in their attempts at recall. Both were clearly disturbed by this effect, and Simon became self-consciously aware of the reasons for his difficulty towards the end of his second attempt at retelling:

DL   Why do you think it was so hard to remember?
Simon   Because...they give the same things over and over
        again but with very detailed and different-each-
        time things.

Both children were highly sensitive to this particular feature of the text. Their parodic intonation when reading and retelling, their amusement at the endless round of menus and meals and the frustrated attempts to give back the story, all testify to their fascination with the curiously cumulative nature of the text. For Simon and Claire, *Where's Julius?* was a story that grew and expanded but never really went anywhere, anchored to one spot (mealtimes) by an excess of detail.

We can only come to see the significance of the fact that *Where's Julius?* is excessive if we are prepared to acknowledge the conventionality of story texts. There is nothing natural about narrative discourse in general or about that species of it that Genette calls 'classical narrative'. It may *seem* natural and unremarkable, for its very ubiquity lends it a certain degree of transparency and obviousness. Furthermore, classical narrative, or classic realist text as it is sometimes called, achieves its effects precisely by effacing the traces of its embodiment in language. As we read we cease to be aware of the words on the page or the book in our hands.

Genette indicates one convention of such story text: '...iterative sections are almost always functionally subordinate to singulative scenes...' In other words, particularised, detailed events are usually set against a background which summarises information that is functionally less important. This is one of the ways in which, as readers, we are invited to make sense of events and build up a sense of verisimilitude. Whether we realise it or not, the information contained in stories is ordered in a hierarchy with some details given more prominence than others. We are never told *everything* about a character, a scene or an event (indeed, how could we be?), but just enough for us to be able to construct as lifelike an image as is appropriate within a particular genre.

Susan Stewart, in her book *On Longing*, puts it like this,

> Realistic genres do not mirror everyday life: they mirror its
> hierarchisation of information. They are mimetic in the
> stance they take towards this organization and hence are
> mimetic of values not of the material world.

Such hierarchies, however, can be disturbed and undermined in a variety of ways, and telling more than is necessary is one of them. Going too far might of course simply be the result of incompetence or inexperience; first novels, for example, are frequently 'overwritten'. But excess can also be a fully literary technique and thus a convention in its own right, a *deliberate* going too far, whose very purpose is to parody familiar literary tropes and raise to consciousness the elaborate decorum and artificiality of the classic realist text.

Although we readily find such excess in the work of those writers for adults whose work has been variously termed Postmodern or Metafictive (see for example the work of Thomas Pynchon or Donald Barthelme) it is still relatively rare in mainstream contemporary fiction. It is also rare in prose narratives for children. Indeed Jacqueline Rose argues that the domain of children's literature has become the (seemingly) natural home for writing of the classic realist kind:

> The writing that is currently being promoted for children is
> that form of writing which asks its reader to enter into the
> story and to take its world as real, without questioning how
> that world has been constituted, or where, or who it comes
> from.   (Rose 1984)

And again:

> Nothing must obtrude, and no word must be spoken, in
> excess of those which are absolutely necessary to convince
> the child that the world in which he or she is being asked to
> participate is, unquestionably, real.

How strange then that we should find here, in a book designed and marketed for those readers at the very beginning of their journey into literacy, a literary device usually found in texts for the most experienced and sophisticated. Rose is concerned with the kind of extended prose text that would be offered to older, more experienced child readers and not with the picture book form as such, but I believe a study of the kinds of picture book currently widely available in schools and libraries would reveal high levels of playful experiment with story forms. Indeed, I have argued elsewhere (Lewis 1990) that the metafictive has come to find a home in the domain of the contemporary picture book in much the same way, though admittedly not to the same extent, as the classical narrative has colonised the children's novel.

Where's Julius?, it seems to me, is an excellent example of a book for the young that refuses to take for granted the settled and time-honoured norms of how stories should be told and written. As we read it we are confronted with a piling up of detail that appears to lack the normal ordering principles that we might expect to find.

> To describe more than is socially adequate or to describe in
> a way which interrupts the everyday hierarchical
> organisation of detail is to increase not realism but *the unreal*
> *effect of the real*.   Stewart (1984)

Thus, in so far as it deals with the content of the individual meals, and in so far as it invites the reader to grasp a sequence of events – that is, it offers a description of the three days of breakfast, lunch and supper – *Where's Julius?* appears to be 'realistic', but it contains an excess of detail, an accumulation robbed of hierarchy and thus of value. The reader is left with little guidance as to how to order or synthesise this superabundant material, for children's stories about home life do not usually bombard their readers with quite so much indigestible data without development or incident.

In attempting to retell the 'story' of *Where's Julius?* both Simon and Claire were drawn towards giving back as accurate an account as they could manage of the written text. A summary would necessitate collapsing singulative scenes into the iterative mode wherever appropriate and, as we have seen, *Where's Julius?* consists almost entirely of scenes which are so much alike that summary treatment would rob them of whatever value and interest they might have. The fascination – and humour – of these scenes lies not in their articulation into a drama or a climax, as we might expect in a more conventional narrative, but in the relentless piling up of surface detail. On reflection it is perhaps not really surprising that Julius should wish to escape from such enthusiastically pedantic parents! The problem for anyone attempting to retell *Where's Julius?* is that there is really only this detail to work with and, as Simon and Claire discovered, accurate recall requires enormous effort.

Despite the fact that it is difficult to retell I would not wish to imply that the book is an effort and a chore to *read*. On the contrary. As one might expect with a

Burningham book, it is actually great fun. If there were only the long-winded accounts of the mealtimes to look at and to read then it most certainly would be a strange book, but we must not lose sight of the fact that it is a *picture* book and that there is a rhythm and a pattern provided by the pictures. It is to a consideration of the pictures that we must now turn.

We might begin to approach this question of the nature and the role of the pictures by recalling that the children were far more confident in their recollections of where Julius was when he was missing than they were about what it was he was being offered to eat. The verbal form of each escapade is not so different from that of each meal – a bald, rather direct statement of where he is. The contents of the meal and Julius's whereabouts are then reiterated as one of the parents carries off Julius's meal on a tray. Why then do the children find this aspect of the story easier to manage? One reason clearly has to do with the fact that each of Julius's adventures is not just verbally recounted but pictorially present to the reader, who has an aid to interpretation and recollection through the visual imagery of the book.

It could be objected that the same argument might be applied to the verbal and visual depiction of the meals. After all, the reader is shown as well as told what the Troutbecks have to eat. However, these two sets of pictures fall into two distinct categories and, in as much as pictorial images will submit to the analysis of narrative frequency offered earlier, those belonging to the latter category (the visual depiction of the meals) may be seen as possessing as little significant singularity as the printed text that accompanies them, at least as far as the movement of the narrative is concerned. To put the matter simply, there is not much difference between the visual imagery of breakfast, lunch and supper. There are the differences of detail noted above, which correspond in a traditional illustrative way with the written text (what Maurice Sendak has called 'narrative illustration' – see Lanes 1981): tomatoes on plates, chops in a grill pan, toast in a toaster; but in terms of narrative function these images are scarcely distinguishable. The large, bold depictions of Julius 'else-where' are another matter altogether.

There is a great temptation, for adult readers in particular, to perceive the pictures in picture books as performing always and only the illustrative function noted above. That is, as 'bodying forth' iconically what is already there in the written text. In addition, the pictures often appear to be the site of operations for a sort of cultural code. Thus we learn from the pictures information *not* given in the printed text: the social class of the characters, the cultural milieu in which they move, the age in which the author or illustrator has set them (eighteenth-century, Victorian, pre-war, sixties and so on). Although the pictures of Julius's adventures do perform these functions, in that they appear to relate directly and unambiguously to the text on the previous pages and show in a way that writing never can what is going on and where and how, they nevertheless differ from the sketchier, less prominent figures in a number of ways. Most notably, they possess precisely that singularity and distinc-tiveness so noticeably absent from the domestic mealtime imagery, and this in itself might be enough to account for the fact that both children were able to recall and retell these episodes with some degree of accuracy.

Once the pattern of the book is established every second turn of the page reveals an image of Julius at work, at play or simply sitting and watching, in locations as geographically disparate as they could possibly be. The pictures are boldly coloured and convey something of the hazy heat of the desert, the breathtaking cold of the

Siberian night and the awesomeness of sunrise in the Himalayas. Such scenes are able to capture and hold the reader's gaze in a way that the embedded illustrations do not.

These pictures then are compelling and distinctive. They lodge in the mind and enable the reader to hold on to an image of what is happening in the tale. Claire's recollection of the 'journeys' came with just a little prompting once she had given up the attempt to tell the story as a story:

DL	...what did Julius do?
Claire	Julius did all sorts of things. He dugged a hole.
DL	Hmmm
Claire	He...made a house.
DL	Hmmm
Claire	He...climbed a pyramid.
DL	Hmmm
Claire	He saw the sun rise.
DL	Hmmm
Claire	He killed the fish.
DL	Hmmm
Claire	He...he threw snowballs at the wolves... and then... Mrs... just a... this is a little bit with Mrs Troutbeck... and at the end when Mrs Troutbeck said, where's Julius? is he doing all those journeys, and then she said, or is he teaching the owls to fly or is he tucking the polar bears in their nice beds? And... Mr Troutbeck said, Sally – which is her name – Ju... today Julius is having tea with us. That's all I can really remember.

Each description is a neat summary of Julius's activity and, interestingly, no attempt is made to recapture the original *verbal* form of each event. Her account of what Julius is doing on the Chico Neeko river ('He killed the fish') is at odds with what the text states, i.e. that Julius is about to 'shoot the rapids on the Chico Neeko river somewhere in Peru in South America'. It seems that here Claire has taken the (verbal) metaphor of 'shooting' (the rapids) literally and is relying upon her memory of the *picture*, where a fish cheekily steals some lettuce from Julius's tray, to find an object for the shooting, as there is no mention of the fish in the printed text, and to shoot the rapids literally would produce a nonsense. She had in fact referred to this image earlier in her retelling, shortly after having given up the attempt to recall the story: 'Well, the last one is him going to kill some fish on a raft he had built.' We had also briefly discussed this picture when I had first read the story to her and her attention and interest then seemed focused upon the fish and the theft of the lettuce leaf.

The only point in her listing of 'journeys' at which Claire attempted to reproduce the characteristic wording of the text was the one place where she had *no* support from the pictures. What she says relates to the penultimate page in the book, where the narrator speculates upon what Julius might be doing and suggests he might be 'helping the young owls to fly in the trees at the end of the road or tucking the polar bears in their beds somewhere in Antarctica'. Claire rendered this as follows:

> Is he teaching the owls to fly or is he tucking the polar bears
> in their nice beds?

In order to give back this form of words she switches tense so that she is no longer simply recalling and listing journeys, but has temporarily resumed the attempt to retell the story and so is once more back in 'performance mode'.

There seemed to be something about these verbally expressed images which appealed to both of the children. Simon too was amused by this final speculation and reproduced it like this:

> I suppose he's...teaching baby owls to fly in the trees at the
> end of our road...or...tucking polar bears in their beds
> somewhere in Antarctica.

The pictures in *Where's Julius?* then seem to fall into two broad categories: those that accompany the domestic scenes and those that atmospherically and powerfully depict the sites of Julius's wanderings. The former tend to be, like the written text, rather similar in outline and not especially memorable. The latter are large and bold and are clearly designed for uninterrupted contemplation. What we have not yet considered is just what kinds of story worlds these two sets of pictures illustrate.

The desire of the children to 'get it right' is, as I have argued, due in part to the structure of the book and to the implicit invitation within the written text. What counts as retelling *Where's Julius?* properly or adequately – at least for these two children – is the recapturing and re-presenting of largely surface detail, larger narrative movements having been suppressed. I have also argued that their repeated failure to retell the story in this way is due to the excessive nature of this surface detail. In contrast, the children were able to recall with some clarity the sites and sequence of Julius's wanderings and they seemed to be aided in this by the large double page pictures interspersed throughout the text. These pictures are clearly not superficial in the way that the mealtime imagery is. They are gloriously gripping images involving action and feeling.

Quite what is going on in these scenes is a question to which we have not yet addressed ourselves, along with the question of how they relate to the text which they follow. Simon and Claire seemed not at all perturbed by the switch from recognisable and familiar domestic play (building dens) to an altogether more indeterminate realm of the fantastic (climbing pyramids). It is, however, important that we ask, and seek to answer, the question of just where Julius *is* at these moments in order for us to understand the nature of the textual game that Burningham plays. The risk is that we may misdescribe *Where's Julius?* at the very moment when we are closest to seeing what is going on. For there is a strong invitation within the text to perceive events as all belonging to the same generic category, that of consistent realism. Our urge to naturalise the tale, to normalise it in this way, is encouraged by an author/illustrator intent upon subverting the very expectations he arouses.

Todorov (1980) tells us that 'a text always contains within itself directions for its own consumption', and the first few pages of *Where's Julius?* appear to contain quite unambiguous directions. As the story begins there is an easy elision between pictures and text. They cohere not only at the level of visual image illustrating print, but also in terms of our understanding of the everyday world. The phenomenon of parents calling for children at mealtimes is wholly unremarkable, as is the deeply engrossing activity of building dens. There are no surprises here. Children are often absent at mealtimes, preoccupied with their play. Even the idea of Julius digging his hole in a field surrounded by cows and wide open spaces does little to subvert this coherence. It merely compels us to modify and extend our minimal knowledge of the Trout-becks' domestic surroundings. But how does Julius make the leap from the twilit plains of rural England to the parched deserts of Egypt in the space of apparently one night? Having accepted the lure of the opening pages we are now in a fix. The temptation is to avoid rocking the boat and to see Julius's bizarre behaviour as existing in his head, as a daydream or fantasy. In other words, to hold on to the set of directions that we began with and embed Julius's behaviour within the form of realism we have been beguiled into accepting.

However, if we make this readerly move there are further problems in store, for we have to account for the presence in Julius's imaginings of his father in shirt, tie and slippers gingerly stepping over the sands and keeping an eye on a marauding vulture. It is, of course, not impossible to accommodate the outrageous, particularly in a children's picture book, but it is very difficult to do it whilst simultaneously maintaining the decorum of the quotidian. An alternative and, I believe, more helpful reading might begin from an acknowledgement that Burningham *changes* the rules part way through. What we need to recognise is the shift in the generic status of the text that takes place when Mr Troutbeck announces Julius's journey up the pyramid: '...he is riding a camel to the top of the tomb of Neffatuteum...' is superfic-ially akin to '...he is digging a hole...' and '...he has made a little home in the other room...' but we are given a clear signal, both in words and pictures, that this is not the same kind of story world at all. The rules here are different. Had *Where's Julius?* begun with a little middle-class boy in short pants wandering the globe we would automatically have located the tale within some rule system that made sense of what was going on, some sub-genre of fantasy. As it is there are plenty of indications to suggest that an alternative reading of *Where's Julius?* might well lie in the regular, systematic alternations of the book (Burningham only changes the rules once – his little joke at our expense) and the juxtaposition of highly detailed, indeed excessive, realism with events and images that stem from the literary realm of fantasy.

The book gains its coherence through this zig-zag movement from the mundane to the fantastic and back again, but with a clear separation between the two modes, a physical separation through the book's pagination and through the ways in which the two realms are presented. It is clear that the bold visual images need not be inter-preted in terms of what has gone before and are not in fact part of the same secondary world at all – the lack of frame or border, the lack of divisive, determining text – despite the fact that the initial movement of the narrative, such as it is, seems to imply that events on the different pages all belong to the same story world.

In short, the book invites the reader to take part in a *game*. Burningham, through the book, *plays* with the reader's expectations: expectations of how a story should proceed, of what can be left out and what should be put in, of how different genres work, of how to read fantasy and how to read realism.

My own first readings of the book left me amused but faintly perplexed by the 'problem' of where Julius actually was. I took this one feature of the story to be a pivotal point around which any interpretation of the tale must move. I also fel. it was less easy to naturalise, in the manner described above, than, say, *Come Away from the water, Shirley*, where the mundane and fantastic imagery can be contemplated literally side by side. However, there is no evidence from any of the transcripts that the children were at all troubled by this aspect of the text, though they certainly found the book funny. No comments or remarks were made at the stage where the book was being read, and during the retellings there was no indication that the children were trying to normalise the text by trying to account for the juxtaposition of incompatible worlds or that they were particularly disturbed or puzzled by its effects. Claire simply referred to Julius's 'journeys' when counting them, and later, when listing them, she drew no distinction between 'he dugged a hole' and 'he climbed a pyramid'. Both children seemed to accept the change in the rules and the alternating pattern without demur.

It is difficult to interpret the children's silence on this matter. It may simply be that they were familiar enough with Burningham's oeuvre, and with books of a like kind, to find them unremarkable. It may also be the case that children who are still learning what it means to read as well as what books can do, are less beguiled by the opening pages than we might suppose. What constitutes a book has to be learned, and that includes the rules by which one might read it. When writers offer contrasting rule systems within one book and play off our expectations in a spirit of fun, such games and playfulness are more readily accepted perhaps by the apprentices than by their masters precisely because they have a less fully formed set of preconceptions. An adult reader might wish for a more determinate answer to the question 'Where's Julius?' than the author is willing to provide, but a child may find such a question less pressing and consequently may not find the indeterminacy too troublesome.

David Lodge, an early enthusiast for Postmodern fiction, claims in his book *The Modes of Modern Writing* that the metafictive techniques he describes only work against the perceived background of more traditional and more widely understood forms of narrative discourse, for Postmodernism is,

> essentially a rule-breaking kind of art and unless people are still trying to keep the rules there is no point in breaking them and no interest in seeing them broken.

Children who are busily *learning* the rule-book are also intrigued and delighted by rule breaking, but books like *Where's Julius?* – and there are many – seem to offer more than the simple pleasure of the topsy-turvy or the nonsense rhyme. They seem to foreground the very textuality of the book itself. The broken rules and subverted conventions draw to the reader's attention the inner workings of the text and put up barriers against any easy entry into the illusory world of realism. *Where's Julius?* can be read as a comical story about a rather strange family, but that would be to miss its most distinctive and, I believe, its most important features. If we are willing to heed its lessons then I think that *Where's Julius?* can teach us a great deal about children's books and about the nature of reading. Furthermore, if the kind of literacy we wish for our children is a *critical* literacy, if we wish them to have some understanding of how different forms of writing work – and work upon *them*, as readers – then we could do far worse than to explore effective and appropriate ways of using books like *Where's Julius?* with beginner readers.

Genette, G. (1980), *Narrative Discourse: an essay in method*, Basil Blackwell
Hutcheon, L. (1980), *Narcissistic Narrative: the metafictional paradox*, Wilfrid Laurier University Press
Lanes, S. (1981), *The Art of Maurice Sendak*, The Bodley Head
Lodge, D. (1977), *The Modes of Modern Writing: metaphor, metonymy and the typology of modern literature*, Edward Arnold
Meek, M. (1988), *How Texts Teach What Readers Learn*, Thimble Press
Rose, J. (1984), *The Case of Peter Pan, or the Impossibility of Children's Fiction*, Macmillan
Scholes, R. (1979), *Fabulation and Metafiction*, University of Illinois Press
Stewart, S. (1984), *On Longing: narratives of the miniature, the gigantic, the souvenir, the collection*, Johns Hopkins University Press
Todorov, T. (1980), 'Reading as construction' in S. Suleiman and I. Crosman, *The Reader in the Text: essays on audience and interpretation*, Princeton University Press
Waugh, P. (1984), *Metafiction: the theory and practice of self-conscious fiction*, Methuen

Children's books
Burningham, J. (1978), *Come Away From the Water, Shirley*, Cape
Burningham, J. (1978), *Time to Get Out of the Bath, Shirley*, Cape
Burningham, J. (1986), *Where's Julius?*, Cape

PART TWO

The Public Face of Literacy

Literacy is not synonymous with education. Learning to read and write in school is neither the beginning nor the end of the variety of social practices linked to these skills. In this section the writers address the English teacher's obligations and responsibilities for teaching reading and writing. They also examine the socially and politically charged 'need to link language and literature, young people's identities, culture and history'. These words are Tony Burgess's, in his critique of Richard Rorty, a contemporary philosopher who argues for 'redescriptions' in a new literary and liberal culture. Peter Traves suggests the emptiness of a system of compulsory schooling in literacy which, while seeming to offer to all extended, purposeful control over the events in their lives, actually delivers to some 'a culturally privileged activity and to others a continuation of the tradition of barking at print'. As Keith Kimberley makes plain, demands for the assessment of pupils' progress and for accountability in teachers' performance cannot begin to be met by the effects of normative testing. Alex McLeod uses Bakhtin's idea of the 'dialogic imagination' to explore what may be at once creative and transformational in learning to write: 'picking for oneself is a very social act'. In contrast, the extent to which literacy is for some children 'a forced march through enemy territory' is woven through the significant examples of Harold Rosen's piece. He looks to the universal skill of storytelling to redress such a notion of literacy and to expand learners' abilities to subvert oppressive practices. John Hardcastle, in the final piece in this section, watches three boys in a London school as they learn to understand and describe their particular historical and cultural inheritance and experience.

TONY BURGESS

Liberal Ironists and English Teachers: the philosophy of Richard Rorty

The last sentence of this essay indicates what has happened in it. As a teacher of English who continues to relate what he knows and does to an analysis of culture and history, Tony Burgess is here concerned to *move on* the philosophical understandings of his colleagues. He does this by tracking his own reflections and awareness through the main statements of a major modern philosopher. As he does so, he makes plain the need to change, extend and particularise theories about 'creativity' and 'responsibility', as these apply to English teaching, so as to include ideas of difference and inequality. Doing so, he claims, will involve educators in making decisions about how to respond to a national curriculum embodying particular political constraints. By extending the scope of what is implied by 'English teaching' this essay also introduces topics that are developed in the rest of this section.

I begin with a rather general argument.

Human minds did not exist before the seventeenth century. The modern conception of mind was invented by Descartes in the course of resolving questions about knowledge. Descartes freed science from religion by identifying an inner space where at least ideas might be known with certainty.

Descartes connected by this manoeuvre three separate questions which have no need to be put together: whether the world exists, whether human knowledge can be relied upon and whether humans have special inner spaces such as minds. His philosophy helped to secularise knowledge, but in doing so created the problem of knowledge in its classical form.

Locke strengthened the psychological orientation which had been given to the problem of knowledge by proposing that through study of how the mind worked more could be learned about what humans could know. Hume inserted scepticism about causes and inferences. The stage was set for Kant to resolve Humean doubts and to secure a foundational role for philosophy among the sciences as the arbiter for claims to know. Kant's solution, however, retained the essentials of the Cartesian mind and of the Cartesian formulation of the problem of knowledge.

> Kant put philosophy 'on the secure path of a science' by putting outer space inside inner space (the space of the constituting activity of the transcendental ego) and then claiming Cartesian certainty about the inner for the laws of what had previously been thought to be outer. He thus reconciled the Cartesian claim that we can have certainty only about our ideas with the fact that we already had certainty – a priori knowledge – about what seemed not to be ideas. (Rorty, 1980, p. 137).

But to 'know' that something is the case is to make a claim in language. It is for someone to put a proposition into a certain kind of logical space in which it is claimed that there are grounds for believing it. The logic of this claim has nothing to do with whether or not a world exists out there, nor with whether the human mind has a particular psychological or physiological composition. The seventeenth century confused 'knowledge of' with 'knowledge that'. Kant's solution took some steps towards an account of 'knowing that' but was still propelled historically by the Cartesian identification of ontology, epistemology and mind.

Rather than spend time disputing these particular classical doctrines, the whole formulation of the problem should be dissolved. What if we were to do this? Twentieth-century culture still clings to a belief in the possibility of grounding knowledge in an independent truth. As creatures of our time, we still want to believe in a truth which is out there in the universe, a truth which is 'Nature's own'. Suppose that we gave up this hope. Suppose that we accepted that truth is a matter of human sentences and not something in the world. We would then be freed to see new possibilities. We would come to value the resources of our culture for different reasons and in a new way.

The argument is that of Richard Rorty, a contemporary American professor of philosophy who, in three books published in the 1980s, has been arguing the case for a new kind of philosophy conceived for new times. Rorty shares with others a critique of traditional epistemology and a critique of empiricist and positivist science. But he has developed a distinctive set of arguments. Rorty is a philosophical pragmatist and a political liberal. More, he is a radical in both directions. He wants us to accept root and branch the lessons of post-Wittgensteinian philosophy. He wants science, philosophy, culture to move on.

Increasingly, Rorty's voice has had an edge which might be called critical were it not at the same time so urbane and were his method in philosophy not one of beckoning to new positions rather than seeking to demolish old ones. His writing has been moving out of philosophy and into cultural criticism. So far the argument may seem to have had relatively little bearing on English teaching. But the gap has been closing in Rorty's more recent writing and it is consistent with his intentions that it should.

A culture which had given up any lingering hope in a truth out there in the universe would re-describe science and would come to take a new kind of interest in literature. Rorty shows us how. In doing so he links the thought of Kuhn, a philosopher of science, with that of Davidson, a philosopher of language. Kuhn has shown (Rorty says) that radical change in scientific theory is a matter of paradigm shift rather than rejection as false of a specific set of propositions. Scientific theories are not so much disproved as abandoned in the light of changed terms in the argument. Davidson's account of metaphor adds interestingly to this account.

A metaphor for Davidson is not the continuation of literal conversation by other means. A metaphor is inserted into literal language like a cough or an interjection. Metaphors are not so much chosen as caused. Once they become mere alternatives within literal discourse they no longer have the same force. Rorty's point is that if we give up the idea of science as a slow accretion of discovered truth we shall be freed to see change in scientific theory as the arrival of new metaphors. We shall be alerted to the radical nature of change in scientific theory (Rorty, 1989, pp. 10–20).

Intellectual life, generally, is less a matter of propositions and sentences than vocabularies. Sentences mean alongside other sentences, and theories trade in whole vocabularies rather than specific truths. Rorty again follows Davidson in putting at the centre of our picture of language not a single object but historically contingent vocabularies developed to describe bits of the world.

> 'Interesting philosophy,' Rorty remarks, 'is rarely an examination of the pros and cons of a thesis. Usually it is, implicitly or explicitly, a contest between an entrenched vocabulary which has become a nuisance and a half-formed new vocabulary which vaguely promises great things.'
> (Rorty, 1989, p. 9)

As with science, then, so with philosophy – and so, more generally, with every-day debates and everyday uses of language.

If there is no ultimate truth out there in the universe waiting to be discovered, it follows that the place of science in culture and with it the place of philosophy should be re-stated. So long as knowledge was thought central to culture, science set the terms for other disciplines. Philosophy kept its 'first' position, given it by Kant, as adjudicator of science's claims to know. But in a culture which had moved on, beyond hopes for absolute truth, philosophy would become part of a 'conversation'. A creative concern to describe and re-describe reality would replace hard-nosed disputes about claims to knowledge.

Rorty's evocation of this culture brings into view a world which English teachers might be supposed to favour. The role of the sciences would recede. Philosophy would cease to hold its former privileged position and would become one among a number of edifying discourses. There would be talk of playfulness with ideas. A central place would be occupied by literature and by literary criticism rather than philosophy. We should appreciate literary criticism (as we are coming to) as a unifying form of discourse, one which connects together novels, poetry, plays and philosophy with other vocabularies of theoretical description.

For this vision of a re-shaped culture to catch on, it needs to be anchored in a version of social as well as merely intellectual conduct. Rorty provides this ethical and political dimension in his most recent book. Here, complementing the radical pragmatism of his account of knowledge, Rorty argues for what may be described as a radically liberal version of social conduct in which a sharp separation is maintained between the public and the private spheres. This argument is approached by Rorty through an original reading of Freud and a linking of this reading to the account of the strong poet given by the American literary critic, Harold Bloom.

Traditionally, ethical discussion has centred round prudence and the justification of moral principles. Faced with what they took to be an unregenerate human nature, philosophers and moralists have chiefly asked how human beings could be brought to accept principles of morality and justice in a manner which saw that this was in their own interests but was also disinterested. To many late nineteenth-century interpreters and their successors, Freud seemed to pose the darkest of all challenges to morality. In showing the appetitive, secret and unknown side of human beings, it appeared that he questioned the very possibility of rational conduct.

Rorty turns this interpretation on its head. Rorty's Freud, by contrast, rather than just revealing human nature's darker side, provided a new way of thinking about the moral self by tracking its formation back to the contingencies of upbringing. Freud demonstrated that it is this pre-formed moral self which needs to be escaped in the interests of a more creative morality. Moral life, on this understanding, is not so much a matter of will or submission to principle, but is like the life of poetry talked about by Bloom, where the problem is to escape the past in order to create new possibilities and new solutions.

Bloom's strong poet is the poet who rebels more strongly than others against 'the anxiety of influence' and against 'the horror of finding himself to be only a copy or a replica'. Rorty's reading of Freud generalises this insight. Rorty proposes Freud as the source of a new awareness: that moral selves must be created through a necessarily private and individual transcendence of the contingencies of an individual past. The argument is best conveyed by quoting at some length.

> The Platonic and Kantian idea of rationality centers round the idea that we need to bring particular actions under general principles if we are to be moral. Freud suggests that we need to return to the particular – to see particular present situations and options as similar to or different from particular past actions or events. He thinks that only if we catch hold of some critical idiosyncratic contingencies in our past shall we be able to make something worthwhile out of ourselves, to create present selves whom we can respect. He taught us to interpret what we are doing, or thinking of doing, in terms of, for example, our past reaction to particular authority-figures, or in terms of constellations of behavior which were forced upon us in infancy. He suggested that we praise ourselves by weaving idiosyncratic narratives – case histories, as it were – of our success in self-creation, our ability to break free from an idiosyncratic past. He suggests that we condemn ourselves for failure to break free of that past rather than for failure to live up to universal standards (Rorty, 1989, p. 33).

Rorty's emphasis on a private individual creativity may seem to have in it some echoes of existentialist thought. But Rorty is not emphasising a heroic freedom, a struggle for an authentic life. This creation of the moral self is not an action which we are condemned to undertake. Rather, his eye is on the private processes which are often neglected in public discussion of justice and the duties of the good citizen. But he also has in mind another cherished hope which should be given up: what he calls the hope of fusing private and public ethics. Here, Rorty's radical liberalism comes into view alongside other radical aspects of his thinking, as he discusses the relinquishing of this further, impossible hope.

Behind the traditional Platonic, Kantian, Christian formulations of the problem of morality lies the hope of fusing private visions of a good life with public social morality. A bold acceptance of the contingent creative nature of selfhood would lead us to recognise that there is no way in which the public and private can be fused. We should come to see, as Freud saw (Rorty says), that there is no bridge between a private ethic of self-creation and a public ethic of mutual accommodation. Both are important and distinct. There is no way of superimposing one upon the other provided by 'universally shared beliefs or desires – beliefs or desires which belong to us qua human and which unite us to our fellow humans *as* human' (Rorty, 1989, p. 34).

Rorty urges us to accept once and for all this gap between private and public ethics. Then we would be able to see how society and the relation between society and individuals look from this position. One implication is that both kinds of ethic would be given their due. Recognising that all people are both poet and citizen in their lives, we would come to value equally the figures of the strong poet and the moral citizen. We would not see as opposed philosophies of private exploration and philosophies of community. We would create social arrangements in which both could thrive. But also, just as the individual, private poet in us needs to be permitted to seek an original life, so public morality can do without too many idiosyncratic visions projected as criticisms of society or as scenarios for the future to which all must subscribe.

In public affairs, we will do best to keep things simple, Rorty thinks. Avoiding cruelty and pain to others will take enough of our time. Rorty is at his most explicitly critical where speaking of philosophers such as Foucault and Habermas who would like to take things further. Habermas is mildly and respectfully chastised for failing to see the value to private thinking of some individually directed philosophies and for reducing all discussion of value to matters of public and political import. Foucault earns something like reproof for demanding 'that our autonomy be embodied in our institutions'. 'It is precisely that sort of yearning,' Rorty comments, 'which I think should, among citizens of a liberal democracy, be reserved for private life' (Rorty, 1989, p. 65). Rorty's point is that by accepting as irreducible the difference between private and public domains we should save ourselves much idiosyncrasy in public places and at the same time protect and benefit from private freedom.

To those who in response say that to give up the idea of a common humanity will weaken social solidarity, Rorty has an answer. Strengthening community should be looked for by other means. Societies will not be bound together by founding community on an unjustifiable belief in a common human nature. Actual sympathy and empathy with other people are needed. The goal should be to expand that sense of 'we-ness' which is exemplified in family identities. 'We-feeling' should be worked at – to the point where, by degrees, other – from different classes, backgrounds, countries – come to be seen as 'like us'.

The function in this for literature and ethnography in creating awareness of others has in it more hope (Rorty feels) than the continuous and fruitless search to ground justifications of social behaviour in an abstract common humanity. As Rorty puts it:

> In my Utopia, human solidarity would be seen not as a fact
> to be recognized by clearing away 'prejudice' or burrowing
> down to previously hidden depths, but, rather, as a goal to
> be achieved. Solidarity is not discovered by reflection but
> created. It is to be achieved not by inquiry but by
> imagination, the imaginative ability to see strange people as
> fellow sufferers. (Rorty, 1989, p. xvi)

Rorty brings the two sides of his philosophy together – the epistemological and the socio-political – in a phrase which he coins to characterise his position: 'the liberal ironist'. The position is liberal because it is concerned to support and protect liberal democracy and 'thinks cruelty is the worst thing we do'. The position is ironist because it claims no final truth for any belief but accepts that any belief may be re-described from another point of view. Rorty himself accepts of course that he is doing no more than offering another vocabulary. 'For liberal ironists,' he comments, 'there is no non-circular back-up for the belief that cruelty is horrible. Nor is there an answer to the question "How do you decide when to struggle against injustice and when to devote yourself to private projects of self-creation"' (Rorty, 1989, p. xv). Rorty would be happy to be judged by the terms of his own argument, for in doing so, his intercolutors would have taken, presumably, the step which the radical in him wishes us to take.

So far, I have been summarising Rorty's liberal ironist position. I have done so at some length because Rorty's work may be relatively unfamiliar. Also, with Rorty as with any other thinker, attempting to grasp the whole position is some precaution against the piecemeal assimilation of particular aspects.

I hope it has been apparent that Rorty's re-description of contemporary culture bears on a number of issues which are of interest to English teachers. He offers us, as English teachers, a description of the place of literature and literary criticism and links this description to connected accounts of language, knowledge, moral identity and society. I feel attracted to the radicalism of an account which urges us to re-draw hierarchies of subject disciplines and to re-allocate social priorities. I have some doubts, however, about how radical Rorty's challenge really is, and in the remainder of this chapter I want to take up some questions and difficulties which are raised for me.

I should begin by acknowledging that some parts of the classical pragmatist tradition are well enough known to English teachers, since many of the concepts of James and Dewey have entered our thinking about 'thinking', almost below the level of consciousness. James sought to close the gap between empiricist and idealist accounts of knowledge through an emphasis on 'experience' – an emphasis which is familiar enough to English teachers as a starting point for thinking about children using language. Dewey attacked the 'spectator theory of knowledge' – the mere passive contemplation of reality. We are used to a view of mind in which 'knowing' is brought close to 'practice', 'experiment' and 'action'.

For Dewey, especially, knowledge was action – a record of successful practice in the world, confirmed by experience. Dewey accepted that it would never be possible finally to establish this as truth, because of any set of propositions further enquiry was always possible. The most that could be hoped for by way of stability and grounding was a temporary interval in the testing of some propositions, where potential counter-arguments were exhausted for the time being. Dewey's was an account, though, which made propositions an instrument of inquiry and thought itself a kind of analogue of the scientific method – an action intended to affect the real world, an act of experiment, of trying it out.

Rorty's liberal ironist culture, by contrast, is concerned with description and re-description rather than action and discovery. Its chief characteristics are awareness, creativity, empathy. In Rorty's new culture, liberal ironists' awareness will lead them to treat lightly all vocabularies (including their own) because they appreciate the impossibility of grounding any vocabulary as final. They will look on culture as continuously in process, an 'endless, proliferating realization' of creativity and freedom. Intellectually as well as morally, the hopes of their new world will lie with the dawning of metaphors coming into being and with the private ethics of self- creation.

Attractive though this vision is, I find myself wanting Rorty to recall more strongly, as Dewey does, that knowledge is not just a matter of its claims for truth or of theory and vocabulary. Illness, language development, nuclear warheads actually happen. Whether in the sciences or in literature, intellectual enterprise seeks purchase on the real world, however impossible it may be to claim final justification for its achievements. It does not follow from accepting that there is no way of finally grounding theories that some theories cannot be found to be better than others in practice. Nor does it follow that we can ignore (or treat lightly in our dealings with it) the real world, which exists independently of our admittedly partial and relative and historically bounded knowledge.

The British philosopher, Roy Bhaskar, puts this point in the following way:

> What we need in order to feel at home in the world is not
> the infantile fantasy that it was made for us; but the mature
> post-Darwinian recognition of the ecological asymmetry:
> that it is more true to say that we were made for it, and that
> we survive as a species only insofar as second nature
> respects the overriding constraints imposed on it by first
> nature. From this nature although it is always historically
> mediated we can never, nor will ever, escape. (Bhaskar,
> 1986, p. 222)

Science is, as Bhaskar adds elsewhere 'the systematic attempt to express in thought the structures and ways of acting of things that exist and act independently of thought' (Bhaskar, 1978, p. 250). Rorty is right to remind us that we shall find no truth which is 'Nature's own', and Bhaskar rightly emphasises that in what humans live by and accept, as their provisional truth they forget Nature at their peril.

I have a worry about Rorty's liberal ironist culture, at this point. My worry is not so much with whether this new culture will be relativist in its view of knowledge. It is more with whether it will be serious enough about its intellectual enterprises and scientific enquiries. I can indicate my difficulties by making more explicit the contrast which I have so far hinted at with Dewey, on the one hand, and with Bhaskar, on the other.

To the one, I want Rorty to show that his vision includes in it more than just private creativity. I have in mind not just an ethic of mutual accommodation, but a Deweyan sense that thinking and knowing may be brought to the tests of experience and put to human use. To the other, I want Rorty to make clearer than he has that the revaluation of literature and science in the liberal ironist culture which he proposes is not simply a return to a pre- scientific 'infantilism' or a form of escapism from human choice and responsibility in the real world. Without such assurances, Rorty's invitation might be thought to be leading us back – rather than forward – to a familiar and ultimately elitist culture of the Humanities, dressed up in different clothes.

I have been suggesting social use and responsibility towards the real world as two indispensable features of a contemporary view of knowledge. Also, I should want to begin from the assumption that uses of our language have been historically constructed, the point which is fundamental to the whole Russian tradition of Vygotsky, Volosinov and Bakhtin. As social human beings, we have at our disposal not language as such but uses of language made possible by cultural resources and by forms of cultural action developed within human societies. Recognising this, I want now to add to epistemological issues some more directly political questions raised for me by Rorty's invitation to liberal ironist culture. Here, Rorty's accounts, in particular of literature and of the liberal ironist position more generally, lack a level of sociological and historical analysis and are, I believe, less innovative and less radical than at first appears.

Rorty's account of literature brings together both the epistemological and the social sides of his philosophy. Literature, Rorty believes, has inherited in a secularised culture the place once occupied by religion and more recently by natural science. Supported by the recognition that truth is created rather than discovered, poets and critics have succeeded moralists as explorers of the moral universe.

Intellectually, then, literature has come to have a new significance within the creativity of pragmatic culture. And on the political side of Rorty's liberal Utopia, literature, alongside ethnographies, will have the major role in extending empathy and in creating community. It is in literature – and also in a philosophy read and written with a more complex awareness of private as well as public functions – that we will find the living record of private ethics and moral self-creation.

Now, this is an account which certainly describes in fresh ways some important aspects of our present literary traditions. My question is, however, whether it is not also rather a conservative account. It could be said that there is little here added to an Arnoldian position linking an idealised account of 'the best that has been thought and said' to an individualised view of culture as the cultivation of the 'best self'.

To bring out what I mean by the conservatism of Rorty's account of literature, I need to comment a little further on his principal emphases. Rorty refers with favour, at various points, to a 'historicist turn of thought'. But he leaves unexamined the connections between writers, their reading publics and the available means of cultural production, when he turns to literature, either as theorist or critic. Rorty's first interest is in literature's role within the private ethics of self- creation, as I have attempted earlier to summarise; and he connects in this the poet's transcending of influence with a post-Freudian sense of moral autonomy as escape from the contingencies of upbringing. But this, like many such arguments, is really no more than a persuasive invitation to a kind of literature (and to a way of reading) which Rorty favours, not an independent theory of literature or of culture. The argument illuminates a strand of twentieth-century literary production, but is silent on how some literary traditions come to be preferred to others or on the connection between literature, literacy and society more widely.

Of a piece with these gaps and silences in the theory, there seems a risk of plain ethnocentricity in the way Rorty formulates his second principal interest: in literature's functions in increasing awareness of suffering and in promoting empathy and community. Whose empathy with whom? Since he has offered no historical and social account of culture, Rorty needs to make it clearer than he does that he envisages more by literature's function in charting suffering than a necessarily selective and random way for members of historically dominant traditions to extend their knowledge of those they dominate. 'Pain is nonlinguistic...,' Rorty comments:

> So victims of cruelty, people who are suffering, do not have
> much in the way of language. That is why there are no such
> things as 'the voice of the oppressed' or 'the language of the
> victims'. The language the victims once used is not working
> any more, and they are suffering too much to put new words
> together. So the job of putting their situation into language
> is going to have to be done for them by somebody else. The
> liberal novelist, poet, or journalist is good at that. The
> liberal theorist usually is not. (Rorty, 1989, p. 94)

As an example of Rorty's theorising of the social and political nature of literature, this is hardly reassuring.

Not to put too fine a point on it, the issue with Rorty on the subject of literature, as with Arnold, is one of class – and more generally of a social and political position which does not address differences in political interest and the unequal power of different groups and different cultural traditions.

The difficulties which I have had with Rorty's account of literature rest, then, on some more general problems about liberal irony, considered as a political philosophy. Politically, as a man of our times, Rorty's liberal ironist seems an engaging but surely a somewhat time-locked figure. He contrasts, as we have seen, with Dewey's explorer and experimentalist. He is a man of private creativity and ready empathy. But we come closest to his nature, I believe, if we see him as a man who is better equipped to withstand dogmatism and cant than to press for change and who is perhaps especially well prepared to resist totalitarian tendencies in twentieth-century culture.

Unlike the eighteenth-century 'man of feeling', whom he nevertheless resembles, his sympathy is motivated by particulars and not by generalities. Like him, and in the manner of the poet Thomas Gray's lines on his own character.

> A place or a pension he did not desire
> But left Church and State to Charles Townshend and
> Squire.

Rorty, I must make plain, does not regard all liberal ironists as male. That is my subversion of him. Rorty complicates such matters by employing in order to write about them a strange system of pronouns which requires them to be alternately 'he' and 'she'. I do not find myself convinced by this of Rorty's feminism. It is unfraternal to remark this, but it is also relevant, since within Rorty's account of liberalism the dissolution of differences in political interest seems what is crucially at issue.

What I find myself wanting to know about liberal ironists is whether they have interests of their own which are ever structurally (not just individually) in conflict. Are some of them ever on the receiving or the giving end of power? To this question Rorty gives no answer. In the face of class or racist or patriarchal or merely male oppression, however, empathy could be said to be either duplicitous or servile. Some answer to the question is needed.

Somewhere between the private ethics of self-creation and the public morality of mutual accommodation, Rorty could have inserted the reality of different political interests. But he does not do so. The reason is, perhaps, that Rorty's social philosophy is here principally concerned with the threat to community which some of his critics might suppose to follow from giving up the attempt to ground social ethics in an account of human nature.

Rorty's worry in this is not an authoritarian one. He does not fear decline in public order. The threat to community which he addresses is whether the result will be that cruelty increases. Even so, this is an idiosyncratic interpretation of the problem created by giving up the attempt to ground social principles in some absolute account of human nature. Presumably for people to act cruelly they must possess or have access to some social power through which they are able to do so. In historically capitalist, racist and unequal societies what citizens seek are rights and equity not solidarity and empathy.   Rorty does not quite say that he starts from the assumption that (give or take some minor differences) there are no major inequities in political interest in western liberal democracies or real contradictions in the exercise of power, provided it is exercised benevolently. He does not say so. But it is a fairly clear inference that this is what he thinks.

I have been setting out in the later part of this chapter some difficulties and disagreements I have with the liberal ironist position of the American philosopher, Richard Rorty. I can summarise my disagreements under two heads.

First, Rorty's pragmatism seems to me to reduce in its own way the presumption of a real world in scientific or social scientific or literary thinking to issues about the relativity of our knowledge about this.

Second, Rorty's account of liberal ironist culture seems sociologically empty and insufficiently historical. Rorty discusses society principally in the ethical context of achieving social solidarity. But his discussion, in general, refuses the social as an independent level of explanation and analysis and leaves out, in particular, class, gendered and ethnic inequalities, social and cultural conflict.

In the world of the late twentieth century, one which has given up the hope of absolute truth, what we need to be shown is not just the necessity of this renunciation but how we live with it. In other words, the test of Rorty's position is not so much the truth of his critique of positivist and empiricist assumptions as the political and intellectual and ethical geography of his alternative vision. As

English teachers, we need more in our account of language and literature than one which offers creativity but takes away responsibility in the world. Also, English teachers need to link language and literature, young people's identities, culture and history. Rorty's account of these matters is, I think, sociologically and historically incomplete.

I hope, however, that my purpose has not seemed merely that of critique. Many of the themes of Rorty's philosophy seem to me of considerable interest. They contain in them parallels with other arguments about literature and about the development of personal identity and culture and are presented in Rorty's work with striking clarity and style. In particular, Rorty's theme of privacy seems to me interesting to pursue within a fully sociological perspective. I have no doubt either that Rorty's thinking would be of interest to English teachers.

I have also had another end in view. This has been to make use of Rorty's work to provide a reminder of the scale of a certain kind of challenge. I have in mind the necessity for us, as English teachers, to continue to develop our own philosophy of English in new times. It is not easy to say so, at a point when an imposed national curriculum is upon us and when the Cox Committee has recently set out a framework for English which will take us much of our time to internalise and disseminate. I shall say so, anyway.

I share the view that the Cox Committee has done quite well in resisting pressures to destroy the heart of post-war English teaching. We have been offered a statement which may yet prove workable if some changes are made on the matter of bilingualism and provided that the political commitment to an irresponsible publishing of results by schools is ultimately abandoned. It would not be surprising if the members of the Cox Committee did not see it as their goal to develop the philosophy of English teaching; and they have not done so.

We. though, have to re-discover our sense of the future and to assemble energies for fresh exploration. English teachers cannot live only within curriculum frameworks. English teaching, as we have known it and valued it, will surely die if teachers cease to look outside their classrooms in order to claim significance for what they do, in culture, in history and in a vision of their times.

I do not wholly agree with Rorty's vision of a liberal ironist culture, as I have indicated. I think he is in danger of re-stating a conservative view of literature and an individualist 'cherishing of private souls' (in Douglas Barnes's apt phrase), to which I am opposed. But I do believe that in offering a vision of the world, larger than but including literature and language, Rorty is beckoning towards a proper task for us to claim, as English teachers, now or at any time. We must continue to prod our own new visions into life.

This essay appeared in *English in Education*, vol. 23, no. 3, Autumn 1989.

Bhaskar, R. (1978), *A Realist Theory of Science*, 2nd edn, Harvester
Bhaskar, R. (1986), *Scientific Realism and Human Emancipation*, Verso
Rorty, R. (1980), *Philosophy and the Mirror of Nature*, Basil Blackwell
Rorty, R. (1982), *Consequences of Pragmatism*, Harvester
Rorty, R. (1989), *Contingency, Irony and Solidarity*, Cambridge University Press

Reading: the entitlement to be 'properly literate'

However we read it, the history of literacy shows that debates about reading and writing come to the fore when societies undergo radical change. Current discussions confirm this, but more often than not the voices of teachers are not heard. In making his case for every child's entitlement to 'proper' literacy, Peter Traves shows by his analysis, arguments and axioms how teachers should seek to regain 'the high ground' in public debates. In their approach to reading, schools are still socially divided, according to whether they regard it as a basic skill or 'a culturally privileged activity inherently superior in its nature to other forms of cultural reception'. The fifteen statements that conclude this piece challenge those who underestimate teachers' skills and sense of responsibility in acknowledging that a fully literate community is more creative than threatening.

> Make a distinction: being able to read means that you can follow words across the page, getting what's superficially there. Being literate means you can bring your knowledge and your experience to bear on what passes before you. Let us class the latter proper literacy; the former improper...
>
> Proper literacy should extend people's control over their lives and environment and allow them to continue to deal rationally and in words with their lives and decisions. Improperly it reduces and destroys their control. They are deluded by the veneer of control they have been granted, not minding that they have lost everything else.
>
> We have too much improper literacy at the expense of properly literate folk!

In the passage quoted above Wayne O'Neil makes a distinction between 'being able to read' and 'being literate', and the difference has to do with power. The literate person, or rather the 'properly' literate person, has an extended and enriched control over their life and environment; their literacy empowers them. It strengthens their capacity for rational thought and enables them more effectively to use their knowledge and experience in the critical analysis and evaluation of the world. Improper literacy, mere reading, on the other hand, is a reductive and destructive state of being, in which the illusion of achievement is substituted for the genuine article, where the potential for power has been thwarted and channelled. Depressingly, he concludes by saying that the education system (he is talking of the US system, in fact) has produced very little real literacy in these terms. I think what he has to say is generally true for Britain, too.

In *The Long Revolution* Raymond Williams observed that there was a majority Sunday newspaper-reading public by 1910, a majority daily newspaper-reading public by 1918, and a majority book-reading public by the 1950s, and yet this has not brought about any basic change in the power structure of our society. We live in a society in which the overwhelming majority of adults are able to read in the terms defined by O'Neil. However, the political potential of literacy seems as far as ever from being realised. We need to examine our own roles as educators in this state of affairs. We need to consider what has happened in education to produce a situation where mass literacy has not resulted in a corresponding demand for greater control over the economic, political and cultural life of society. Public education has not produced an empowered people. Education has served to control and repress the aspirations of the general population, and the teaching of reading has had a central part in this.

Ironically, we have little choice but to face up to the political implications of reading because the Right is forcing the pace in this respect. The aim of this essay is to help those who want to win back the ideological high ground from the Right. I shall begin by briefly setting the context within which our approach to reading is made. I will illustrate this by looking in some detail at the early reading experience of one child. Finally, I will try to offer some positive suggestions about what reading – and that includes our definition of reading – should look like in our schools. In other words, I will be addressing the issue of entitlement, the entitlement far too many have been cheated out of. In pursuing this theme it will be necessary to discuss wider political concerns. Literacy in its proper sense cannot be disentangled from politics. Our opponents recognise this even if we do not.

It could be argued, rightly I believe, that literacy and other educational issues have always been fundamentally political in their nature: however, the difference now is that they are the subject of very explicit political debate and action. Education is very high on the agenda of political discussion at the moment, and literacy is at the centre of that discussion. In the third term of a Conservative administration, education may well be described as the cutting edge of the radical New Right. What I mean by that is that far more than, say, the Poll Tax, it is in the discussion of education that we see the most explicit examples of Right-wing ideology. In particular it has become the focus for a populist crusade couched in terms of Choice, Consumerism, Common Sense and Decency, terms which are very much to the fore in New Right rhetoric.

Literacy has an important place in this, and has been crucial in terms of fixing the debate. I use the word 'fixing' firstly to describe the way in which literacy is an issue used to *place* the debate, to decide the ground on which it will be contested; secondly, to describe the way in which it has been used to *fix* or *distort* the debate, to *fiddle the books*, so to speak. The phrase 'Children don't read as well as they should' or even more often 'as well as they used to' is probably the single most effective cudgel with which the education system – and teachers in particular – have been beaten. It has played a major role in creating the sense of crisis so necessary in order to allow the Right to push for the effective dismantling of a comprehensive, publicly-funded education system. It has been extremely effective, whereas the responses to it have been bewildered, confused and generally unsuccessful.

The responses from within education have tended to refer to facts and figures which 'prove' that literacy has increased and is continuing to increase. The government has found with the National Health Service that facts and figures can be singularly unimpressive in the face of a general sense of decline and crisis. We have fared no better on literacy, nor do we deserve to do so, as this is a relatively feeble line of defence. It is feeble because it is evasive. It evades the issue of achievement and the sense that many teachers share with the general public that children are not in fact as literate as they should be and that under-achievement is a major problem. It is, of course, easy to understand why we have evaded the issue. We are under attack. We are held *personally* to blame for this under-achievement. Consequently, the climate is not right for open discussion and honest assessment. Furthermore, we know that the under-achievement is *in spite of* and not *because of* the efforts of teachers, at least in so far as hard work and a genuine desire to do the best possible for the students is concerned. I would also argue that we are held back by a failure of definition. A failure, that is, to define what we mean by being literate when we are talking about reading. We quite rightly reject the crude definitions implicit in the majority of popular and media attacks, but we have not been able to put in their place a definition that is at once intellectually rigorous and generally accessible.

In order to help focus some of the issues I would like to concentrate briefly on the experience of one child, my elder son, Richard. I hope that this will anchor the arguments on to the firmer ground of a specific reading history.

Richard's pre-school and nursery experience of reading was a very positive and fairly rich one. Although he went to school unable to 'read' in the sense of being able independently to decode the print of books, he behaved as a reader in almost every other respect. He lived in a house where there are many books and where both adults read a lot and with obvious pleasure. It's a house where books and the experience of reading are talked about seriously but without any overwhelming sense of preciousness. He enjoyed being read to, talked about the stories and wanted more books. He memorised stories and large chunks of the phrasing from books and then delivered them back enthusiastically in a readerly tone of voice. His experience at William Patten Nursery School reinforced all this. It was a very different experience when he started at a local east Enfield school.

The school is in the middle of a council estate, and this was used as an excuse to set very low expectations for the pupils. There was a systematic policy of effectively excluding parents from the school. There was also extensive use of the appalling *One, Two, Three...Away* Reading Scheme. Richard started at the bottom of the scheme and stayed there. Within a term he was able to place and grade virtually every child in his class in terms of where they were on the hierarchy of colours within the scheme. Those at the bottom were often given boxes of words on cards to learn before being allowed to go on to the delights of Roger Red Hat and his jolly friends in the village with three corners in the books with no stories. He had seen himself as a reader. He now described himself not only as a non-reader but as generally stupid. Though he continued to enjoy being read to at home, there can be no doubt that the year's experience in school has left a deep and scarring wound on him as a reader and a learner.

He has moved since then to another local school, also on a council estate, but with quite different expectations and attitudes. He is now in the Juniors and is making steady progress, but he still sees himself as a 'poor reader' and takes little pleasure in the school reading he does.

Its effect on his parents was less important but equally dramatic. Despite the fact that his mother was attending a course in reading run by Margaret Spencer and his father was an English Adviser, his parents managed to make all the available mistakes. These included enforced reading through the books which he brought home, shouting gems such as 'Look what it says!'; 'Yes, you do know that word – come on, what is it?'; 'You're not looking at the words, stop guessing from the picture'. A great many tears were spilt, on both sides. We knew what we should do, what enlightened theory told us to do, but these were 'mere rags that flew off at the first shake'. It was, as anyone who has had a child go through a similar experience will appreciate, a painful and sobering time.

The implications of this child's experience seem clear enough to me. First of all, it shows very forcefully the central place that literacy occupies in education. The behaviour and attitudes of child, teacher and parents illustrate this. Teacher and parents were anxious, and this anxiety rapidly communicated itself to Richard. As parents, our expressed concern was that he should not be put off reading by this early experience, but there can be no doubt that this was accompanied by nagging fears that his chances of an enjoyable and profitable education were under real threat. As teachers we both knew how hard it is for children who struggle as readers.

Secondly, it suggests the enormous pressure on pupils to demonstrate visible, measurable success as readers within a few weeks or at most months. We are, after all, talking here about a child of six. The successful readers could be identified with ease by the colour grading of the book they were on and they gained a great deal of general kudos from their perceived status as readers. The unsuccessful readers, equally easy to identify, were already being looked upon as problems, as potential failures. The assessment made of a child's reading ability, even at an early age, is often generalised into a description of the child's overall intellectual potential. This generalisation is then shared by teachers and parents and, worst of all, can be internalised by the child.

Finally, it suggests the dominance of a particular and highly limited definition of what it means to be a reader. It is a mechanistic definition that has evolved more for the comfort and convenience of educators and publishers than in response to well thought-out models of reading and readers. It is a definition that concentrates heavily on the capacity to read relatively decontextualised print out loud. It pays little or no attention to the broad and complex web of behavioural and intellectual patterns that underpin real reading. It presents a complex process as a series of ever higher hurdles over which the child either leaps or falls, or, in a minority of sad cases, before which they shrink with fear. The question, 'What are the dominant definitions of literacy available to us?' is one I would like to take up briefly now.

I am not concerned here with the academic definitions of literacy available to specialists. Rather I am interested to explore tentatively those available in common parlance, those ideologies of literacy most deeply embedded in our society. It seems to me that we tend to discuss literacy in two main ways. Probably the most common way we talk about reading is as a skill, a functional activity, which is acquired in order to negotiate the day-to-day demands of print in our society or in order to go on to pursue higher, more complex intellectual activities. In this definition, reading is not a truly intellectual activity: it is fundamentally passive in nature and is a fairly low-level skill. Nevertheless, it is a crucial skill to acquire, hence the demands for 'back to basics' education. I think that the word 'basics' says a great deal about this conception of literacy.

Alongside this definition there is another in our society. The second kind of description sets reading up as a culturally privileged activity inherently superior in its nature to other forms of cultural reception. In recent years, this has crystallised around the 'books versus television' argument. This culturally privileged view of reading is enshrined in the hierarchy of reading activities and texts, with the analytical study of good or great literature set firmly at the top. These two broad definitions sit in an ill-defined relation to each other and reveal some of the underlying contradictions in the dominant ideologies, not only of literacy but of learning and knowledge.   In education these two versions of reading are represented in classroom practice. The reading schemes and tests, and the tendency to talk about 'reading problems' and reading ages, embody the skills definition of literacy. Furthermore, most of the reading activities done particularly in Secondary Schools underline the functional emphasis on literacy. Most of the reading from eleven onwards tends to be done in order to do something else – usually writing. It is a process to be gone through so that something more important, more tangible or more useful can be accomplished. Such a view can be reinforced by even the best-intentioned of English teachers.

The culturally privileged version also has its place in schools. Teachers often share Mr Baker's mission to wean kids off television and on to books. It's there in the hierarchy of texts when matched to the hierarchy of examinations, and GCSE has blurred the distinctions only slightly. It used to be only the classics at 'A' level, good books for 'O' level, virtually anything for CSE. Yet despite the fact that lip service is paid to the cultural prestige of reading it remains a curiously marginalised activity in terms of the time and resources given to it.

If these definitions are the dominant ones available to us, then we need to think about the implications of that fact. I think it is easy enough to see the kinds of classroom practices that are built upon these views of reading. It is also relatively easy to see why they have such a powerful appeal to the popular imagination. It is even simpler to assess their attractiveness to the Right. It is much more difficult to see what kind of definition we might put in their place. It is more difficult because it would have to do a much more complex task. It would have to be grounded in what we believe to be true about reading, readers and reading acquisition, but it would also have to be expressed in a way that would make it accessible and appealing to non-professionals. It needs to be a definition that has theoretical integrity but which also helps in the struggle to win back the high ground in the debate.

The first thing we need to do is to accept that the public sense of under-achievement is fundamentally realistic. This does not mean that we have to accept the precise details of public criticism or even the general description of the debate as it is usually phrased. What is does mean is an end to the lame dependence on figures of improvement, or pathetic stickers which insult readers by saying, 'If you can read this sticker – thank a teacher.' If that's what literacy and education have achieved over a period of at least ten years per child and several billion pounds per year, perhaps we should pack up and go home. We need the courage to admit what most of us as teachers and/or parents intuitively feel: that despite the enormous effort and concern of teachers, the education system is failing large numbers of children and that failure includes inadequate literacy.

However, by itself such an admission would be very likely to produce despair. We need to go beyond this. We need to re-define the popular discontent so that it ceases to appear to us as ill-informed and often malignantly destructive criticism. (I think that the attacks by the Right are malign. I'm less sure that they are ill informed as I believe them to be politically shrewd manoeuvres.) We need to see the discontent as part of an unsatisfied aspiration for full educational entitlement. The failure of the Left has been in its inability to offer models of society within which these aspirations might be more fully satisfied. Consequently, large parts of the population have turned to the Right, who offer a crude but tangible fulfilment of parts of these aspirations, while at the same time denying the possibility of their fuller and richer realisation. The desire for full literacy is part of this. In the past, in this country, and in many parts of the world today, literacy has been regarded as one of the key routes to power by ordinary working people. Literacy was not simply a desirable and useful sub-skill, it embodied the struggle for full economic, social, political and cultural enfranchisement. This is as true today as it ever was, and we need to be making this the central tenet in our argument and build it into our definition of literacy. Such a definition would describe literacy as an active, critical, potentially disruptive but empowering process, enabling all people to describe, analyse and contribute to the cultural, political, social and economic life of society. Furthermore, it helps give the power not only to contribute to but also to change society. To be literate in these terms is a vital part of being socially and politically enfranchised in the broadest sense.

This is what we need to place against the Right-wing sub-skills version of literacy which attempts to portray parents and students as consumers, and skills and texts as consumables. The consumer image is a potent one. The Right implies it embodies choice and value. In fact it is an image we need to work to our advantage. As a consumer you get what you pay for and no more. The goods are put in front of you and you buy what you can afford. You can never have any real role in defining and shaping the product itself. What it hints at, and what is quite explicit in many of the Right Wing Think Tank proposals is an education system in which there will be a very basic model of education available for most of society and a fuller one for the wealthy and privileged. Of course, to a large extent, that is what already exists, but there was at least a general consensus that it was not wholly desirable. The Right now feels confident enough to question that consensus and is able to propose that inequality should be enshrined in the principle of 'you get what you pay for and no more'. Our job is to expose this and to oppose to it a definition of literacy that is coherent and accessible. This definition would build upon the best available practice and theory. It would involve in the process a change in the ownership of theory. It would be necessary for the theory to be produced in a genuine partnership between everyone involved in education. The academic producers of theory would still have a vital role to play but their virtual monopoly of theoretical production would have to be broken, so that teachers, pupils, parents and others would cease to be consumers and become genuine producers.

If we could establish what literacy means in terms of entitlement, then part of the Right's stranglehold would be broken. At present, they use the language of demand.

They demand that children reach certain measurable levels of attainment. Failure to do so will be blamed on the schools. Entitlement shifts the ground of the argument. Children are entitled to a defined range of reading experience in order to become as fully literate as possible. In order to do so, definable levels of resourcing in terms of teachers, training and materials will need to be provided. However, in order to make that demand, we will need to have our arguments, our definition of literacy ready. We will also need to find more effective ways of disseminating our ideas. The Right has identified education as a key area of ideological conflict. Within education, language and literacy occupy an important place in their thinking. Anyone who doubts their unscrupulousness, the extreme nationalism and narrowness of their thinking, or their anti-intellectual and ignorant but politically shrewd populism, should read the Centre for Policy Studies document written by Dr Marenbon. He is chillingly confident that his is a voice that will be heard, and the title is a carefully chosen one – *English, Our English*. We cannot cede the popular ground to people like him.

One point at which a start might be made would be to ask what being literate should mean and, as a consequence, what kinds of literate activities ought to be given value in schools? My brief offering below is to list a series of things students should be entitled to in their education with regard to reading. I don't claim any kind of originality for any of these points, and others will add to them.

They represent many of the things that have been taken for granted by a considerable number of English teachers for many years. Still, they need to be stated and restated in a way that will make them more accessible to teachers and non-teachers. We need to use every effective means at our disposal to persuade pupils, parents, teachers, governors, politicians and the wider general public that what we want to offer in terms of literacy is richer and more convincing than the crude 'basics' propagated by the Right and unfortunately generally accepted as the working definition of literacy by the public and much of the educational establishment. We must assert on all occasions the concept of 'entitlement' against that of 'basic standards'. Our aim should be to press fiercely for an expansion of literacy and what literacy means rather than feebly to defend a measured inching-up on the scale of basic reading skills. Here then are fifteen assertions which might provide a starting point in an entitlement campaign:

1.   Being literate must involve the capacity to deal with the day-to-day demands of print in our society. This is not the ultimate goal of literacy but it has to be one of its staging posts, part of the process at least. It is a disgrace if we attempt to justify the existence of even a small minority of people who have been denied this capacity in our society.

2.   Pupils must be able to cope with the reading demands placed on them by the education process. Too often children are denied access to whole areas of the curriculum on the grounds that they cannot read well enough. The child's entitlement is to receive the levels of support and help necessary to sustain them as readers right across the curriculum and right through their educational career. One implication of this is that the importance of reading in terms of general educational success ought to be recognised in the resources given to it. At present insufficient time, money, personnel and training are devoted to reading in our schools.

3. Literacy involves the recognition that readers employ different reading strategies according to the nature of the text and the purpose of the reading activity. This is inherent in the reading demands placed on children in school, but it is not an insight that is achieved by magic or innate intelligence. From very early on, children ought to be offered a wide range of reading experiences for a wide range of purposes. Where particular reading skills need to be developed and where structured practice will help in their development, then such work needs to be undertaken in a methodical and coherent fashion rather than in the piecemeal and random manner that is true of most schools at present.

4. Readers should know something about the processes by which they make meanings from print. Hitherto, this has been largely the preserve of a small band of literary theorists. Books like *Making Stories* and *Changing Stories* show how students can be engaged in enjoyable activities that begin to make explicit the processes of making meaning.

5. Texts work to achieve effects on their readers. Literacy should involve the capacity to see how the rhetoric works. Again, we already know of activities that can do this for students.

6. Students should be made aware that print carries values. These values always have a relation with wider ideological structures. Literacy involves the confidence and capacity to explore this relation.

7. Every reader has a history of experience as a reader. Part of the process of literacy is an awareness of that history. Students should see that history valued by being made explicit in talk and writing. A reader's history is not simply a record of what they read and when, it is the complex web of experiences that constitute our memory of reading. It includes where they read, under what conditions, with whom, how they responded, and so on.

8. Reading can be a source of pleasure. The nature of that pleasure is varied. It is important that the principle of pleasure should be a high priority in a school's approach to reading. At present very little time is given to reading for pleasure, particularly in the secondary sector. This should not be the exclusive concern of the English department. The whole school ought to be involved in presenting an image of reading as a potential source of pleasure.

9. Students should be encouraged to be adventurous in their reading, both in what they read and how they read it. This is a challenge to more limited conceptions of relevance. We should make fewer assumptions about what will interest children at particular ages or from particular backgrounds. Students should be encouraged to develop a more extensive sense of cultural ownership through their reading. Schools ought to develop in children a defiance of cultural boundaries that will allow them to gain powers of choice over what they choose to read, watch, write, listen to, make. Choosing not to read Milton or Ngugi because you don't enjoy their work is real choice, choosing not to because you think they are for someone from a different class or culture is not.

10. Being literate ought to involve a sense of choice over what is being read. For many students school ought to be a place for developing that power of choice. All too often, however, schools give students little or no experience of choosing what is read.

11.   It is important that readers value what they bring to the process of reading in terms of their language, culture, intellect and values. They need the opportunity to test their own resources against the resources of the text. Marenbon and Baker would have them sitting in awed insignificance before the works of geniuses.

12.   As an extension of the last point, readers need to relate their own values and experiences to what they read. There must be literature available, and reading practices should be encouraged, which build upon what the students already know and believe. Conversely, there needs to be literature that takes them beyond the confines of their experience, their culture, and which offers a challenge to their values.

13.   The experience of reading in school should help students to be aware of what is peculiar to the reading of print. It should also help them to see that it has much in common with the processes of making meaning from other forms of cultural production.

14.   Literacy involves all the language modes, therefore reading ought not to be divorced from other language activities. Children should engage in activities which encourage them to see themselves as producers of texts to be read by themselves and others. Writing and reading are inextricably bound together. The reader rewrites the text she or he reads, and the writer is constantly reading and re-reading the text under composition. This can be made explicit in the way we ask children to engage in activities connected with reading and writing. Talk about reading, about the text, and the general experience of reading, should be far more commonplace than it is in our schools, and such talk should include the reading material produced by the children as writers as a legitimate subject for serious discussion.

15.   Finally, schools must aim to produce in readers a sense of power over the whole process. We should be producing readers who not only see the vast potential for pleasure in reading but who are also aware of its potential for power. Literacy is not an achieved state. It is a process in which human beings can vastly increase their creative and critical faculties or can merely be passive consumers of someone else's products. The former is obviously our aim: the nurturing of critical human beings using literacy as one means not only of achieving a richer and fuller individual life but also of achieving social growth and genuine democratic power.

Our opponents have recognised the power of literacy and wish to keep access to it a strictly limited process. Consequently, they market it as a sub-skill to be purchased, a commodity to be added to the individual's value as labour. Only for the few will there be a route through literacy to power. We need to expose the poverty of what is on offer and at the same time counter it with an image of literacy that will tap the dormant sources of energy in the aspirations of parents, pupils, teachers and the rest of society.

This essay appeared in *The English Magazine* 20, Summer 1988.

O'Neil, Wayne (1977), 'Properly literate' in Martin Hoyles (ed.), *The Politics of Literacy*, Writers and Readers

KEITH KIMBERLEY

The Third Limb. Assessment and the National Curriculum

The public face of English in education is new, officially at least, and delineated by the novel, centralised initiative of the National Curriculum. Its constituent features are framed by statutory orders, laws about standards, programmes of study and tests. At the centre of this web of hierocratic prescriptions is the Secretary of State, with powers to make teachers accountable, notably in the matter of 'Standard English'. Keith Kimberley's ordered account of how this situation came about, and the nature of the authoritarian control of English teaching which it has generated cuts a clear path through the obscurantist prose of official documents.

Some developments have taken place since 1989, when the article was originally written. Key Stage 1 SATs (Standardised Assessment Tasks) were piloted in 1990 and drastic reductions followed, limiting the areas of core subjects which were to be assessed through SATs and requiring cutbacks to the scale of SATs themselves. At Key Stage 3, Maths and Science SATs were piloted in 1991, with English and Technology to follow the year after. The conduct of assessment arrangements has been given to local authorities, with the examination boards to be involved in moderation. Exemplification for the National Curriculum is being developed by the NCC (National Curriculum Council) and other agencies.

But the fundamental difficulties and conflicts which Keith Kimberley identifies rumble on. Against the background of many teachers' apprehensions about the first unreported run for Key Stage 1, Kenneth Clark, Secretary for Education, has been in correspondence with SEAC about short, sharp tests and terminal examinations at Key Stage 3. How teacher assessment should be reconciled with SAT assessment remains problematic. Maths and Science curriculum orders are being reconsidered, with a view to cutting down and re-ordering the proliferation of Attainment Targets and Statements of Attainment inherited from National Curriculum working parties.

Keith Kimberley's account analyses the contradictions which are still being worked out in contemporary educational politics and he offers a continuingly relevant vision of an education worth fighting for and still to be achieved. He shows how the best challenge to crude forms of comparison and to an assessment-led, narrowing curriculum lies in the proven strength and reliability of teacher assessments. The exemplary detail of this account suggests what teachers of all subjects have to encompass, and how a critical analysis of administrative confusions can release a powerful view of the way ahead.

...the leg went hopping over the rocks with the arm
swinging from the hand that clung to the top of the leg. The
other hand clung on top of that hand. The two hands, with
their eyes, guided the leg, twisting it this way and that, as a
rider guides a horse.
    Soon they found another leg...

The Iron Man, Ted Hughes

It may be that the writer of *SEAC Recorder Number 3*, the newsletter of the Schools Examinations and Assessment Council (SEAC), did not have this section of Ted Hughes's *The Iron Man* in mind when describing, as three interdependent limbs, the statutory orders for attainment targets, programmes of study and assessment arrangements. But for me there is something in this uncomfortable, disjointed image which refuses to go away.

Of course, in the story, the Iron Man reassembles himself after the temporary set-back of falling off a cliff and goes on to save the world; turning it to peace and putting it in touch with the music of the spheres. *The SEAC Recorder* piece entitled 'Beyond TGAT', having conjured up a vision of a set of parts which are being progressively assembled ('advice in stages to the Secretary of State...leading eventually to Statutory Orders about the assessment arrangements'), does not evoke confidence in the same sort of humanitarian outcomes. In fact, from what we know is intended by the Government, we may predict far less beneficial long-term effects on students, teachers and schools.

First let us consider what we are being told by SEAC. The dominant piece of information is a reminder of a fact that many of us have so far only imperfectly grasped: in the course of 1990 the assessment arrangements will have been codified into statutory orders, put out to consultation and become law. For some of us it may come as something of a shock to be obliged to think of the assessment part of the National Curriculum package as having the same legal force as the two parts which have grabbed most of the public attention so far (the attainment targets and the programmes of study), but those who read the first Task Group on Assessment and Testing (TGAT) Report when it came out in 1987 and have thought about the effects in practical terms on the students will be unsurprised.

We also need to pay attention to what we are being told about the process by which the statutory orders are being drawn. The SEAC mode of operation is to negotiate the assessment arrangements with the Secretary of State bit by bit and to make this correspondence publicly available. (Visitors to SEAC's headquarters at Newcombe House can collect a set. Otherwise you can ask for these important – if tediously bureaucratic – exchanges to be sent to you by post.)

SEAC's role, as defined by the 1988 Education Reform Act, is to offer advice to the Secretary of State on the development, implementation and operation of the whole National Curriculum assessment system. The Secretary of State has full power to accept, reject or modify the proposals as he thinks fit. Moreover, while SEAC does appear to consider it necessary to consult LEAs, examination boards and other interested parties, it is not obliged to reflect their views. At the end of the day, the Secretary of State can, if he so wishes, make key decisions which conflict either with the advice of his appointees on SEAC and/or any further views which may have reached him filtered through SEAC's consultation procedures.

This concentration of power in central government provides the context for any current discussion of assessment and English. Whatever else we may wish to consider in relation to the teaching and learning of English, we need to hold on to an understanding of the underlying functions which the national system of assessment and testing has been designed to perform. The accompanying diagram indicates both the ways in which the assessment of individual students is to be controlled and the ways in which data gathered about individual students is to be used to trigger other mechanisms which are consequences of the 1988 Act. It is a complex set of arrangements: bureaucratic but at the same time intended to bring about dramatic changes in teachers' and schools' fortunes; authoritarian but with a veneer of local autonomy for schools and 'choice' for parents.

The statutory orders for assessment, and the powerful roles of SEAC and the Secretary of State in implementing them, are not an additional item tacked on to the National Curriculum as, it might seem, an afterthought. They are, rather, the centre of the system and the means by which the inter-relating mechanisms of the Education Reform Act are to be brought into play. I include here a brief résumé of the recent history of developments in assessment, which may be useful at this point to show how National Curriculum and assessment initiatives set in motion by Sir Keith Joseph in 1984 when he was Secretary of State took on a sharper and more specific form in the years 1986–8. You may remember that Sir Keith in his speech to the North of England Education Conference called for the raising of standards through the setting of explicit objectives for the curriculum, national criteria for the GCSE, moves towards a system of criterion- referencing in exams at 16 and a reorganisation of the examination boards. His successor, Kenneth Baker, stepped up the pace of change dramatically, moving from consultation and research conducted through the HMI and the examination boards to re-shaping the curriculum and its assessment, using carefully vetted groups of people thought to be free of vested educational interests.

July 1987: As a prelude to legislation, a consultation document, *The National Curriculum 5–16*, was circulated, which proposed that there should be assessment of all students in state schools at 7, 11, 14 and 16 and that these results should be reported towards the end of the year in which the majority of students reach one of the age points. It was envisaged that 'much of the assessment at ages 7 (or thereabouts), 11 and 14, and at 16 in non-examined subjects' would be done by teachers 'as an integral part of normal classroom work'. It was expected that GCSE would provide 'the main means of assessment' in the foundation subjects at 16 for virtually all students, on the basis of a revision of the national GCSE criteria to select the attainment targets. It also proposed that, 'at the heart of the assessment process' there should be nationally prescribed tests, given and marked by teachers in the classroom but with arrangements made, probably with examining groups, for external moderation.

At the same time, the Secretary of State set out terms of reference for subject working groups and set up the Task Group on Assessment and Testing (TGAT). This was instructed to advise him on:

> the practical considerations which should govern all
> assessment including testing of attainment at age

(approximately) 7, 11, 14 and 16 within a national curriculum; including the marking scale or scales and kind of assessment to be used, the need to differentiate, so that the assessment can promote learning across a range of abilities, the relative roles of informative and diagnostic assessment, the uses to which the results of the assessment should be put, the moderation requirements needed to secure credibility for assessments, and the publication and other services needed to support the system – with a view to securing assessment and testing arrangements which are simple to administer, understandable by all in and outside the education service, cost effective and supportive of learning in schools.

TGAT was also instructed to:

take into account the need not to increase calls on teachers' and pupils' time for activities which do not directly promote learning, and to limit costs.

October 1987: TGAT was given further guidance which distinguished assessment purposes concerned with students' learning (diagnostic, formative, summative of attainments, recording achievement) and purposes concerned with publicising and evaluating the work of the education service and its various parts in the light of the pupils' achievements.

This supplementary advice emphasised the use that was to be made of the assessment of students as a performance indicator to gauge the efficiency of the education system as a whole. It was pointed out that this would require procedures for ensuring consistency and comparability between different approaches to assessment, including testing, and for aggregating results.

December 1987: In its main report, TGAT proposed a national assessment model which would chart progression across ten levels, covering ages 7–16. Anxious to avoid a 'top down' approach it proposed that the new system should be phased towards GCSE rather than down from it. Criteria and scales devised were to relate to 'expected routes of development'. Subjects were to be seen as made up of a number of profile components which in turn were made up of a cluster of attainment targets. In addition to teachers' own assessment of normal classroom work, there were to be externally provided tests:

to elicit a particular response in a standardised manner, and to rate this, using standardised methods, so that the pupil assessed would be assigned a score, grade, or category...the national system should employ tests for which a wide range of modes of presentation, operation and response should be used so that each may be valid in relation to the attainment targets assessed. These particular tests should be called 'standard assessment tasks' and they should be so designed that flexibility of form and use is allowed wherever this can be consistent with national comparability of results.

TGAT proposed, as an integral part of the plan, a group moderation procedure that was to provide a means of using teachers' professional judgements as a means of aligning teachers' assessments with the results of national tests. It suggested that the publication of assessment results should take place:

> if, and only if, this is done in the context of reports about that school as a whole, so that it can be fair to that school's work and take account so far as possible of socio-economic and other influences.

March 1988: TGAT produced a further series of three short reports. The first of these included a statement on the way in which levels were to be established:

> Initially, the norms now expected for particular ages will be used in helping to identify criteria appropriate for the system of ten levels; but once devised, the system will rest on the levels and criteria alone, through which different pupils may progress at different paces.

The second supplementary report elaborated this mechanism for the establishment of criterion-referencing, making a virtue of employing what was described as a 'rough and ready' approach in its construction:

> ...it does not depend on empirical evidence of a particular linear, or other, pattern of learning for its initial construction, although the definitions of the levels may need to be reviewed in individual cases in the light of information about the actual distribution of pupils' performance when the national curriculum and assessment system are in operation.

They did not discuss whether this procedure might be problematic, being apparently more interested in generating an internally consistent system than in keeping sight of information external to it.

This historical sequence gives the main elements which made up the overarching framework within which the English Working Group (Cox) operated and the terms of reference which they accepted as given. They have said that they had insufficient time to examine assessment issues as fully as they would have wished, though they were able to offer some general advice on what they thought were positive forms of assessment and commented on the specific proposals made by the Secretaries of State. Broadly speaking, the important things for us to note are that:

1.   They endorsed the idea of a linear form of progression over ten levels, despite their acknowledgement of the development of language use as recursive and the subject as process-orientated.

2.   They made up, with a high degree of conscientiousness, abstract statements of attainment for each of these levels, even generating a further sub-division of criterion – the strand – in an unsuccessful attempt to be fully systematic.

3.   They recognised that, as a consequence of having specified the levels in such

specific detail and insisting on each student demonstrating competence 'in all the strands of an attainment target', there could be some apparent lowering of standards in English compared with other subjects (14.34).

4. They proposed a combination of elements for assessment at 16 (coursework assessed by teachers + some coursework undertaken in controlled conditions + SATs including end-of-course assessment and written examinations) which showed a lack of understanding of GCSE, and the coursework mode of assessment in particular.

It is worth remembering that these developments, which may substantially change the assessment of English, did not occur in a vacuum. A very great deal of English teacher energy has gone into discussion of assessment in the last 30 years. Both the National Association for the Teaching of English and the London Association which preceded it, undertook pioneering work, which informs much current practice in assessment. English teachers on examination boards and in their own schools have continually searched for effective forms of assessment which would allow children to demonstrate what they know, understand and can do. Over the years, English teachers, with others, have been instrumental in bringing about: the demise of the barren comprehension task in examinations and the multiple choice test (Sir Keith also helped this one on its way out); a broadening of the range of kinds of writing thought worthy of assessment; the inclusion in examinations of the assessment of speaking and listening; the replacement of subtractive by positive forms of marking; the advent of reliable forms of impression marking; coursework alternatives to the timed test; a major rethinking of the principles for choosing literary texts and so on.

In many schools today, the English department has a commitment to many of the following: ways of describing students' achievements for the purpose of whole-school assessment, which avoid using crude grades and which reflect a wide range of linguistic and literary competences, including some in other languages than English; use of portfolios of individual students' writing as a means of demonstrating how understandings and skills develop over time; student self-assessment schemes; assessment of units of work in which the assessment objectives have been discussed at the beginning as well as at the end of the work; syllabuses which require 100% coursework modes of assessment for English and English Literature at GCSE; and other rich, and flexible, ways of gathering and reporting information about students.

These are a touchstone which may help us to keep our heads clear in these times of rapid, sometimes dogma-driven, change. Whereas with respect to assessment the emphasis for English teachers up to now has been on finding satisfactory ways of making descriptions, the task assigned to the English Working Group was to dream up a set of prescriptions.

In its strongest form, criterion-referencing leaves no room for manoeuvre – you either achieve a target, or level, or you don't. Thus, if each strand in the English Statutory Orders is to be seen in this way (as is proposed by the English Working Group) the typical English classroom is going to be focused on meeting detailed, abstract criteria which have little relationship to the kinds of classroom conversations and opportunities for reading and writing which we have in the past found to be most productive. Attention will be less on the programmes of study than on how the achievement of a particular level is going to be assessed.

Weaker forms of criterion-referencing allow for compensation and some use of general impression, as all those who have completed adequately all the items in a driving test but still failed to convince an examiner of their general competence as a driver know only too well! For all practical purposes of assessment in English, student, teacher and parent are in need less of information as to whether every single detail in the specified National Curriculum has been achieved, than a general sense of what the student can achieve across a range of opportunities in, and through, language.

As I tried to make clear at the outset, the difficulty is knowing exactly where we are now. The National Curriculum Council's Consultation Report barely discusses questions about the nature of the subject and the assessment implications of dividing it up into a hierarchy of levels. The framework for responses to some extent precluded such discussion; but we should note that the terms of reference issued by Kenneth Baker in June 1989 were quite general, asking for a report on practicability, levels, coverage and precision. The NCC's Report reduces the results from the consultation procedure to a set of statistical statements, for example:

> Three quarters of all respondents indicated endorsement of
> an approach which retained 100% coursework, that
> involved writing under 'controlled conditions' as the GCSE
> currently requires. Problems associated with the
> implementation of SATs concerned over half the
> respondents.

These are indicative but, even as statistics, extremely unreliable, since they do not reveal how they have balanced the responses from individuals with those from LEAs and associations. More damaging, they fail to acknowledge adequately that substantive arguments have been put forward which, if accepted, would entail a major restructuring and simplification of the attainment targets.

Much of the NCC's effort has gone into sharpening and clarifying what they term descriptions of performance in order to remove imprecision in the statements of attainment. It has also increased exemplification at each level and opened up possibilities for the use of exemplar material at a later date. The Report's very brief separate section on assessment rejects the Secretary of State's proposal for a higher weighting at Key Stage 4 for reading and writing at the expense of speaking and listening. Beyond this, as far as assessment is concerned, the NCC has merely endorsed comments made on the Working Group's Report by SEAC.

The positions adopted by SEAC in relation to the English Working Group's Report are of interest in that they demonstrate how little is yet finally decided at the level of individual subjects. Inter alia, SEAC committed itself to further work on:

> the nature of, and relationship between, ordinary
> coursework, controlled coursework and end-of-course
> assessment;

the most effective means of reporting the positive
achievement of pupils attaining levels 1–3;
the question of the separate certification of literature.

It expressed an intention to offer subject specific advice on determining levels of attainment in the attainment targets and it noted that progression, particularly in the knowledge about language strand needs further work.

This last item, almost alone, hints at the kind of analysis which might challenge the general consensus which appears to accept that the TGAT model can be applied to English (it is up to teachers in other subject areas to decide whether it works for them) and that all that is required is some refinement of descriptors. As LATE said in its responses to *English for Ages 5–11*, and repeated in its responses to *English for Ages 5–16*:

> The move to operationalise the TGAT proposals with respect to English immediately reveals the difficulties involved in the construction of levels of attainment for the subject. We are aware, as probably are the members of the Working Group, that these hierarchies are crude and arbitrary. More than this, we doubt whether a developmental order can be proposed which does not have major problems within it...

> The danger is that the lists will be self-justifying, establishing and creating the products they describe. Once defined within the Act, these hierarchies will set a supposed order of development to which teachers will teach and against which children will be tested...

LATE is surely not alone in thinking that the whole structure of content should be discussed, both in terms of its internal coherence (what sense can be made of the levels and strands as a system) and its relationship to what is known, but in the National Curriculum often ignored, of children's development as speakers, readers and writers.

I make no excuse for having concentrated so far on the building blocks of the system and the ways in which they have been, and are being, shifted around. Neither, in the context of talking about assessment do I feel the need to make positive, balancing statements about the achievements of the English Working Group and the NCC (though as we have seen there are some causes for commendation). The task, ultimately, is not to assess how much it has been possible to achieve in a difficult climate, or to identify some of the actors' liberal and humane views of English, but to search out the heart of the system. Criterion-referenced assessment (especially if very detailed and requiring the full attainment of each separate criterion) is bound to produce an assessment-led curriculum (whatever TGAT, the English Working Group or the NCC might say they prefer). This is what they are designed to do. They intended to narrow down what it is possible to do in the classroom, to the achievement of specific objectives, and not others.

What then will prove to be the principal assessment issues of the 1990s, if we assume that for the time being we have to work within (if not accept without challenge) a system which requires the assignment of children to levels at each of the Key Stages? Some crystal ball gazing, based on the fragments coming out from SEAC and elsewhere, may not be inappropriate. I find it difficult to foresee any other scenario than teachers having the major role in the assessments related to the National Curriculum. Whatever the Prime Minister's distrust of teachers, the cost of assessing seven million school students by external means of any kind is going to be the deciding factor. Work on just what teachers can reasonably be expected to do in the time available has not been pursued by SEAC with the same enthusiasm and resources which they have devoted to SATs' development. Material has been produced to raise primary teachers' awareness of assessment issues through INSET, and a similar project, to do the same for secondary teachers, has been set in motion.

What is still missing is clear information on what guidelines will be laid down as Orders for how teachers will be expected to assess students who are reaching the end of a Key Stage.

The one part of the procedure that has already been decided by SEAC is that only information concerning a student's performance in relation to the National Curriculum will be statutorily recorded in a Record of Achievement. The wider description of achievements, to which many schools have become accustomed, will remain optional and up to schools and LEAs to include if they wish. In reporting at the end of Key Stages a school, as a minimum, will have to give parents a set of grades for the subject overall, and for profile components within it, on the 10 point scale. Parents will be able to ask for further information by requesting full details of their child's progress in reaching each attainment target, which will have to be provided by the school within 15 days (The Education (Individual Pupils' Achievements) (Information) Regulations 1990).

Despite these pressures, teachers will, of course, continue to assess their students in a variety of ways during their teaching – as they always have done – and will stubbornly resist check-list approaches. However, there will be a high level of anxiety caused by the lists of attainment targets and levels of attainment, particularly for those teaching at the end of Key Stages, and anxiety about how well the children are doing. Headteacher and/or parent pressure will probably ensure that the levels of attainment also impinge dramatically on other years as well. Additionally, the National Assessment arrangements, as a result of Angela Rumbold's recommendation and now confirmed in the draft regulations being circulated, include a regulation requiring schools to report students' grades to parents every year. In-course assessment by teachers is the only reliable way in which some of the most important attainment targets can be assessed. Attainment targets specifying range can only properly be assessed over considerable stretches of time and in varied circumstances. For example, a statement which specifies:

> Read a range of poetry, fiction, literary non-fiction, eg
> letters, diaries, autobiographies, and drama, including some
> works written before the 20th century and works from
> different cultures

relies on a teacher building up knowledge over time, as does the assessment of writing in a wide variety of forms – though in this case (perhaps in both) a portfolio of writing could be brought together, as additional evidence, at the end of a Key Stage.

For the present, the most powerful strategy which appears to be available to all teachers concerned with language is to demonstrate, to all who will pay attention, the strength and reliability of teacher assessment and record-keeping. The best way of preventing the statements of attainment coming to dominate practice will be to show the narrowness of such approaches by comparison with broader descriptions of students' language achievements – including their bilingualism, where appropriate. The ILEA Primary Language Record has provided a vigorous and creative model. Secondary teachers have time to adapt it to their own different circumstances and time constraints, but its philosophy has considerable potential at this level also. The Centre for Language in Primary Education's new guide: *Patterns of Learning: The Primary Language Record and The National Curriculum* provides a compelling counter-argument to any teachers who feel that life must be dominated by the attainment targets.

> Any teacher would need to know more about a child's
> progress and development in language and literacy than
> could be gathered from the English attainment statements,
> which provide only minimum descriptions of progress in
> language. Because of this lack, in this publication we suggest
> a model of learning which is in some important aspects
> broader than that presented in the National Curriculum
> document...(p. 5)

In the longer term, given proper initial and in-service training, and adequate local support and resource provision, the extra responsibilities for assessing students in relation to the National Curriculum will prove an important extension of teachers' professional skills. Indeed, it is possible to envisage a system, at some future point, which will rely chiefly, or entirely, on these methods to help teachers to make judgements against a set of National Curriculum statements. Indeed, for all those purposes of assessment which face towards teaching and learning, professional teacher assessment, checked by comparison with other teachers and subject to local or HMI inspection as to full delivery of the attainment targets and programmes of study, could prove quite satisfactory in giving all students access to their curriculum entitlement.

You will recall that TGAT was given the task of inventing a model which could face one way towards learning but the other towards accountability. It was in an attempt to achieve this that it looked for a device which could achieve some measure of comparability nationally and settled upon the SAT. In the TGAT system, teacher assessments were to be combined with SAT assessment through complex (and expensive) moderation procedures, which acknowledged that teachers would need to discuss individual students in some detail. This has since been rejected at Key Stage 1, being replaced by a review procedure within individual schools – possibly involving an external moderator – with some cases being referred to a local moderating group. In this procedure, it was suggested that SAT results should be used for recording and reporting purposes where they were available; that is to say that the SAT assessment would be 'preferred' to the teacher judgement. These arrangements are being placed in the hands of LEAs for Key Stage 1.

Since then, some changes appear to have occurred. At Key Stage 1, according to *The Independent* (11.12.89), the length of time taken to administer the SATs, the part played by oral work and the cost of any form of external assessment arrangements have led to a decision that the teachers of 7-year-olds will be 'in charge of all assessment'. Talk of the SAT assessment being 'preferred' is claimed to be at an end, but the report also noted that Ministers have not yet decided on the teacher role with respect to marking and standardisation of SATs at the other Key Stages. Whether this reflects a more pragmatic line of thinking throughout the system or merely reflects a flexibility which has to be employed in relation to the assessment of 7-year-olds, remains to be seen.

SEAC is necessarily going to have to rely substantially on the SATs development groups and the information that they are able to bring back from the classroom as to what can be achieved, and under what conditions, by SATs. Teachers will play a major role in their development, since there is no way to determine what a student can do at a particular level other than by working with teachers in a wide variety of classrooms. There are few ground rules for the construction, and operation, of SATs and thus for upper primary and secondary teachers no simple answers to the question: 'What will SATs be like?' At Key Stage 1, SATs have now been trialled on a massive scale throughout the country but, at Key Stage 3, the SATs development teams are still at an experimental, research-focused stage. No work is in progress with respect to Key Stage 2, and activity at Key Stage 4 is limited to the work of a GCSE task group whose job is to bring GCSE syllabuses into line with the Attainment Targets. The strategy apears to be to get systems up and running at Key Stages 1 and 3 and then to see what further is needed and how the arrangements can be aligned.

The SATs development group at Key Stage 3 has to face some intractable problems. 'Flexibility in form and use', was advocated by TGAT, 'wherever this can be consistent with national comparability of results.' But this is an understatement of the two conflicting functions. They have been given a pretty free hand to find ways of gathering information about students across attainment targets and across levels within attainment targets, as a check on what is already known by the teacher. The easy part of this is to concentrate on the face towards the students' learning. The difficult part is to achieve a satisfactory level of comparability.

Both of the development groups concerned with English seem to share a general dislike for crude attempts at discrete skill testing and to espouse the TGAT proposal that there should be little 'discontinuity between teachers own assessment of normal classroom work and the use by them of externally provided tests' (TGAT main report para. 49). By and large, they have so far been involved in exploring SATs that integrate the profile components. They are exploring possibilities for assessment within sequences of work, taking up to five hours over a period of two or three weeks, which allow opportunities for assessing a number of aspects of the National Curriculum. There are, however, differences in philosophy and stance towards assessment.

My personal view is that there is little possibility that a single SAT, even one that creates a wide variety of opportunities for reading, writing and talking, can hope to gather information from more than a cross section of the whole English curriculum at Key Stage 3. Such SATs as are being tried out at present seem more likely to produce information with respect to a number of more generalised assessment objectives than with respect to each strand in each statement of attainment. Such evidence may provide the means to calibrate the kinds of performances that children are capable of achieving in the classroom against the National Curriculum specification or, alternatively, may suggest ways in which that specification will have to be revised in the cold light of classroom realities.

For TGAT, standardisation was considered to consist of finding a common format of tasks, assessment arrangements, and reporting of results. By this it was intended that there should be clear rules for the administration of the task; standard formats for marking; and that any 'tests' should be tried out on a national scale prior to use. Though it is possible to predict that SATs may be constructed which combine good classroom practice with such regularised procedures for their administration and marking as TGAT proposed, it is less clear that any such SATs should be considered more than rather approximately comparable nationally. Even taken together with teacher assessment, some as yet unspecified form of moderation; non-statutory guidance from NCC and SEAC; future availability of exemplar material, INSET on assessment and so on, the information gained and turned into 'results' will be neither objective nor (pace Sir Keith) absolute and should only be used for purposes of evaluating the education system with great care – if it should be used at all!

External assessment is not a new issue at 16. We are well accustomed to procedures which, at considerable cost in both money and time, achieve some degree of reliability and comparability. Moreover, we have a newly reformed examination of recognised worth. Even in relation to the accountability issues, most teachers have come to terms with the publication of examination results – though the ways in which results should be reported are more open to dispute. League tables do not provide fair comparisons.

But important issues are unresolved, and what seemed settled a year ago is again in doubt. For example, there is no challenge to the general principle that GCSE will be the chief means of assessing achievement at 16, but it is not yet clear what provision there needs to be for students who do not, for whatever reasons, take GCSE. Level 4 has been set by John MacGregor as the minimum level of attainment at which a GCSE award can be made, in conflict with the wishes of SEAC, which wished to assess across the full National Curriculum range. It appears that GCSE English, as a 'core' subject, will be obligatory for all students, but it is less certain what will happen to English Literature in the fight for curriculum space. Meanwhile SEAC still ponders over dual certification.

From September 1992, GCSE syllabuses will all have to conform to national criteria revised in the light of the National Curriculum. These criteria are already in draft form and provide an important midway point between the detail of the National Curriculum and the level of detail needed for writing syllabus assessment objectives. Examination boards had to get their revised syllabuses in to SEAC for approval by March 1991.

Following the line of his predecessor, the Secretary of State, John MacGregor, insisted that the general criteria must require in all subjects 'a balance between coursework and a terminal examination'. In his view the balance may vary from subject to subject, but a terminal examination (what a horrid term!) 'should always contribute significantly to the final assessment'. This has to be read as an attack on 100% coursework modes of assessment, which are known to give offence to some Far Right members of the Conservative Party. Our response has to be: prove to us

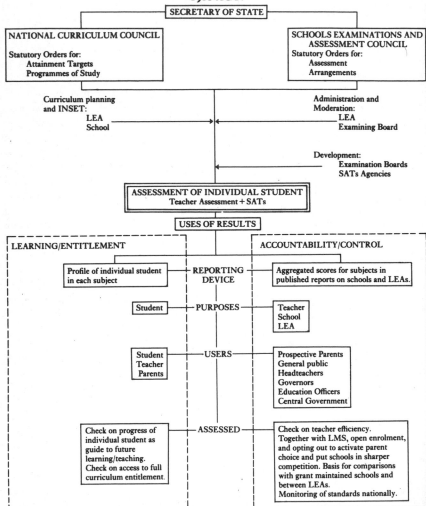

ASSESSMENT OF SCHOOL STUDENTS
RELATED TO THE MECHANISMS OF THE
1988 ACT.

SECRETARY OF STATE

NATIONAL CURRICULUM COUNCIL

Statutory Orders for:
    Attainment Targets
    Programmes of Study

SCHOOLS EXAMINATIONS AND
ASSESSMENT COUNCIL
Statutory Orders for:
    Assessment
    Arrangements

Curriculum planning
and INSET:
    LEA
    School

Administration and
Moderation:
    LEA
    Examining Board

Development:
    Examination Boards
    SATs Agencies

ASSESSMENT OF INDIVIDUAL STUDENT
Teacher Assessment + SATs

USES OF RESULTS

LEARNING/ENTITLEMENT

ACCOUNTABILITY/CONTROL

Profile of individual student
in each subject
— REPORTING
DEVICE —
Aggregated scores for subjects in
published reports on schools and LEAs.

Student
— PURPOSES —
Teacher
School
LEA

Student
Teacher
Parents
— USERS —
Prospective Parents
General public
Headteachers
Governors
Education Officers
Central Government

Check on progress of
individual student as
guide to future
learning/teaching.
Check on access to full
curriculum entitlement.
— ASSESSED —
Check on teacher efficiency.
Together with LMS, open enrolment,
and opting out to activate parent
choice and put schools in sharper
competition. Basis for comparisons
with grant maintained schools and
between LEAs.
Monitoring of standards nationally.

that there is a better, or more reliable, way to demonstrate the range and variety of a student's achievements in English at 16!

LATE was blunt in its criticisms of the English Working Group on this matter:

> ...they should have built their recommendations around the 100% coursework option. We are aware that the Secretary of State has made it clear to SEAC that he wants there to be end-of-course examinations in all subjects. The Working Group should have been saying loudly and clearly that this was not needed for English.

As we saw above, SEAC has recently committed itself to do further work on 'the nature of, and relationship between, ordinary coursework, controlled coursework, and end-of-course assessment'. This is a debate to influence.

Anyone who has borne with me this far will have some understanding of why I set out with an image of the three limbs hopping in ungainly fashion over the rocks. At times it seems that only the waves washing away this awkward conglomeration of pieces can provide a satisfactory way forward. More realistically, of course, we have to live with, bring under control and rebuild this set of devices.

Some, like the idea of a National Curriculum, have emancipatory potential. This is true of assessment arrangements also, though there is not space to elaborate the idea here. Children and young people, their parents, headteachers, employers, local communities, central government, all (in different ways) have rights to the kind of information which assessment can provide. At issue is: what should it be? how should it be gathered? and how should it be used? Thus there are battles both in the short term, over such matters as the nature of SATs and the future of 100% coursework, and in the long term about the nature of the system as a whole.

As the wider set of mechanisms slowly begins to operate, I have two major areas of anxiety. The first concerns the way in which the system could – if we allow it – become self-justifying, sealed off from the real world, and naturalised (generally be thought reliable, scientific and objective). Professor Cox ensured that his group's report emphasised the provisional nature of its proposals, but it is easy for such perceptions to be lost when they are converted into legally binding orders for which there is no review timetable. The second concerns the effects that the system will have if operated over time. If you're doing badly, the effect of being assigned to levels at significant stages in your life is unlikely to make you work harder and strive more. The whole mechanism may well depress rather than raise expectations.

Both of these anxieties call for a complex programme of action. Arguments' need to be developed in staffrooms, unions, subject associations, parents' and governors' meetings. Specific issues need to be pursued with John MacGregor, with SEAC, with examination boards, with SATs development teams, with LEA advisers. Alternatives need to be thought through and shared with all who will listen. Research on the effects of assessment practices on students, classes, schools, need to be documented and published. Mounting evidence of discrimination against particular groups of students could be a powerful argument for reappraisal of all the arrangements.

In the end, no amount of detailed abstraction in a written specification, such as we have in the National Curriculum for English, removes the need for success in the central teacher-student activity, in which students first become engaged and then intrinsically interested in knowledge, ideas and experiences beyond their own. The positive work of teachers with students in maintaining high expectations of what all students can achieve has to be at the heart of a national system for the assessment of students if it is to have any chance of success. If it is not at the centre of things, the abstractions will remain outside the grasp of very many students. SEAC and the Secretary of State should consider, first and foremost, how they can ensure that teachers feel good about their role, their subject, their working conditions, and the value placed on them by society. No other course is open to them if they want – as they claim – to raise standards.

This essay appeared in *The English Magazine* 23, Summer 1990.

Hughes, Ted (1968), *The Iron Man*, Faber & Faber

ALEX McLEOD

Critical Literacy and Critical Imagination: writing that works for a change

Ever since his participation in the research which led to the publication of *The Development of Writing Abilities* in 1976, Alex McLeod has explained and exemplified his conviction that writing in secondary schools is at its best when pupils deal with topics that matter to them as they sort out their views of themselves and of the world. Recently, he has been responsible for the British part of an international writing exchange between London students and others in California. Here we see him generating from his reading, from his writing of a poem and from the examples offered by his students a theory of social action which has its roots in classrooms. In doing so he illustrates his conviction that imaginative and powerful writing is not a privileged activity for a small number of 'cherished private souls' but possible for all, and a necessary goal for democratic English teaching.

Only I ask you now to realize
When everyone is learning how to write,
What happens if you shrug, and drop your voice.

Raymond Williams (1983, p. 258)

Writing that matters is social action, and that applies both in and out of school. I begin with the assumption that classrooms are good places to consider questions about what's going on in the world, what's wrong with it, how it might be different and what the future could be like.

My thinking about this started in Britain and continued in California. Here is a view from one of our more interesting playwrights, Hanif Kureishi. It was written in one of the worst winters of the present administration.

> Britain is such an unpleasant and cruel country to live in at
> the moment – and the best and most sensible are leaving if
> they can afford to – because variety and criticism in all their
> forms, sexual, political and cultural, are being seen as
> aberrant, as unnecessary, in the paradise of money being
> established. Creativity, the human imagination, culture
> itself which is a live thing or it is nothing, are being stifled.
> In these dark times such expressions of the human spirit are
> hated – or put in the Theatre Museum.

Kureishi is giving imagination a social and political context, and I propose to develop that point of view. Of course the word is open to widely different interpretations. How you use it probably depends on what kind of psychology you work from, what kinds of literary theory you find suit you best, and also your theory of writing and learning to write. I see imagination as a process by which people most energetically engage with – and ask questions about – their lives and the circumstances that shape their future. I will pursue that assertion by discussing some writing, mostly by school students.

I think of writing as essentially a social activity, though sometimes it seems to be taught as if its social function were not important. Here is the view of Marilyn Cooper and Michael Holzman in their introduction to *Writing as Social Action*,

> What we mean by social is that writing is located in the
> social world and, thus, is fundamentally structured by the
> shape of that environment...If we wish to change writing
> activities within our society, we must look not at what we
> think happens within our students' heads but rather what
> happens between our students and us, between our students
> and other social groups with which they interact...Writing is
> a form of social action. It is part of the way in which some
> people live in the world. Thus, when thinking about
> writing, we must also think about the way that people live in
> the world.

I have chosen my examples to show some of these interactions. In schools the first and nearest of the 'other social groups with which they interact' are their peers. We have seen how writing in classrooms at its best grows out of those interactions in which students bring their talk about their lives and their experience of each other into a particular focus – and they write something that matters for them (Hardcastle 1985, McLeod 1986, Dyson 1989).

Before I pursue that line of thought further, I need to remind myself, and you, that as we do not all talk in the same way, we are not likely all to write in the same way, though there are some forces that try to constrain us to do so. I offer here a comment by James Baldwin on the languages of England:

> It goes without saying, then, that language is also a political
> instrument, means and proof of power. It is the most vivid
> and crucial key to identity: it reveals the private identity,
> and connects one with, or divorces one from, the larger,
> public or communal identity. There have been, and are,
> times and places, when to speak a certain language would be
> dangerous, even fatal. Or, one may speak the same language,
> but in such a way that one's antecedents are revealed, or
> (one hopes) hidden. This is true in France, and is absolutely
> true in England: The range (and reign) of accents on that
> damp little island make England coherent for the English
> and totally incomprehensible for everyone else. To open
> your mouth in England is (if I may use black English) to
> 'put your business in the street'. You have confessed your
> parents, your youth, your school, your salary, your self-
> esteem and, alas, your future.

So I now declare these things: with Baldwin, that 'language is a political instrument, means and proof of power'; with Kureishi, that imagination is being stifled, and where it is not quite stifled, as in school, it is still undervalued and inadequately understood, and I take up Williams's declaration in that poem with the answer I think he was looking for – that it's time 'to stand, and raise your voice'.

Could it be that language as 'means and proof of power', which Baldwin found so potent, is where we should begin? How can I take you from Kureishi and Baldwin to writing in school? Baldwin contributed to a new consciousness – not only for people of colour, but for the courage of gay men. Kureishi's films and plays challenge the oppressive certainties of a dangerous era. Williams urged us to believe that in such a world, there are needs that only imagination can meet.

> There are periods in a culture when what we call real knowledge seems to have to take priority over what is commonly called imagination. In our own image-conscious politics and commerce there is a proliferation of small instrumental professions which claim the sonorous titles of imagination and creativity for what are, when examined, simple and rationalised processes of reproduction and presentation. To know what is happening, in the most factual and down-to-earth ways, is indeed an urgent priority in such a world. A militant empiricism claims all; in a world of rearmament and mass unemployment seems rightly to claim all. Yet it is now the very bafflement of this militant empiricism, and especially of the best of it, that should now hold our attention. It can quickly identify its enemies among the hired image-makers, the instrumental projectors of the interests of wealth and power. *But now, very clearly, there are other deeper forces at work, which perhaps only imagination, in its full processes, can touch and reach and recognise and embody.* [my emphasis] If we see this, we still usually hesitate between tenses: between knowing in new ways the structures of feeling that have directed and now hold us, and finding in new ways the shape of an alternative, a future, that can be genuinely imagined and hopefully lived. There are many other kinds of writing in society, but these now – of past and present and future – are close and urgent, challenging many of us to try both to understand and to attempt them.

Williams is proposing, then, that only imagination could move us towards 'finding in new ways the shape of an alternative, a future, that can be genuinely imagined and hopefully lived'. And I am proposing that this is something that we *can* do in school. I am not setting out to prove that imagination is being stifled, exactly, but the way imaginative work, writing especially, is set up and received frequently amounts to suffocation – or at least to consignment to a conservatory or to an elegant but unproductive garden, rather than to a hothouse of ideas. I want specifically to disagree with the popular belief that imagination is an individual product which springs from the soul or the heart or the gut – whatever it is that people sometimes seem to think that they write with when they are talking about creative writing. I also disagree with the approach which sets imaginative writing in school apart from informative, discursive and persuasive writing. Informative writing without imagination is likely to be dead. And who would want to claim that a poem, a play or a story is not also informative and persuasive? Jerome Bruner suggests that,

> The imaginative application of the narrative mode leads...to good stories, gripping drama, believable (though not necessarily true) historical accounts. It deals in human or human-like intention and action and the vicissitudes and consequences that mark their course. It strives to put its timeless miracles into the particulars of experience and to locate the experience in time and place.

Now put that beside a suggestion from Janet Emig:

> We know that words are events affecting other events; and that if students are truly to learn to read and write, they must witness literacy making a difference, first to themselves, then to others...
> What is it we must imagine? Alternative social, economic and sexual structures and arrangements since so many we have are obviously bankrupt.

I hope that Bruner and Emig would think that I am heartily agreeing with them both when I select and juxtapose these statements. Take first, 'making a difference'. Suppose we follow the possibility that imagination, dealing with 'human or human-like intention and action, and the vicissitudes and consequences that mark their course' is one of the things that can make a difference, and line that up with 'alternative social, economic and sexual structures'. I look at my own reading through some parts of my life, and think about those books that did make a difference to me, as I am sure they did for many. I'll cite just a few: *Germinal, The Ragged-Arsed Philanthropists*(*), *The Grapes of Wrath, The Fire Next Time* and *Their Eyes Were Watching God*. And, of course, re-reading can sometimes be just as potent. Shakespeare's sonnets, after I discovered that most of them were written for a male lover, I came to think of almost as personal property, as if, in a different sense, he had written them for me. I am not, of course, suggesting that writers like Bruner and Emig and Williams don't make a difference, too; they do it so well because they have the power of imagination as well as theoretical analysis and a precise sense of what it is important to say. Moreover, Williams wrote novels and poems as well as political and cultural theory.

But I am proposing here that it is not necessary to be a Tressall, a Baldwin or a Hurston, let alone a Shakespeare or a Zola, to write and 'make a difference'. I am thinking here about the kinds of writing that we hope to encourage in school. Imagination *and* argument are both undervalued, or restricted to safe subjects. I want to see more writing that combines the two. Even if this writing makes its impact

---

*Raymond Williams points out that this was Robert Tressall's title for the book which appeared in a heavily abridged form as *The Ragged-Trousered Philanthropists* (Williams 1982).

only within the classroom where it was composed, it is still potentially persuasive, because classrooms can be places where writers grow. What matters first is the way emerging writers' ideas are engaged, and then their sense that – as I have proposed elsewhere (McLeod 1986) – writing can be a way of beginning to take control of their own lives. Their thinking and talking and writing emerge and take shape in the interchanges in a lively classroom, in the crossfire of opinion, evidence, argument, question and justification. These are generated from the ways they enjoy their reading and share it, from film and tv, from news and observation, from interpretation and participation, from school curriculum and students' experience as they contemplate their past, their present and their future.

Imagination, like argument, I see growing first as a conversation. Imagination is socially constructed, not something magically generated from within. The 'conversation' we might be having now finds its way into the array of conversations in the past: an intertextuality of thinking.

> Internally persuasive discourse – as opposed to one that is
> externally authoritative – is, as it is affirmed through
> assimilation, tightly interwoven with 'one's own word'. In
> the everyday rounds of our consciousness, the internally
> persuasive word is half ours and half someone else's. Its
> creativity and productivity consist precisely in the fact that
> such a word awakens new and independent words.
>
> M.M. Bakhtin

The imaginative process, as I understand it, may sometimes seem more like the conversation we have with ourselves when we're reading a stimulating book than the one we might have when we're holding up a strong point of view in a discussion. But not always. It can emerge from an actual conversation. In the dialogues and conversations of classrooms the conditions can be ideal, because classrooms are essentially places where people talk to each other and listen; so perhaps critical imagination – what Williams called 'imagination in its full processes' – can actually be encouraged and included in school activities as something more like an actual conversation.

My first example is a transcript of a dramatic monologue. Judy Logan, who teaches English in Everett Middle School, in the Mission district of San Francisco, asked her seventh-grade class of 13 year olds to prepare and present the lives and thinking of famous women and men in Black History. The students undertook extensive research, learned their 'texts' and eventually made a presentation, in role. They were invited to look for clothing their 'model' might have worn, to use props if they needed them, and to speak as if they *were* the person they had chosen and had been invited to address this actual class. Christine chose Rosa Parks. Here is her presentation:

> Hello, everyone. My name is Rosa Parks. Children, when I
> was young, my name was Rosa Macauley. I was born in a
> small town named Tuskegee, Alabama, not far from
> Montgomery, on February 4th, 1913. My momma's name
> was Leona. She was a teacher for a while. My daddy, he was
> a carpenter. I had only one brother. His name was

Sylvester. We lived on a small farm on the edge of
Montgomery with my Grandparents. I attended the
Montgomery Industrial School for girls. My favorite class
was sewing. I would make handkerchiefs and aprons and I
could sew a dress for myself from an easy pattern.

In two long paragraphs Christine outlined Parks' childhood and adolescence,
referring to the Klu Klux Klan, to segregated facilities and shops, and then to the
buses. She continued,

I finished my education at the United Alabama State
College, a school for children of all ages. One week before
my 20th birthday, I got married to Raymond Parks. Now
my name was Mrs. Rosa Parks. I joined the NAACP,
National Association for the Advancement of Colored
People, because I wanted...I was very uncomfortable with
the rules they put out for Black people. And I wanted to
defend myself and my race. I...there were many young
people in the group, and I helped them learn about their
government. Later I joined the Montgomery Voters League.
I wanted to join them because I wanted to help my people
have the freedom to vote. I tried my best to avoid the signs
marked colored. I would walk up and down stairs instead of
using elevators, and I would rather go thirsty than drink out
of a water fountain marked colored. And I would rather
walk a mile to work and back again than ride a segregated
bus. The buses were the worst, children. You would have to
get on at the front, pay your fare, then get back off and use
the back door to get back on. On December 1st, 1955, I was
coming home from work. And children, I was tired. So I
decided to take the bus. I got on the bus and I sat right
behind the white section. Soon the bus got full. Then a
white person got on the bus. And the driver came over to
me and said, "Lady, get up so this man can sit down." Now
children, my feet hurt, and I decided right then and there I
was not going to get up for anyone, anywhere, at any time
just because the color of my skin was different. So I just said
no. The driver told me how he was going to have me
arrested, but I just sat there and paid no attention to him.
He had me arrested, and his policeman put me in their jail.

Now none of this was easy for me, children, but with the
help of God and the NAACP, I was able to get out of jail
and prove to the courts that the bus company's rules were
against the laws of the United States Constitution which
says that all people should be...all citizens of the United
States, must be treated fairly. It took a very long time to do
this, children. During the meantime, in Montgomery, Black
folks boycotted the buses. We decided to stop paying money

to the bus company. So that...so we walked, children, and
we kept on walking; for a year, men, women, children, and
old folks walked in the streets of Montgomery until the
United States Supreme Court said that the bus company's
laws must change. It was a long, hard struggle, children,
and it still goes on for many different kinds of people. If we
could fight it then, we can fight it now. Let's carry on,
children.

Christine's oral presentation adds an extra dimension to her critical imagination.
She wrote it first, after careful reading and discussion with her teacher and her
friends. She was in a classroom where ideas and culture, books and lives, thinking and talking and writing, are shared. Her teacher believes that her students
should use their imagination when they write and, to her, writing is, indeed, a
form of social action. It is, as Emig put it, writing that makes a difference. All the
students in her classroom were asked to present a woman or man they admired,
and in the process they learned for themselves and taught each other, as they
planned and talked and presented – and then talked again about the presenta-
tions. The class is socially and ethnically mixed, and this diversity is regarded by
the teacher as an added resource in the classroom culture. She regularly finds
public audiences, outside school, for her students' writing.

Now let me return to my themes of 'critical imagination' and 'making a
difference'. Persuasive writing is worthwhile even if it does not reach an audience
of millions. First, the writer and her readers are sharing a sense of purpose – the
articulation of a commitment to humanity – that is greater than the sum of
individual achievements. They are learning what writing can do, can achieve, in
nurturing the thinking of a group of people who already have their ideas on the
move, and as they continue, the growth and movement of ideas will increase.
Their reading of books, their response to television and film, and essentially their
reading of the world is enlarged. Second, in classrooms like this one, they are
learning that becoming a writer, a mature writer, includes becoming able to
make one's own decisions. In the world of work and profit, writing is only valued
if it is of a kind which people do because someone else asked them to do it and,
moreover, to do it in a restricted and rule-bound way. I'm making a plea for
writing as taking control.

By now you may be wondering – at least I hope you may – does this person
do any of this himself? We know all about those teachers of literary theory and
literary criticism who haven't dared write anything themselves that could conce-
ivably be called literature – however defined – for years. Probably not since they
left primary school. Teachers of writing seem to be a little more daring. There
have been a few exciting poems in *Language Arts* in the past few years. That's a
good sign.

I'll make a modest claim. I think that my academic writing, such as it is, has been
fed by the kinds of imaginative processes I've talked about here. It has certainly been
fed by my responses to the critical imagination of both school students and college
students, but most importantly by the class of working-class boys in Hackney,
taught by John Hardcastle, with whom I worked for four years. Occasionally I write
a poem myself. I offer you one here to show that I have tried out my ideas about

critical imagination. It's a political poem, about forced emigration and language, but its context is one that is not widely known outside Scotland.

I offer it now because writing it made a difference to me, and I hope to those of my friends who read it. In writing it I wanted to make a connection between my sketchy knowledge about my own family history, and some of the issues I care about most in schools: language, history and the effects on children and their families of moving from one country to another. I had been learning, in frequent visits to the Isle of Skye, about the forced and frequently violent clearances of the Highlands of Scotland, their impact on Scottish and then on English history. I decided to try to relate those historical events to the remarkable diversity of cultures and languages in Britain today – and how they came about. So a theme of the poem is the languages of people migrating, and the economic imperatives that either force them to move, at gun point, or drive them to move in search of work and hope.

I had visited some ruins in a small glen that runs down to the sea on the west coast of Skye, and I had recently learned that in 1842 the entire community had been forced to leave – placed on a ship and transported to Newfoundland. There are only sheep in Ramasaig now, descendants perhaps of the sheep whose welfare and value mattered more to the landowner than the tenants and crofters did. This had not been my own family's experience, but they must have been perilously close to it. The Ramasaig people spoke Gaelic, and I thought about the languages of Canada and then about the languages of Britain – and the world. Borrowing Bruner's phrase, I was thinking about the 'vicissitudes and consequences' of changing one's life and language – and inevitably one's future – by moving or being transported to another country. But I also believe that the variety of languages spoken in Britain today has broadened and enriched our culture. So perhaps I am, with Emig, imagining alternative 'social, economic and sexual structures'.

RAMASAIG: 1842 – 1986
Cainnt mhàthaireil agus darna cànain
[The learning of a first and second language.]

Ruins of bothies near the shore,
Grass covered humps of granite and gravel:
There couldn't be much else.

Island horizon, Barra, Uist, Benbencula.

The bailiffs who burned the thatch
Talked plain enough English.

'If that old woman inside won't come out
She'll burn. Her fault. Her choice.
A fine ship is waiting in Harlosh.
It will take you all, mothers, fathers, babies, grandmothers,
To Nova Scotia.'

Island horizon, Barra, Uist, Benbecula, Lewis.

'No, you have no choice. There are no exceptions,
Except women over sixty-five, who have no family
To provide for them.

They can go to the workhouse
In Glasgow.'

Island horizon, Barra, Uist, Benbecula, Lewis, Canada.

Here was a little town
Of folk who fished, and grew their food,
And told old tales, in winter nights...
Sang, maybe, if the parson hadn't told them yet that music
belonged to the Devil.
And the lord's will must be done.

Lords Macleod and Macdonald, not the friendly one above.

On those ships, more died than lived.
Merchant venturers of London, Bristol and Plymouth
Had learned to sail on profitable voyages
Providing tourist rates for folk from Mali, Senghor, Accra
To Trinidad, Haiti and Carolina.
For them, the auction block
For the young girls and lads of Ramasaig, who knows?

Island horizon, Barra, Uist, Benbecula, Lewis, Canada,
Heaven or Hell.

Hell, most likely,
Sickness and death
Atlantic gales, at sea
And on that barren land,
Ruled by those English laws.

Only themselves to talk their own tongue with,
To sing its songs of love and loss, and old heroic deeds.
And maybe the tales of lies, told to get them there.

Island horizon, Barra, Uist, Benbecula, Lewis, Newfoundland.

Now, a time has come
For new words, new worlds, new plans, new hopes.
Now we claim our tongues. They are our history.

Our languages are tales of struggles we have won
And those we will win...soon.

Soweto, Brixton, Bronx, Botswana,
Sylhet, Mangere, Cairo, Mullumbimbi, Managua.
Can we make good, make plain, make strong
The power, the will, the hope
That all our tongues have taught us?

Island horizon, Barra, Uist, Benbecula, Lewis, London,
Soweto, Brixton, Bronx...

[June 1987]

I wish to thank Catherine Macdonald, and her mother, Mrs Macdonald of Lewis, for the Gaelic translation of 'learning a first and second language'.

Let us return now to how these ideas work out in school. I have two more examples of student writing to share with you. The first comes from a fourth-form class taught by John Hardcastle in Hackney Downs School, London.

A class discussion was videotaped. It was one of many that we made in the course of the four years in which John invited me to join him for half a day a week. Previously, the agenda for all videotaped discussions had been agreed beforehand, but this time John Hardcastle decided to keep it open, knowing that in the past months a number of important questions had been considered, and several of these he thought were continuously present, becoming part of the classroom culture (Hardcastle 1985). He got the discussion moving by reminding the class of some of these questions; among other things he mentioned racism, and at one point raised the question of the time in their school lives when the black students started going round nearly always with other black students, and the white with white. This is how the discussion continued:

Participants:
Kevin (Skerritt), Sunday, David and Robert are black.
Simon (Youens) and Ricky are white.
JH is John Hardcastle, the teacher.

Kevin	We don't exactly all go hang around...most of us black...but then Youens, sir...he know both cultures and he keep everybody together. He knows Ricky, and then he knows us...in a way he keep both sides together. [several voices together]
Sunday	Ask Simon what he thinks it means. [Simon shows embarrassment.]
Kevin	Just say it out Simon man. Say it out...what you think...innit?
Simon	About what, sir? About what?
Kevin	About what I said. Don't be shy...
Simon	Then put a question to me and I'll answer...
JH	Well, Kevin says that the way the class operates you keep everything together. To some extent I agree with that.
Kevin	In a way...in a way...
JH	I don't think you keep things together on your own, because I think although you work in that way...as a white kid...It's more unusual for a white kid to be able to operate with the black kids...to understand a lot of the things that are going on, but I mean it's also...Sorry?
Simon	It's...if you grow up with them...if you start from an early age...like mixing with black people, right

early...'cause that's how I started...when I was about three...

[there is a diversion at this point, but soon David returns to the question.]

David   I think I know what Skerritt's trying to say, but I don't think it's Simon that really keeps them together...

Kevin   I don't mean that...

David   ...because I don't believe in this class that anyone is really racist. I believe they might have certain views but no one's racist. They can get along. They've got their own opinions about race and...

Kevin   They must get along because they've grown up together...innit? From the first year...

[The discussion continues on this and related topics. After a time it turns to language, and specifically to white people who take on black dialects and speech styles.]

JH   What do you feel about things like...sometimes teachers talking like black people...like sometimes Simon does it. Simon does it in...

Simon   I only do it for a joke.

Kevin   You do it good though Simon.

JH   He does do it extremely well. How do you feel about that?

Kevin   It doesn't really worry me...

Robert   It doesn't really affect them...it doesn't really do...

Kevin   Can't hurt nobody's feelings...

Simon's own personal history is making an unseen contribution to this dialogue. His father had grown up in Hackney, and in fact was a student in this same school. He went to live in South Africa and married. Simon was born there, but before he reached school age the family decided to leave and to live in England. Simon has been to visit relatives in South Africa and has written about what he saw. He was regarded by most of the class as an expert, especially on apartheid. This would not in itself explain his continuous friendship with black students, continuing through his secondary school years, but it may well have contributed to his known position as someone who 'mixes with both'.

Some months after the video discussion Simon returned to some of the questions raised here. This is how it happened. The students were now in the fifth form and nearly all their writing topics were chosen by them. The selection process usually began with a review with John Hardcastle of a piece they had just completed, and a consideration of several possibilities for what they might embark on next. Recalling the exchange on video, John suggested to Simon that he might write about an occasion when the conversation would be largely in creole, and Simon readily agreed to write about a Hackney Friday night with reggae music.

RAVING FOR A WHITE BWOY

Friday nights and Saturday nights are strictly raving times.
When I get home from school I get on the phone to my friends
asking what we are doing tonight.
'Hello Alex. Is what happen?'
'Well heavyweight are nicing up the session at the college, you
wah come?'
'Alright.'
I get dressed, nothing too fancy, not for heavyweight, cause
people come with stink bret and vim armpits. No, I just put on
my tracksuit, and I'm ready. Heavyweight starts at 8 so we'll
reach there at 10.
'Alex you ready?'
'Yeah man.'
'Lets chip round to the others.'
8 of us step down there, there we meet 10 other people we
kinda go around with. We allocate a spot in the giant hall.
Heavyweight have brought quite a lot of weight. The usual
people are there, Rethlee, Spencer, Colman, the usual bunch
of gangsters.
'Give me a draw pan that there twig, wait nah.'
A lot of my friends are in. Heavyweight run one slate and all
my friends start skanking. Yeah heavy. Challenging starts up.
The winner is heavy, the loser is saff. Leyton boys are heavy
skankers they can do some impossible moves. As a white bwoy
you would think I am a sheep in the middle of a pack of
wolves but this is not true. When I go out I hardly ever get
laughed at and I have never been harassed or beaten up,
anyway all you have to do is keep your nose out of trouble.
Coming up to 11 it's nearly time to go, heavyweight puts on
kouta and everybody starts skanking, the BO level starts
getting higher, "Jesus Christ!" my friend said. "Don't these
people believe in deodrant?" I say. "Come lets go before we
die of lack of oxygen". We step out of the college feeling ire*,
"Let's go down to the hunger-cure."
After we killed the hamburgers we stepped home.
"Later spa," my friends said...

*pronounced 'Eye Ree'

[There is more. Simon wrote about Saturday night as well, when he went to a
party. In typing I have retained his spelling because obviously some of the
non-standard spelling is deliberate and necessary. I have made a few minor
changes in punctuation to make reading easier.]

Locating this writing in its cultural context is complex, because so many different currents of thought and action are operating in one event. In Cooper and
Holzman's terms, it is writing as social action, even if it never went outside the

classroom, because it is making a statement, in a culturally diverse class, about the languages and dialects spoken there and in the students' lives outside. Simon is admired for his ability to transcend ethnic boundaries and, by implication, for his ability to comprehend and potentially remake them. His writing did in fact go beyond the classroom. It went to the Board of Examiners for the Certificate of Secondary Education. (This was the last year before GSCE.) They thought it was a remarkable achievement, but they would not agree to the Grade 1 his teacher thought he deserved for the Course Work folder. It's worth noting here that Simon was one of two white students who watched a BBC programme on racism and came to school angry about it. 'It made out that all white people are racist. We are white and we're not racist.' – a response that made an important addition to the discussion about aspects of racism in Britain that was part of the continuous agenda of the class as long as they stayed in school. Many examples of students in London schools learning each other's languages and dialects have been recorded, especially by Roger Hewitt (1986). If schools and teachers encouraged this cross-fertilisation more consistently, they might be delighted by the results.

How is imaginative writing thought about? Barnes and Barnes (1983) and Medway (1986 and 1990) suggest that the diet of personal and imaginative writing that school students are offered is usually on a severely restricted range of topics, and probably not those the students themselves are happy with, and would choose for themselves. If this happens, what is called 'creative writing' is neither imaginative nor creative. It just becomes routine and will certainly not encourage students, in their writing, to explore their most significant thinking. More seriously, students may not be encouraged, imaginatively or otherwise, to engage with issues that they feel really concern them, and which may well concern them even more in the future. But imagination is a critical weapon. The personal should never be equated with the trivial. Serious fiction demonstrates that obviously enough. Many of the most highly acclaimed novels of our generation acquire their power from the imaginative recreation of personal experience. Autobiography is not just a matter of remembering important occasions and nice or nasty things that once happened. It is also a way of making a commentary on the state of the world, about things as they are. Bruner (1990) puts it like this,

> Although autobiography is the most personal kind of
> writing, it is where you locate yourself in a culture. There is
> no sharp cut between fiction and history, between the
> personal and the social.

This is just as true for high school students as it is for famous writers. In many schools, emphasis on the personal, and on the imagination, has frequently in the past been associated with a narrow view of personal experience, and reveals considerable misconception about what imagination is and does. A writer's imagination feeds on experience and interaction, and at the same time feeds on the personal relationship of writer and reader, as well as writer and teacher. Fostering imagination, which I see as an essential role for writing teachers, should not be equated with those theories which suggest that the 'creative' writer turns inward for inspiration which is personal, individual and essentially the opposite of social concern and critical thinking.

Barnes and Barnes in 'Cherishing Private Souls?' include a report on a survey they had undertaken of writing by fifth form students. In conclusion they observe that:

> Few teachers involve their pupils in writing to persuade,
> explain, analyse, criticise, plan or justify: most of the writing
> done was decontextualized in the sense that one could not
> conceive of it having been addressed to someone for a
> purpose other than earning a grade; though a minority of
> pupils were probably writing for themselves. In sum,
> English teachers should be giving reality to Friere's dictum
> that education should be 'the means by which...men and
> women deal critically and creatively with reality, and
> discover how to participate in the transformation of their
> world'. (p. 51)

Medway (1990) proposes,

> What is needed, then, is to bring thinking back into
> personal writing, so that it presents not only re-enactments
> of experience but also related thoughts which might
> constitute initial moves in arguments – or in inquiries or
> speculations or explorations. Writers need to posit ideas as
> well as represent things. Conversely, as well as writing
> about experience being set up in such a way as to initiate
> argument, so argument needs to be about issues that matter
> to writers and relate to their experience, however broadly
> defined. The best context will be one in which participants
> share a common social experience.

One of the most significant parts of their 'common social experience' is the classroom and its culture. Cultural processes inside classrooms, and their relation to cultural processes and cultural products in the students' lives outside school, have rightly become subjects of scrutiny. Here is an example from another London school.

Dalia was, when this piece was written in 1987, a fourth-form student in a school in the London Borough of Hammersmith. Her parents are Egyptian. Her grandfather is a writer, in Egypt. Dalia was born in London, but lived and went to school for three years in Egypt, where she learnt to speak, read and write Arabic fluently. In the 1986/87 school year her class took part in a writing exchange with a school in the Bay Area of California. Her teacher, Sue Llewellyn, had been the English teacher of this class since the class had come into the school four years earlier. 'I knew them very well indeed,' she said, 'and that's why I chose this class when I was asked to take part in the exchange.'

Early in the year the two classes exchanged extended autobiographies and other writing about their schools, their lives and their interests. Later the teacher in California suggested that both classes might take on controversial issues, and Sue willingly agreed, as this fitted in well with the way she regularly organises work in her class. They read novels, poems and plays together, including, in this year, *Romeo and Juliet*. Sue is also their drama teacher. They have an hour a week in the drama studio, and she regularly takes them to London theatres. In English classes the students are usually seated round tables in groups of three or four, but the tables can be quickly moved if Sue wants a whole class discussion, when the arrangement is a square with all the students able to see one another. They are a lively class of mixed ability and diverse ethnicity. It is easy to get a serious discussion going. Typically, students' topics for writing will arise out of these discussions.

When Sue suggested that they write on controversial issues, there was no shortage of suggestions. These topics were eventually chosen: *Oppression of Women, Rape, Drug Abuse, Teenage Pregnancy, Racism, AIDS, Conflict with Parents, Euthanasia, Animal Rights, Ecology, Nuclear Power, Nuclear Arms, Acid Rain, Police Harassment of Black People.*

Dalia wrote about AIDS. In that year newspaper reports and tv programmes about HIV and AIDS were frequent but often inaccurate and misleading. Students often discussed them, and usually seemed to be better informed than some popular daily papers. Dalia was the only member of her class to write about AIDS. She undertook her own research, and obtained informative booklets from government sources and from the Terrence Higgins Trust, a national organisation which distributes information and organises support for people who are HIV positive or who suffer from AIDS related infections. First she wrote a factual informative piece. This is the first paragraph of a 350-word essay:

> A topic that has been dominating our newspapers recently is
> AIDS – Acquired Immune Deficiency Syndrome. It is
> caused by a virus which can attack the body's defence
> system. If this happens people can then develop AIDS itself
> and become ill, slowly dying from an illness which they
> cannot fight off. First of all people just thought that AIDS
> was caught by homosexuals and drug abusers, but it was
> soon found out that AIDS can be caught by anyone. (...)
> AIDS kills and there is no cure. This is why it concerns me.

Dalia worked so hard and so efficiently that she had completed her assignment when many other members of her class had a good deal still to do. She does most of her writing for English at home, including redrafting and revision. Sue suggested that she might like to tackle the same subject in a different way, as a fictional narrative, perhaps, or a dramascript. This was the result:

> *Inside Mr D.*
> Son, get off that white cell and come over here! Hurry up, you
> should have multiplied ten minutes ago. Now listen son, next
> time you get at that white cell cling to it until it backs down.
> Your aim is to break down the immune system, not make
> friends with it, OK? No, not like that. You just haven't got it,
> have you? Too soft, that's your trouble. Stick your chin up,
> that's right, be proud that you are on the way to being a great
> AIDS virus. As my old uncle used to say, 'Who cares about
> cancer and hepatitis B, the greatest of them all is good old
> HIV!'
> 'You don't know what HIV is? Silly boy! It is written on a

doctor's paper when one of those weak people has AIDS. You don't know anything, do you? I bet you don't even know how we managed to get inside this person's body! You don't know? Gosh, every son of mine should know that. Sit down, I'll explain, so listen very carefully. Now, we are inside Mr D's body. He is a good man, is Mr D. He has a wife, three children, a good home. He seems like a sensible man, but when he went on that business trip to America, he faltered. He ended up in bed with that blond girl. He shouldn't have betrayed his wife, silly man. If he was going to, he could at least have used a condom. He didn't bother. He thought she was a nice girl, but little did he know she had AIDS. She caught the virus from that long affair with her boss. We do spread well, don't we?

Dalia's in-role monologue is about twice this length. She concludes:

This story was written by Bill the AIDS virus, as his autobiography. He leaves readers with a final message. "If sex without a condom has a certain allure, remember very carefully, for AIDS there is no cure."

Dalia is an accomplished writer. She achieves very high standards in all her school subjects. In English, she has been encouraged continuously to write for real audiences and not just for her teacher. Her AIDS writing was entered in a competition. She was given a prize, and parts were printed in a local newspaper, but the most challenging sections were cut because they were considered too controversial to print. In this case the school domain, which included her fellow students and another class in California, provided a more generous audience than the public domain. Surely it should become general practice for imaginative writing by school students about significant issues to be published wherever possible, without censorship.

The three examples I've cited here are all taken from ethnically and socially diverse classes in inner-city schools. Schools have many things wrong with them, but one thing they have, which is not found so ready-made in communities outside, is a forum where people whose lives and cultures are very different can be engaged in dialogue over long periods of time. The interaction is continuously recharged by the events of the curriculum and by events in the world, local and national and international. Christine and Simon and Dalia are voices in a continuing conversation about history and racism and anti-racism, about humanity and democracy, about knowing and caring and wanting a better future.

Just imagine that the goal for education really was the nurturing of new generations, who can think and decide and act for themselves, who plan and behave democratically, who care about the kind of society they live in as well as about their own future. The approach to writing that I have outlined here also involves my certainty that 'thinking for themselves' is a very social act. Those processes we often choose to call 'independent thinking' or 'original ideas' are *dependent* on and have their *origins* in the interaction and response to the thinking and the ideas of other people. The hope, naturally, is that what goes on in the small forum of the classroom will have some wider effects. Here I draw on some words of Myles Horton, whom Studs Terkel described as 'America's most influential and inspiring educator'.

Horton died in 1990, almost at the same time as the publication of his autobiography.

> I think it's important to understand that the quality of the process you use to get to a place determines the ends, so when you want to build a democratic society, you have to act democratically in every way...A long range goal to me is one that grows out of loving people, caring for people, and believing in people's capacity to govern themselves. The way to know they have these capabilities is to see something work on a small scale. I've seen it in the labor movement, I've seen it in the civil rights movement, I've seen it in the anti-war movement. Since I know those things can happen on a small scale, I assume that if we ever got wise enough and involved enough people, it could happen on a bigger scale. (Horton 1990, p. 227)

One place where it could happen on a larger scale is school. Although Horton doesn't mention schools, it was in his own 'school' in Tennessee, known as the Highlander Project, that Martin Luther King Jr. and Rosa Parks had some of their political training, along with hundreds of famous and unknown heroes and heroines of the civil rights movement, peace campaigns and struggles for freedom, inside the United States, in Nicaragua and other countries where the US exerted its power.

So where might all this take us? I have tried to make constructive use of some of the ideas I share with Horton and Baldwin and Williams, and I hope with many others. I want them to work for me when I think about what goes on in English classrooms, and especially about what gets written there. That's why I've focused on the need to re-value the power of imagination, and to think of that power as one of our best resources, if we are, with Raymond Williams, 'to find in new ways the shape of a future that can be genuinely imagined and hopefully lived'.

This essay originated in a lecture in the University of California, Berkeley, 1990.

Bakhtin, M.M. (1981), *The Dialogic Imagination*, University of Texas
Baldwin, James (1985), 'If Black English Isn't a Language, Then Tell Me, What Is?' in *The Price of the Ticket: Collected Non-Fiction*, Michael Joseph
Barnes D. and D. (1983), 'Cherishing private souls? Writing in fifth-year English classes' in R. Arnold (ed.), *Timely Voices: English teaching in the eighties*, Oxford University Press
Bruner, J. (1986), *Actual Minds, Possible Worlds*, Harvard University Press
Bruner, J. (1990), 'Folk psychology and other narrative codes', public lecture at San Francisco State University, March
Cooper, M. and Holzman, M. (1989), *Writing as Social Action*, Heinemann
Dyson, A. (1989), *Multiple Worlds of Child Writers: friends learning to write*, Teachers College Press

Emig, J. (1983), 'Literacy and freedom' in *The Web of Meaning*, Boynton Cook

Hardcastle, J. *et al.* (1983), 'Growth, community and control in secondary school writers' in B. Kroll and G. Wells (eds), *Explorations in the Development of Writing*, Wiley

Hardcastle, J. (1985), 'Classrooms as sites of cultural making' in *English in Education*, no. 3

Hewitt, R. (1986), *White Talk Black Talk*, Cambridge University Press

Horton, M. with Judith Kohl and Herbert Kohl (1990), *The Long Haul: an autobiography*, Doubleday

Kureishi, Hanif (1989), article in *The Guardian*, January

McLeod, A. (1986), 'Critical literacy: taking control of our own lives' in *Language Arts*, 63/1

Medway, Peter (1986), 'What gets written about' in A. Wilkinson (ed.), *The Writing of Writing*, Open University Press

Medway, Peter (1989), 'Argument as social action' in R. Andrews (ed.), *Narrative and Argument*, Open University Press

Williams, Raymond (1982), 'The ragged-arsed philanthropists', Tressall memorial lecture in *Writing in Society*, Verso

The Politics of Writing

Throughout the history of writing the author of the text, the one whose version of ideas or events remains in the written words, has always been more important than the scribe, the one who makes copies. In the history of compulsory education, children's writing in school has been predominantly scribal. Only recently have they been expected to compose as they write. In doing so, the implicit assumption has been that they will follow the formal rules of accepted modes of organising knowledge. This essay challenges this idea of reproduction by emphasising the 'creative stylising variants which children produce and the imaginative energy they bring to their new powerful texts'.

This essay is the prosing of a hefty fistful of notes for a lecture I gave in Detroit in 1983 to the National Council of Teachers of English. It bears the marks of a certain podium style, but I decided to let that stand. In view of the recent burgeoning of genre theory and more particularly of a pedagogy of genres, mostly Australian – (see, for example, Kress 1987 and 1989, Reid 1987) it seemed to me worth making this available.

Learning to write in our culture is a significant part of the process of the socialisation of children. It has been claimed that learning to write is much more than this, that it leads to profound changes in the human psyche, abstract, context-free thought, rationality, powers of criticism, detachment – in sum a totally new way of looking at the world (see Goody 1977, Olson 1977, Ong 1982). And all that at the mere cost of learning to read and write. Since I am concerned here specifically with learning to write, let me cite Olson's well-known essay, 'From utterance to text' (1977) as typical.

> ...the invention of the alphabetic writing system gave to
> Western culture many of its predominant features including
> an altered conception of language and altered conception of
> rational man. These effects came about, in part, from the
> creation of explicit, autonomous statements, statements
> dependent upon an explicit writing system, the alphabet and
> an explicit form of argument, the essay. (p. 262)

On the other hand, if we turn to Michel de Certeau (1984) we find a much more hostile note being sounded,

> To write...is to be forced to march through enemy territory.

I shall come back to this disturbing and outrageous notion, but for the moment I shall assume that you find the idea a little odd (at the very least) and perhaps lunatic. Certainly it does not match the enthusiasms of Olson and others who hint at no such thing. But if you find the idea odd, I ask you to recollect having to write a piece of formal prose recently: a report, an official letter of some length, the minutes of a meeting or, better still, a letter of application for a job. My guess is that you experienced some tension between what you wanted to say and what you knew were the expectations of how you should say it. A self-censorship produces a calcified prose you would gladly disown.

There is, after all, a common way of treating socialisation, especially socialisation into a specific kind of literate culture. We all know that from the moment of their birth all children have to be changed from little animals into social human beings. One way (not mine) of looking at this process is to say quite simply that the complex organism we call society, heterogeneous and elusive as it may be, is sustained, confirmed and reproduced by a set of norms and rules, and that basically a child's socialisation consists in learning those rules and governing her practices in the light of them. There are obvious refinements on this model, the incorporation of some diversity of norms and rules and sub-systems; but in general, as Agnes Heller (1982) puts it,

> professionalism (in the social sciences)...views society as it
> exists, the status quo as a datum...(it) is concerned to
> investigate but not to change, at most to improve the way
> society works.

To put it another way, the social system is looked upon as lying in wait for us with a whole apparatus of practices, values, beliefs and so on, and we are irresistibly drawn into them. Let me say very briefly what I think is wrong with that model. First, the social system always confronts us at a particular moment in history. Then, because power is unequally distributed, some practices will be given high value not because of their intrinsic merit but because they are validated by the powerful. Third, many of the most important practices in the culture help to keep the powerful powerful, though they are never presented that way but rather as universal or value-free or in their final state of evolution. Finally, the model does not offer us any understanding of the conflict of values and of practices except as deviance or maladjustment, and so on.

To come down to earth from those generalisations, let me cite an instance of how the discourse of social scientists has its parallel in everyday discourse in one of its most common locations, school. I borrow the example from Henry Giroux (1983).

> Mrs Caplow is a kindergarten teacher working on a unit
> devoted to citizenship. The aim of the unit, she says, is to
> teach 'respect for the law'. As part of her scheme she
> appoints a 'sheriff' from among the children. The sheriff
> interprets this by pushing and shoving the children who
> step out of line. Here is an exchange conducted for the
> researcher's benefit.

Mrs Caplow:	David, can you tell Mr Rist why you are wearing a star.
David:	Cause I the sheriff.
Mrs C:	Can you tell him how you got to be sheriff?
D:	By being a good citizen.
Mrs C:	David, what do good citizens do?
D:	They check up on others.
Mrs C:	Well that's not all they do.

(Mrs C repeats the question for Frank)

Frank:	Good citizens obey the rules.
Mrs C:	That's right, Frank, good citizens obey the rules, no matter what they are.

I quote that exchange because it makes brutally explicit what for most of the time is conveyed by much more oblique means: the tacit assumptions behind everyday discourse and practices which naturalise the way society works, and are familiar to us, perhaps, as the hidden curriculum. Such assumptions include, for example, beliefs that society, as we know it, is in a state of achieved perfection, or, if it is not, that it has never been bettered and never will be and that we must play our cards right to ensure that no inferior form asserts itself, that the 'rules' are in no way problematic and that society is not a legitimate site for conflict, since it is neutral and even-handed: the same rules apply for all.

What has all this got to do with writing? What about all those things we hear so much about like conferencing, redrafting, paragraphing, the use of journals, topic sentences, and so on? Perhaps you will have glimpsed a way of reading what I have been presenting which points in that direction. Mrs Caplow can be read in this way. A good writer (citizen) obeys the rules no matter what they are. And I don't just mean grammatical rules, spelling rules and so on, but also discourse rules. One of the very few writers to have taken a sociocultural view of writing, Gunther Kress (1982), puts the matter gloomily when discussing genres, which we might call forms of discourse or kinds of writing (1982). These different kinds of writing, he says,

> ...are fixed, formalized and codified. Hence the learning of genres involves an increasing loss of creativity on the child's part and a subordination of the child's creative abilities to the demands of the genre. (p. 11)

or, later in the book,

> ...just as there is a fixed number of sentence types so there exists a small fixed number of genres within any written tradition.

Now Kress is aware that kinds of writing are related to our social system, but he never works out satisfactorily what that relationship is. The idea that writing is fixed, formalised and codified needs examining more closely. It is only partly so. There is not a fixed number of genres. Note in passing that Kress does not reveal this magic number, although, if there are so few, it should be an easy business to do so. Moreover, the writing police – editors, employers, writers of school manuals and self-appointed controllers of other people's language – try to promote this world of fixed genres, so that discourse itself in all its heterogeneity comes under the yoke of sets of rules. For all their intimidation they never quite succeed. Kress clearly perceives that learning to write is a form of socialisation, but he sees this in a determinist way. According to him there is no escaping the iron rules.

> Learning language is one of the highly developed rule
> systems...Learning genres...represents the child's
> socialization into appropriate and accepted modes of
> organizing knowledge. It is important to recognize that
> genres have this constraining effect and that they are
> conventions. (p. 123)

So we are back to the rule of law and order, with this important difference, that Kress sees the source of that law and order and does not give it his stamp of approval. One interesting remark he makes is that 'Other conventions can be imagined: indeed it is one of the main points of this book that children constantly invent their own modes of organizing and knowing which, however, do not become recognised as such but rather are categorized as errors'. It is my argument that to behave as though adult forms of writing are fixed and codified is to accept the messages which power delivers and to ignore what actually happens. The legitimised forms of writing are in fact constantly being eroded and undermined – and not just by children – just as are other powerful social norms, the family, for instance. Writing is a site of conflict, and ferocious play goes on within its boundaries. Old forms die out and new ones appear, others are in a state of flux. This is especially true if we stop thinking of typical prose and look at other forms. A few examples. First, consider obsolete and obsolescent forms. I take off the shelf beside me *A History of Leicester*, J. Throsby, 1791. It begins with the now obsolete sycophantic style of dedication complete with special layout (see opposite).

Dedications are now either omitted entirely or go like this,

> For Boyd, Elizabeth, Greta without whom I could not have
> gotten on (Heath 1983).

Where is the code which specifies the rules governing those texts? What is the fixed, formalised, codified set of rules for writing a philosophical work? Would the rules (how many?) enable you to predict a passage of this type?

> Once upon a time there was a man; we tell his story. Once
> upon a time there was a King, and he had three sons; we tell
> their miraculous stories. Once upon a time there was a
> hunter...

This is taken straight from Agnes Heller's *A Theory of History*. Of course, there are many, many texts which we could group together and through analysis show to

> To the
> Right Honourable
> George Townsend
> Earl of the County of Leicester
> Baron de Ferrars of Chartley
> Lord Bourchier, Lorraine, Bassett and Compton
>
> My Lord
>
> As the following sheets are the first published attempt at a
> regular history, the writer looks up to your Lordship in
> particular, as Patron to his labours. Your Lordship's
> supereminent station in the Antiquarian Society and your
> illustrious descent from the renowned Earls of Leicester
> show the propriety of this address
>
> He is,
> My Lord
> with due deference
> John Throsby

be governed by a code; but we would find that the rules are by no means as rigid as some would maintain (for instance, dogmatic manual-writers and codifiers). The rules are constantly being abandoned, subverted, mocked, ignored, sometimes as a deliberate act of refusal, sometimes as intuitive innovation. And finally, the rules are tightest where very direct controls operate and a certain measure of power is in the hands of certain controllers – editors, employers, teachers, who themselves came through a formation likely to make them eager rule-obeyers.

There is a long history to the evolution of this state of affairs. It has yet to be written. For the moment let us take a look at one corner of the field. *Harvard Educational Review*, which in practice is an enlightened journal and tolerates some diversity, informs its contributors that

> All copy, including indented matter, footnotes and
> references, should be typed double-spaced and justified to
> the left margin only. The author should be identified only
> on the title page. Manuscripts should conform to the
> publication guidelines of the APA (for technical and
> research articles), the MLA Handbook (for theoretical,
> descriptive, or essay-style articles) or The Uniform System
> of Citation published by the Harvard Law Review (for legal
> articles). For general questions of style authors should
> consult The Chicago Manual of Style.

The recollection of lengthy transatlantic telephone calls from *Harvard Educational Review* reminds me just how seriously all this is taken. No wonder Enzensberger once remarked that we can see an attempt in our society to industrialise the mind.

The attempt to drill students into conforming to certain supposed rules of discourse amounts to nothing less than the imposition of a code of unquestioning obedience. It turns them and us away from asking the important questions. Eagleton (1983) puts this simply,

> The language of a legal document or scientific text may impress or even intimidate us because we do not see how the language got there in the first place. The text does not allow the reader to see how the facts it contains were selected, what was excluded, why these facts were organized in this particular way, what assumptions governed this process, what forms of work went into the making of the text and how all this might have been different.

In other words, concealed beneath the surface of the most humdrum document, which we would take for granted as a satisfactory not-to-be-tampered-with means for achieving its end, there is always a deeper social process at work. As students proceed through our schools and possibly into higher education they are unlikely to be encouraged to probe their own writing and that of others for the workings of this deeper social system. One form a writing workshop might take would be the interrogation of a set of texts like these:

> (a)   Contrary to the impression we may have given in this column on 16th March, the Acme Thunder Railway Guards' Whistle marketed by Mailpost is made by J Hudson and Co. (Whistles) Ltd., a British firm which has been manufacturing whistles for more than 130 years. The whistles offered by Mailpost are replicas.

> (b)   We are seeking to appoint an Officer in Charge to our Hostel for 20 emotionally and mentally distressed young adults at 15 Homerton Row, E.9. Applications are invited from mature, experienced men/women with qualities of management. The successful applicant...

> (c)   Mum, Back at 11.30. Don't lock garden door. Leave caviar and champers in fridge. Chaz.

Jay Lemke, in a fascinating paper (1982), asked a set of questions which might be applied to any text and which we might use to deconsecrate them:

> Who is doing what to whom in this text?
>
> How?
>
> What other texts and doings stand in what relevant relations for the meanings made and the acts performed by this text?
>
> What social systems are maintained or altered by what relations among the set of texts to which we may assign this one?
>
> What social interests and their conflicting discourses are

being served or contested in this text and through its
intertextual relations?

How does the text contribute to the maintenance and
change of the linguistic system and the patterns of use of
that system in the community?

To ask questions of this kind is, as Lemke says, 'to strengthen our ability to dispel
the sense of givenness and inevitability...and better arm us to contest them'. It
might lead us to consider more carefully what we ask our students to write and
how we respond to anything which is fresh and liberating. We need to look at
every form of writing as a specific form of social practice embedded in our social
system and impregnated with its own social history. Our kind of scientific writing, for example, is the culmination of three centuries of the development of
science as an institution and is therefore likely to be thought to have attained a
state of immutable perfection. When we have served an apprenticeship in any
particular genre of writing we are neither inevitably nor inextricably enmeshed
in its rule system. But greater awareness of that system and how it works can
enable us to begin to free ourselves from some at least of its oppressive features.

Over the last fifteen years there has been a significant shift in research energies directed towards investigating language in schools. Writing has been discovered. We are in the process of redressing a strange imbalance (another piece
of social history). When we began our writing research at the Institute of Education in 1966 there was available a whole library of work on reading, whereas
worthwhile work on writing consisted of a mere handful of books and mono-
graphs. We now have the results of large funded projects, a proliferation of
models of the writing process, analyses of students' written texts, maps of functional diversity, blueprints for patterns of development and much more. A dis-
criminating study of this literature can teach us a great deal. But in preparing this
paper I set my face against reviewing fresh material. For all the insights and
useful findings there has been a consistent failure to address the issues I have
been exploring. There has been no attempt to question the goal (good writing?
mature writing? competent writing? genre writing? and so on). Largely, the goals
have been taken for granted, no matter how elaborated they have become, and
the debate has focused on the route. To put it simply, the unspoken proposition
is, 'We know what good adult writing looks like: so let us research the best ways
of attaining it. If we know what kinds of acceptable language are used in our
society then we can devise better ways of training students to use them.' In terms
of the old pieties this is part of the process of preparing children for society. Since
there are many kinds of writing, we will need to establish priorities. Up pop the
old favourites – the business letter, the job application, the essay. Should we add
advertising copy? Kress is almost alone among those addressing writing in
schools in pointing out that

> To become proficient in the genre one has to become
> absorbed of these contents [ie ideological and cognitive
> contents, HR] and of the institution itself. Effective teaching
> of genres can make the individual into an efficiently intuitive
> and unreflective user of the genre. The genre and its

> meanings will come to dominate the individual...and this is
> so whether he be scientist, bureaucrat or short story
> writer...Is that what we want? (p. 125)

I do not hear that question being asked by most of those engaged currently on work on writing. I grumble once again at Kress's assumption that the more we are drawn into the system the more inevitably we accept its hidden agenda. The literate culture is full of examples of writers who conduct unceasing guerrilla warfare against it. How for example do you write for an audience of educationists about writing? Easy. Follow this model. It comes from a collection of papers (Freedman and Pringle 1980). This writer slips into the mode like a homing bird.

> A common assumption shared by many rhetoricians is that
> the act of composing is linear. Gordon Rohman, for
> example, distinguishes three stages in the composing
> process: first the pre-writing, then the writing, and finally
> the re-writing. Pre-writing, like Aristotelian invention,
> is...(Butturf and Sommers in Freedman and Pringle p. 99)

And so it continues. However, what we do find in this same volume in which one contribution after another obediently follows the tradition (as indeed does this essay for the most part!) is a contribution from Don Murray (1980) which begins by cheerfully defying the code, the rules and expectations.

> Emptiness. There will be no more words. Blackness. No,
> white without colour. Silence.
> I have not any words all day. It is late and I am tired in the
> bone. I sit on the edge of the bed, open the notebook, uncap
> the pen. Nothing. Or.
> Everything has gone well this morning. I wake from sleep,
> not dreams.

All this leaves me in an uncomfortable position. Yes, the Don Murrays of this world, established and secure, may be able to thumb their noses at the conventions, but their ways are scarcely a credible recipe for the teaching of writing. Suppose we do have an understanding that writing is an interlocking set of social practices shaped by the context of the society we live in. What are we expected to do about it? The students eventually have to get jobs, don't they? If they don't toe the line, they are finished. And how could we possibly change our teaching to accommodate the alternative view? The first part of my answer, as I have been suggesting, is that the Kress picture insufficiently accommodates the subtle diversity of possibilities within the written language and the promiscuity of genres. These possibilities are present from the moment a child starts to write. The real issue is whether we exploit these possibilities and help students to avoid being drawn inexorably into the embrace of house styles. The one theorist who sheds a helpful light on this matter is Bakhtin. He alone provides a base which shows how every act of writing can potentially break the code within which it is operating. In his book, *The Dialogic Imagination*, he argues that two forces are always at work in language use: he calls them centrifugal and centripetal. The centripetal describes all that which pulls us towards a centre of prescribed norms, genre conventions, discourse etiquettes, and so on. The counterforce is centrifugal, which pulls away from the normative centre. Bakhtin writes,

> Every utterance serves as a point where centrifugal as well as centripetal forces are brought to bear. The processes of centralization and decentralization, of unification and disunification, intersect in the utterance.

Linked with these concepts is Bakhtin's contrast between authoritative and internally persuasive discourse.

> ...in one the authoritative word (religious, political, moral, the word of the father, of adults, of teachers, etc.) that does not know internal persuasiveness; in the other the internally persuasive word that is denied all privilege, backed up by no authority at all and is frequently not acknowledged in society (not by public opinion, nor by scholarly norm).

Authoritative discourse for Bakhtin demands

> our unconditional allegiance – permits no play within its borders, no gradual or flexible transitions, no creative stylizing variants. It is indissolubly fused with authority. All is inertia and calcification.

Bakhtin's elaboration is much more complex than this, but I have cited enough to show that his ideas open up new possibilities for students and teachers alike. We can see in every act of writing those two forces at work. We can never totally escape the centripetal pull: we cannot jump out of the language system and its practices. On the other hand we do not have to elevate that system into an object which has achieved perfection. On the contrary, it is necessary to insist again and again on the need to disrupt the authoritative voice with the unheard voices of our students, to help them engage in the difficult struggle (so difficult for all of us) to articulate, develop, refine and advance their meanings as against the mere reproduction of the words of the textbook, the worksheet, the encyclopaedia and the guides. To insist on this involves squaring up to the oppressive power of authoritative language. Millions of notebooks, examination papers and 'essays' are crammed with words which are in essence no more than transcriptions, the forced labour of submission. The very least we can do is to emancipate ourselves from the notion that there is only one good and proper way, and that that way is quite rightly prescribed by others, because they are paying the piper or because we have bowed before their assured authority without question.

What I find cheering is that many who would not subscribe to the views I have expressed or at any rate to the idiom in which I have expressed them know all that in their bones. They are the centrifugal teachers. See the writing in *Beat not the poor desk* (Ponsot and Dean 1982). In the early days of the Writing Project in the UK John Richmond (1986) shrewdly set out in diagrammatic form seven 'Key Ideas' about writing and placed them tellingly against 'what often happens in schools'. I should stress that he also extends an invitation to amend, add and disagree. He does not in fact address the issue I have been trying to elaborate. Yet if we write it in as a subtext, each of the key ideas can be seen in sharper form. Let me try this with a few of them.

> Writers as Assessors is one of his key ideas, which he
> enlarges on. The development of a critical sense, the ability
> to get outside your own or someone else's product, to make
> judgements, is an essential half of the reflexivity between
> creation and criticism. Writers need it.

Agreed. But what is the platform from which the criticism is to be launched? Any well-indoctrinated students – including very young ones – may have internalised a set of criteria which will lead them to place their own efforts solely against the authoritative model. Are there binding rules for the structure of a story? Or a lab report? What kind of teaching emancipates students from that punishing form of self-criticism?

> Collaboration is another of Richmond's key ideas. The
> process of interaction, conversation, mutual support and
> criticism grants orientation and critical space to the writer as
> well as the benefits of others' ideas.

This is better still. For here is the moment when the large social processes filter into everyday exchanges, but also when the culture and values of the students have a chance to emerge, though only if teachers nurture and validate centrifugal moves. There is a huge discourse of experience which is largely censored out, and collaboration is one way to let it in. It must be added that if what is being collaborated on is itself suspect (the imitation of a piece of inflated descriptive writing, for instance) collaboration will contribute very little or nothing.

In applying any of these key ideas it would help if we bore in mind Bakhtin's reminder,

> language is not a neutral medium that passes freely and
> easily into the private property of the speaker's
> intentions...expropriating it, forcing it to submit to one's
> own intentions is a difficult and complicated process.

'We never write on a blank page but always on one that has already been written on,' says de Certeau (p. 43). To write is to engage with social history, the social history of discourse, but it can never be the total history, only the writer's particular links with that history. What is pre-inscribed on the page is different for each one of us. Never to have encountered the classic folk tale or blank verse is to have these forms erased from the page. There is gain and loss. On the one hand the writer is released from the tyranny of the model and on the other is more limited in choice and support. As the pen moves and pauses the writer is making choice after choice, powerfully affected by the already inscribed invisible texts. With each specific piece of writing the invisible consists of the matrices of particular genres, a selection of lexicon, formalities, mini-structures, stylistic devices and so on. What asserts its presence will be different if I am writing a fable, a pseudo-folk story, some notes for a lecture, a set of instructions, a letter to my wife. Indeed, one of the ways of forcing the writing to submit to my intentions is to call up the 'inappropriate' model or to mix one tradition with another. This is a possibility, whatever the work in hand. But there is one mode which lends itself to this tactic more than any other, narrative. Of course, we all know that there are profoundly established stereotypes; but there are two properties of narrative which leave it open to the play of infinite possibilities: we inherit an enormous range of resources, and within the text of any one narrative there is infinite space for play, juxtaposing strategies and tactics drawn from any kind of discourse. Here, for instance, is Helen, aged eleven, demonstrating the use of these possibilities.

The Hero Howard

Howard was the city's most cowardly man. He had one
ambition and that was to marry the King's daughter,
Princess Victoria. She was a beautiful girl with silky brown
hair. She said, 'Whoever kills Great Hadden, the fierce,
fiery dragon, I will marry.'
On hearing this, Howard decided to kill the dragon. He
went to the library and asked for books about killing
dragons and marrying princesses. The librarian looked
rather surprised and told him to go to the children's
department, thinking he was looking for books for his
children. He came out of the library with a big pile of fairy
tales to read.

(Later in the story the librarian writes Howard a letter. It is couched in perfect bureaucratic prose.)

The play of language here depends on the intertwining of two sets of social meanings, which have accreted around specific genres (folk-tales, realistic short stories, farcical tales, official letters, kinds of conversation) and by these means have coaxed a new meaning out of the text. Helen has successfully refused to make the forced march through enemy territory and has set off on a jaunty discourse journey of her own.

As a last step, let me suggest – pursuing the possibilities of narrative – how all students from the youngest to the oldest might be helped to make that journey. John Scurr School is a primary school in the heart of the inner city. Two thirds of its pupils are Bangladeshi and speakers of Sylheti. It is a school where story-telling by the teachers occupies an unchallenged place in the curriculum, and that includes bilingual story-telling. In a class of ten- and eleven-year-olds, which I now know quite well, I told an Italian folk story, 'The Land Where No One Ever Dies'. It is a subtle and ironic tale of time and death. I proposed that the children should re-tell the story in writing. My only suggestion was, 'Tell it which way you like. Change anything you like.' I watched the children with some misgiving as, after a generous amount of time they had written very little, per-haps some five to ten lines. With no prompting from me they promised they would finish before my next visit. Two weeks later I returned to do some more story-telling. Joe, the teacher, put a folder in my hands. It contained all the children's re-tellings. In them you can find dozens of ways in which they have shifted the genre, frequently by filling the story with contemporary dialogue. Most striking perhaps is the very shy little girl, who changed the chief character of the story from the inevitable young man to a young woman, who, instead of setting out on her own, takes the whole family with her!

Let me shift the context. We are still in the inner city but this time in a class of fifteen-year-olds. There is a strong contingent of students of Caribbean origin, and the rest are as ethnically diverse as they come. Here the teacher has designed a whole unit on re-telling, which includes much discussion of ways in which stories can be changed (see Rosen 1988, 1991). This unit is based on Greek legends, a surprise perhaps, given the context. At one point she tells her very lyrical version of the Orpheus story. Here too they move outwards from the told version, using every possible ruse to shift it to their own telling, changing events, characters, language, dialogue, points of entry and exit, omitting and adding.

Narrative, but more especially re-telling, is one way of wriggling out of the coils of the quasi-official written codes, because it invites cunning. The story is given, established, approved. Within its confines it is possible, while nodding agreement, to defy it: defy it to just the extent we wish. A nice paradox then appears in the ways we all operate. The beauty of re-telling is that while it appears to desert invention (the old rhetorical term) it lets it in by the back door. At the intimate level of the classroom a micro-culture of shared discourse can assert itself.

This essay originated in a lecture delivered to the National Council of Teachers of English in Detroit, 1983.

Bakhtin, M.M. (1981), *The Dialogic Imagination*, University of Texas
Butturf, O.R. and Sommers, N.I. (1980), 'Placing revision in a reinvented rhetorical tradition' in A. Freedman and I. Pringle (eds), *Reinventing the Rhetorical Tradition*, CCTE and L and S Books, University of Central Arkansas
de Certeau, M. (1984), *The Practice of Everyday Life*, University of California Press
Eagleton, T. (1983), *Introduction to Literary Theory*, Basil Blackwell
Giroux, H. (1983), *Theory and Resistance in Education*, Heinemann Educational
Goody, J. (1977), *The Domestication of the Savage Mind*, Cambridge University Press
Heath, S.B. (1983), *Ways With Words*, Cambridge University Press
Heller, A. (1982), *A Theory of History*, Routledge & Kegan Paul
Kress, G. (1982), *Learning to Write*, Routledge & Kegan Paul
Kress, G. (1989), 'Texture and meaning' in R. Andrews (ed.), *Narrative and Argument*, Open University
Lemke, J. (1982), 'Thematic analysis: systems, structures and strategies' in *RS/SI*, vol. 3
Murray, D. (1980), 'The feel of writing – and teaching writing' in A. Freedman and I. Pringle (eds), *Reinventing the Rhetorical Tradition*, CCTE (see above, Butturf and Sommers)
Olsen, D.R. (1977), 'From utterance to text: the bias of language in speech and writing' in *Harvard Educational Review*, 47 (3)
Ong, W. (1982), *Orality and Literacy*, Methuen
Ponsot, M. and Dean, R. (1982), *Beat not the Poor Desk*, Boynton
Reid, I. (ed.) (1987), *The Place of Genre in Learning: current debates*, Deakin University
Richmond, J. (1986), *About Writing*, no. 2, Spring 1986, National Writing Project
Rosen, B. (1988), *And None of It was Nonsense*, Mary Glasgow
Rosen, B. (1991), *Shapers and Polishers*, Mary Glasgow
Throsby, J. (1971), *A History of Leicester*

'What was necessary to explain'

Young people forge their identities as actors within history. In this essay, John Hardcastle sets what he calls 'the stubborn particularity' of individual children's lives within the changing cultural settings of school and the wider world, where what is shared is also marked by tension and by absolute inequality. Three boys – Tony, Ahmed and Derrick – learn through their own writing to understand the influence of the colonial experience and successive migrations of labour on their own lives and their families' lives. Hardcastle is intent on recording 'the kinds of complex differentiations to be made if we are to grasp the relationship between language and lived experience'.

For a number of years I occupied a classroom along a narrow corridor in an all boys comprehensive school in East London. The corridor was a main thoroughfare and during the course of a school day most of the school population eddied around my doorway. The majority of children came from families of Caribbean origin, though this was to change as more children from Asian and Turkish families entered the school. Tony came from a Jamaican background. Born in London, he went as a small child to live with his grandmother in rural Jamaica. There he attended a village school. After several years, Tony's mother visited Jamaica and brought him back to London. Family pressures were such, however, that by the time Tony was ready to enter secondary school he no longer lived with his parents.   The language spoken in Tony's London home was Jamaican creole. Yet whereas Tony's family came from Jamaica, the majority of children in his class came from eastern Caribbean backgrounds, though the children themselves were London-born. Parents, then, spoke language varieties, including French and Spanish creoles, which were quite distinct from the London Jamaican creole being acquired by many of their children. Initially London Jamaican creole was learned, in most cases, as a supplement to, or as a conscious alternative to, the white working–class vernacular which I was accustomed to hearing in the playgrounds, or along the congested corridor between lessons. Recall, however, that Tony had left London for the Caribbean before starting school, and that he subsequently spent several years living with his grandparents in the Jamaican countryside. His experience was not typical. It was more usual to meet children, born in the Caribbean, who remained with grandparents until their own parents were sufficiently well established to bring them over. In such instances, depending on their age and educational experience, children were more likely to code switch or shift between a Caribbean creole (or Caribbean Standard English) and the London vernacular which they rapidly acquired. My main interest in what follows, though, is not in describing language varieties in London schools. Rather, I am seeking to suggest the kinds of complex differentiations to be made if we are to grasp the relationship between language and lived experience. And, where speech is intimately related to questions of social identity and affiliation, as part of the dynamic of social and cultural formation, I wish to show something of the ways that language, as social practice, permeates the fabric of social and cultural relationships within classrooms.

Let us begin, then, with a story written by Tony when he was fourteen. The immediate context was a sequence of lessons where the class were asked to produce a sustained piece of writing. Pupils were given a free choice of theme and approach. They could, if they wished to, ask for help with planning and organisation. Now Tony had experienced considerable difficulty with written tasks since his entry into school. He lacked confidence. Very often he was quick to show signs of frustration and impatience. For an 'open' assignment such as this one his teachers would have predicted that, according to the usual run of things, he would need a great deal of support. However, on this particular occasion, Tony set about the task with uncharacteristic independence. He wrote at greater length than he had done before, producing four pages of a first draft, which was virtually free from false starts and crossings out. His story opens with a description of how the main character, Paul, was taken to Jamaica by his father when he was six months old. Subsequently, his mother realises that a terrible mistake has occurred: there is not enough money to pay the return fare for the child.

Paul

This is a story about a boy who was born in England but went to the West Indies when he was very small.

One day Mr Clark wanted to go to the West Indies to see his family that lived over there but his wife didn't want to go over there because they only had Paul about five months and he was still brest sucking so that mean she will af to stay home and look after it. Now it was about in the middle of the year now and Mr Clark was going to book his fare to Jamaica when his wife said to him would you like to take Paul with you and leave him over there until you are coming back. So Mr Clark agreed with his wife Mrs Clark. Now it was time for Mr Clark to leave the country to Jamaica to see his family over there with Paul his baby boy. So Mrs Clark said bye bye darling to her husband and her son and kissed them goodbye. Then suddenly she remembered that her husband had only paid to go over there because he didn't have enough money to pay for him and his son to go there and back.

So that means that either him or his wife has to get a job quicker to get enough money to come back in the country. You can guess who had to work the hardest it is his wife because she could get a job quicker than he can over here and another reason is because he is over Jamaica and it is hard to get a job over there especially if you don't know where to look for them so thats why it is going to be harder for him.

The events of the story, as they unfold, appear to correspond at certain points with episodes from Tony's own life (that is in as far as they were known to his teachers) though, significantly, not in all respects. Tony's narrative materialises along the blurred margins separating autobiography and fiction. As readers, we have no sure way of distinguishing between the representation of actual events, as he remembers them, or as they have been told to him, and scenes of pure invention. But then, such lack of clear definition may allow him to retract, to reshape and to change the selection and the evaluation of significant moments, as he attempts to give previously unrecounted, and newly recollected, events a kind of restored coherence. In recalling and reordering incidents from his past, and in inventing imaginary episodes, he concentrates his energies on arranging the elements of the story into new, meaningful patterns, which, no doubt, carry implications for his current sense of self.

Tony shows that he has a grasp of basic economic realities. At the time when he was living in rural Jamaica it has been estimated that one half of the population earned ten dollars a week or less. Patterns of employment are such that the heavier burden falls upon the mother. Financial and material hardships provide the underlying causes of family separations. In one sequence in the story domestic quarrels are frankly and harrowingly portrayed, although we must be careful to keep in mind that these may, in fact, bear little correspondence to actual events. Tony was living with his grandparents by this time and consequently could not have witnessed them. Yet he shows genuine insight into seemingly intractable problems. Simply, how do families manage to keep together, and to endure material hardship, divided between Britain and the Caribbean? Tony was taking the first steps. Here he had discovered a theme which fully engaged his interest, and one which made the writing worth the effort. Moreover, he had touched upon social realities about which his teacher knew less than he did. Carolyn Steedman (1982) has argued from the perspective of a feminist historian that we may read children's writing 'for evidence of individual psychologies in certain social circumstances'. The eight-year-old working-class girls who wrote *The Tidy House* were able, she maintains, to manipulate and rearrange the symbols of their social realities, precisely because of their ability to know such symbols and their meanings. The resource of written language, with its potential for symbolic representation, afforded the girls opportunities to make and to discard representations of their daily lives. Thus they were able to construct theories about how things which were familiar to them came to be as they were. I find this a powerful argument. But questions arise. How are the symbols and their meanings carried in the culture? How are they distributed and how transmitted? How were they made available to these eight-year-old girls? And how and where did they learn to manipulate them?

Tony, I think, was engaged in a similar way, working with the symbols of his social realities and putting together a version of personal history that made sense for him. As he wrote he drew upon the conventions of autobiography as he knew them, and he had met these in different settings and at different moments in his development, both in and out of school. I have in mind, here, possible differences, say, between autobiography as it has been fashioned within traditions of expressive writing in English classrooms in London, and personal narrative, written and spoken, which he had learned in his grandparents' village in Jamaica. Such differences would be marked, no doubt, by variations in internal organisation or in the compositional structure. I am also making a more general point, however, which is that autobiographical traditions have different distributions within the wider culture. The value placed upon them varies according to context. And – over and above this – they have been elaborated variously within different social histories, which have been shaped in this specific instance by colonial and post-colonial relationships of domination and subordination. It is a matter of social history that some people's stories have been articulated and valued while others have been relegated to the margins. For Tony it was never a matter of choosing between alternatives, school and community, London and Jamaica, as ways of representing the self. His exposure to different traditions of personal narrative was uneven, both in time and intensity; and the opportunities and motivations for him to learn and to employ their resources occurred intermittently at points along his developmental path.

Here Tony writes about his misfortunes in Jamaica,

> In Jamaica Paul is in the lowest class in his school. Another
> thing that he is doing is going into peoples house and taking
> things. There was a donkey what we had, and Tony was
> playing with it and it kicked him just above his eyes and
> after that lots of other things happened to him over there...

The slip which occurs where Tony shifts from a third to a first person narrator reveals his imperfect control. Such errors are common with less experienced writers. Although we cannot be sure, the incident with the donkey appears to be drawn from memory rather than from invention. Tony has difficulty maintaining a consistent narrative voice, but the greatest challenge he faces is the management of two separate sequences of events as the story switches back and forth between London and Jamaica. By and by, though, he moves towards the moment when Paul is reunited with his mother.

> Now he is nine years old and his mother is going to send for
> him...Now it is time for her to leave the country for Jamaica
> to see her family and to bring back her son...the plane she
> got on was a BOAC. Now she is in Jamaica and she is going
> to get a taxi. It is about two o'clock and she has reached the
> house where her family lives...All the family came down to
> see her and to help her to bring her things up to the house,
> then, after a while, someone showed her her son and told
> her 'that is him playing with the chickens, looking at them
> when they are laying their eggs...'

Tony plots the mother's journey in some detail, drawing her securely towards the reunion. And yet overall the pattern of the family's complicated movements is uncertain. As we have noticed, Tony's experience was not typical. It was more usual for children born in the Caribbean to remain with grandparents until their parents were sufficiently well established in London. It seems worth recalling here that the role of grandparents as carers has been a feature of social arrangements in the Caribbean for generations prior to the post-war migrations to Britain. Such arrangements were common, for instance, when migrant workers took employment building the Panama Canal, constructing the Costa Rican railways or cutting cane in Cuba and the southern USA.

Between the 1850s and the 1920s one hundred and fifty thousand Jamaicans moved abroad to work, often for short periods. Then, when the depression came, the cane workers were no longer needed in Cuba and the USA. Thus they returned, increasing the levels of unemployment in Jamaica. Tony's story, then, may be placed within a wider frame and read, for all its singularity, as evidence of a history of Caribbean migrant labour. In significant ways his individual experience may be connected to the broader picture in order to enlarge Tony's understanding of his own, and his classmates', lives.

Tony had discovered for himself themes which have been treated extensively in Caribbean fiction and poetry. Themes of departure, absence, loss and separation derive a peculiar power once they are linked to history. Here, for example, is a passage from George Lamming's semi-autobiographical novel, *In the Castle of My Skin*, which centres round growing up in a small village in Barbados. G, the main character, buries a pebble on the sea shore, hoping to retrieve it the following day. Lamming writes,

> I selected the spot and placed the pebble under the leaf on the even slope. A day had passed. There was no change in the weather, and the waves were as quiet as ever on this side of the sea. They rode up gently, tired themselves out and receded in another form towards the sea. But the pebble had gone. The feeling sharpened. It had really started the evening before when I received the letters, and now the pebble had made it permanent. In the evening I had read the letters and it seemed there were several things, intimate and endearing which I was going to see for the last time...

The episode marks a moment in the passage from childhood into adulthood. It serves to make G more keenly aware of the experience of loss. At the same time it marks an attempt to achieve, at a symbolic level at least, some kind of continuity in the face of disjunctions and separations to which G's life, and the lives of the islanders, seem fated. The feeling the loss of the pebble evokes is given piercing definition. It is exactly the feeling that recurs when G's friend, Trumper, leaves for the USA.

> ...Later when Trumper came to say that he was going to America I couldn't bear to look him straight in the face. He had always dreamt of going to America and the dream had come true. He was happy and I was glad for him. He left on a wet morning three years before I left the High School; and although an important difference in our fortunes had forced us apart I went to see him off. We stood on the pier together and watched the ship which was anchored in the distance. There were hundreds of them leaving for America, and I saw them all less real than Trumper but with the same sickness which the feeling brought on. It seemed I wasn't going to see any of those faces again. Later I returned to the pier and watched the big ship sweep through the night and out of sight across the sea.

I have tried to suggest through my brief discussion of a single episode from *In the Castle of My Skin* one interpretative background against which Tony's achievement might be understood. As he wrote his own semi-autobiography he was moving towards an engagement with essential themes of migrant experience: separation and disjunction. Earlier, I attempted to show that the manner of his writing was new. He showed greater confidence, and the piece seemed to signal a qualitatively different phase in his literacy development. I have also indicated that the origins of the piece are opaque. Antecedent factors leading to the composition may not be directly attributed to a pre-planned programme of study devised by his teachers. By referring to the intermittent character of Tony's meeting with personal narrative in a variety of settings I am seeking to register the importance of extended perspectives, which will enable us to see learning histories over time. Tony did not appear to conform to a linear developmental pattern. An organised learning environment was needed which would afford many entry points and which would be capable of accommodating different learning histories.

Tony was an inexperienced reader, and *In the Castle of My Skin* is a demanding text. But if he could not engage with Lamming in a direct way, Lamming's novel might still have informed the learning environment in which Tony looked to make progress. And his English teacher, mindful of children's long-term developmental paths, might begin to envisage intermediate stages, guiding them towards eventual goals. As it was, Tony's achievement, though considerable, remained incomplete. In order to extend and develop from this beginning he needed to be able to take from the cultural materials surrounding him, and to go on to construct representations which were capable of supporting his own active engagement with meaning. I wonder, for example, what Tony might have taken and made from Christine Renault's film *Rue Cases-Nègres*, which is about growing up in rural Martinique in the 1930s, and where the relationship between the main character, Jose, and his grandmother, who cares for him, is central. To deny children the symbols which have the capacity to represent their own and their communities' past and current experience is to deny them the opportunity of understanding their lives and the possibility of changing them.

There is a growing body of work, undertaken within traditions of ethnographic research, which usefully brings to the attention of teachers different linguistic and literacy practices across communities. The investigation which Shirley Brice Heath conducted in the Piedmont Carolinas region of the USA is probably the best known. For nine years Shirley Brice Heath looked at 'literacy events' in white middle-class (Mainstream), white working-class (Roadville) and black working-class (Trackton) communities. She collected evidence to show that each community has its own distinct rules for social interaction and knowledge-sharing in literacy events, and that communities are not only literate in different ways, their children – whether from Mainstream, Roadville or Trackton – enter school with different expectations of print. Her study reveals the mismatch between community and teachers' notions of literacy development, and she is able to show through the analysis of rich empirical evidence that schools tend to privilege norms corresponding to notions of literacy held within the white, middle-class community. Mainstream's ways of achieving literacy are so deeply rooted that they appear 'natural'.

Her method, then, is to get behind literacy events, such as reading a bed-time story, and to go on to uncover the rule systems which make them possible. And her emphasis upon 'ways of taking', by which she means enculturation, reminds us that what is crucially at issue is nothing less than a mode of cultural formation.

Hilary Minns, a primary headteacher in Coventry, is a sensitive and perceptive observer of literacy events. She acknowledges her debt to Shirley Brice Heath where she describes the way that Jaspal, a four-year-old Sikh child, enters school,

> Jaspal has been surrounded by quite different literacy
> practices in his home ever since he was a baby. These
> practices are embedded in the set of institutions and
> relations that form his culture: the religious life of his family
> and community and the domestic life, work and leisure
> occupations of those around him. Jaspal's parents have a
> conscious desire to prepare him for school and at the same
> time they want him to understand Sikh culture and beliefs.

The literacy events in which Jaspal takes part at home are seen to provide cultural continuity and coherence for a child, who will encounter different ways with words at school.

Hilary Minns describes a moment where Jaspal's father is reading to his child after a day at work. The child interjects, but the father returns firmly to the text. Hilary Minns writes,

> Why does he feel the need to do this? Possibly he is tired
> after a day at work, perhaps too, the effort of sustaining a
> conversation in English – the second language for all the
> participants – is too much, and I think there may be another
> reason which lies within the father's own ways of listening
> to and making sense of texts. He is used to taking the role of
> the listener himself at the temple, through the priest,
> without interruption. He associates the modes of reader and
> listener, in other words, with the ritual relationship of
> reader authoritatively mediating texts and the listener
> receiving actively but without interrupting, and it may seem
> appropriate for his children to do so when he reads to them.
> So although his responses may appear repressive to some
> infant teachers, they are in fact a gift of cultural inheritance
> to Jaspal and his sister.

She goes on to say that what is being held out to Jaspal, as part of a broader process of enculturation, is, in fact, a means of seeing his community as in control of cultural and literacy practices, which connect the Sikh community in Coventry with the distant homelands of parents and grandparents. The role being advocated for the teacher/ethnographer here is one which attends to differences, and in particular to the systematic nature of differences of language and culture, in order to bridge more effectively the practices of the home and the school, and thus achieve a total literacy environment.

For Jaspal, growing up in Coventry's Sikh community, his cultural inheritance is an unsolicited gift. Sikh values and beliefs permeate his life, shaping and constituting his response to the world and thus his identity. The boundaries demarcating home and school are clearly drawn. But whereas it is important to see Jaspal learning to participate in literacy events at home within a rich and complex cultural environment, it would be a mistake to see Tony, by contrast, separated from his parents and grandparents, as somehow culturally impoverished. Some accounts of minority cultures idealise and essentialise, in ways which abstract culture from material history and current social circumstances. Such accounts tend to place culture beyond historical making and – implicitly – change, with the result that their authenticity appears to reside in distant (and 'natural') homelands, and not where it is actually made and lived.

London classrooms, such as the one in which Tony wrote, are places where cultures come into direct contact, cross and re-cross, drawn together in the inner city in new and changing relationships. And the ethnic composition of school populations alters, sometimes rapidly, in significant ways which introduce fresh and sometimes conflicting educational expectations, assumptions and imperatives. In contexts such as these what constitutes tradition or custom, or simply what is taken for granted, is often thrown into relief and challenged in ways teachers cannot always foresee or control.

Here is Ahmed, a fifteen-year-old, London-born, Pakistani boy, writing to his teachers about negotiating the cultural and social relationships of an inner-city classroom. He speaks of his difficulties in trying to find a point of entry into class discussions. At the same time, he criticises what he sees as the neglect of Asian history in the school's Humanities programme. He recalls a heated debate which had taken place in the classroom eight months earlier. At issue on that occasion was the extent of the coverage of Caribbean history in the syllabus. The debate was sustained for an hour or so by both black and white students, with minimal intervention from their teacher. It was committed and intense, but neither acrimonious nor divisive. At one point Ahmed was invited by one of his classmates to put forward his own point of view, but he declined to do so. Then, after several months of deferral, he decided to set out his reasons in an open letter.

> *What was Necessary to Explain*
> Many students had joined into this interesting discussion and
> had put forward such strengthy points, which were arguable
> and they were able to continue the discussion for some time...
>
> Anyhow, although it continued for some time, there was
> me, a Pakistani present and another friend of mine, Iqbal, who
> is half Indian and half Pakistani. Me and Iqbal sat within the
> overpower(ing) majority of white and black. The thought of
> this had influenced me of being left out and therefore had
> convinced me of staying out of the discussion. I'm not sure
> whether this stood for Iqbal. But anyway, for me, there were
> many reasons for my staying out of the discussion. The first
> reason being that I am a very shy type of person, already
> known by my teacher, and I just could not adjust myself to

talking in such large crowds. Although there is an exception in
small groups I become very talkative, I felt that within such
large crowds, whatever the point of view was lodged within my
head, I always thought of the point of view as being wrong and
not right.

Ahmed writes here about his experience of marginalisation. He sits alongside
Iqbal, while the others, 'the overpower majority', make their 'strengthy points'.
Perhaps we should try to look beyond his self-description as a 'shy person'
towards differences of interactional style, but then, even if we were to identify a
dominant mode of speaking and listening, questions remain as to the processes
by which some modes prevail over others. Over time the class established ways of
talking to itself about important issues; yet, as we have seen, these discussions
were not always (if ever) open to all on an equal footing. These ways of talking
were made and remade within the conflicts, tensions, friendships, affiliations and
allegiances constituting the internal social relationships of the classroom. And it
is from within these interactions, in a paradoxical fashion, that Ahmed begins to
articulate a sense of social and cultural identity. He goes on,

At the moment, not knowing the actual basis of my country,
I seem to feel that if I were to return for a visit, or stay there
for a year or so, then I suppose I may feel stupid not
knowing any history of the country...
    As already it has been noticed that the population of
Asian pupils in school has risen (and therefore will rise
every year) and I suppose the demand for history/culture
will rise to a point where it would have to be taught as one
of the important topics...
    ...Just recently I have realised that I have realised that I
have been one of the first generation of Pakistanis present in
the school.

Ahmed carries forward a dual sense of himself. Firstly, there is his immediate
and personal experience of exclusion and his difficulty in finding a point of entry
into the main currents of classroom discourses. Secondly and remarkably, there
is a perception of his representativeness as one of the first generation of Pakistanis present in the school.

Ahmed began to see himself caught up in the broader currents of history. As
one of the first members of his family to be educated wholly in London he was
aware of cultural discontinuities. This awareness kindled his desire to know
more about his own history and his cultural heritage. At the same time, as one of
the first Pakistanis to enter the school, he was faced with the task of making sense
of an inherited culture in a new and sometimes alienating environment.

If Ahmed noticed the singularities of his own experience, his personal sense
of exclusion, and, concurrently, his representativeness, then his engagement
depended upon a sense of connection between his own situation and that of other
members of the class. The insight was gained initially within a classroom, where
many perspectives, some of them conflicting, intersected. From within these
tensions his thinking emerged. Over the intervening months (the discussion took

place in June, and the writing appeared in the following March) Ahmed's thoughts took shape, though this was not to be his final statement. Although it revealed a depth of understanding it is incomplete. He went on to develop his thinking and, significantly, to insert himself within subsequent discussions: to put forward his views and, when he judged it to be necessary, to disagree with the majority. In my brief account of the dialectical process through which Ahmed's self-understanding continued to develop, I have tried to suggest the movement of his ideas, arising from social interaction, submerging within individual reflection and then, at a subsequent stage, resurfacing in the flow and counterflow of classroom discourse. And perhaps Ahmed's intervention disturbed the surfaces of 'daily domination', as he moved from the margins into the mainstream of classroom interaction. But here I am using Ahmed's story to stand for much larger processes. In short, I am arguing that new cultural practices are to be forged from within the social relationships of classrooms, and these are subject to the pressures of wider social and cultural determinations.

Whereas Ahmed took up these issues fairly late in his time at secondary school, Derrick became a confident advocate for the inclusion of African and Caribbean literature and history in the syllabus much earlier. Derrick's father, a musician, came from Georgetown, Guyana. His mother was from Greenock in Scotland. By the late sixties, the family had settled in north-east London. In the sixth form, as one of the first generation of students to take the London Board A level which included 'New Commonwealth' writers, Derrick studied the poetry of Edward Kamau Brathwaite as well as Chaucer and Shakespeare. *Masks* is a long poem which deals with Brathwaite's personal engagement with African history, and in particular the eight years he spent working in Ghana before returning to the Caribbean. Commenting on the long process of coming to recognise continuities between Africa and the Caribbean, which had shaped his responses at the deepest level he writes,

> ...obscurely, slowly but surely, during the eight years that I
> lived there, I was coming to an awareness and
> understanding of community, of cultural wholeness...I came
> to a sense of identification of myself with these people, my
> living diviners. I came to connect my history with theirs,
> the bridge of my mind now linking Atlantic and Ancestor,
> homeland and heartland... And I came home to find that I
> had not really left. That it was still Africa; Africa in the
> Caribbean. The Middle Passage had now guessed its end.
> The connection between my lived but unheeded non-
> middle-class boyhood, and its Great Tradition on the
> eastern mainland, had been made.

On a warm afternoon Derrick and a small party of sixth-formers met and talked with Brathwaite about *Masks* during a visit to London. Most, though not all the students, were from a Caribbean background. At one point Brathwaite recalled a moment of recognition when he saw for the first time the correspondence between West African and Barbadian ways of setting out produce in open markets. The larger, more abstract vision of continuities within the African diaspora was made concrete and graspable. Later, I recall, Derrick, secure in his own identity, asked searching questions, which were implicitly about tendencies within Black literature to construct romanticised versions of ancestral homelands. Derrick continued his studies at university. After graduation he went on to develop theoretical work around shifting representations of the mixed-race 'light-brown subject'. Here, movingly, with restraint and economy, he describes his own social and ethnic formation.

My parents arrived at Finsbury Park, North London, at the beginning of the 60s – one a Black man from George Town, Guyana, the other a white woman from Greenock in Scotland. Apart from their hopes, anxieties and dreams for the future, they brought with them two different but inextricably linked colonial histories. They arrived at a stage already set though constantly unfolding around tensions of Sex, Colour, Class and Race – tensions set in motion long ago and most recently so graphically exposed by the Notting Hill race battles of '58. A scene where the cultural/political apparatus had already begun laying down the geography of the re-cycled 'Colour Problem'. In the middle of this my parents, and many others, defied the prescription for separation/segregation. They came together and in so doing they broke the taboo, they threw white patriarchal society's nightmare back in its face. This they confirmed and celebrated with the birth of a brown child.

We need to look again at the brown child in photographic discourses from the 50s and 60s. It is not enough for us to concentrate on the codification of white (mother)/Black (father) for an understanding of the complexity of Colour. This can only be a beginning. With our arrival there is a shift away from the binary opposition of black/white, masculine/feminine, the threat/the threatened, to a position where the single brown body might hold all of these tensions simultaneously...Looking through family albums at snapshots from the 60s and 70s, our hair is the focal point for an insight into the cultural/social forces that were at work on us 'beyond the frame'. Our hair is usually the primary signifier of our difference – so it was combed, cut, manipulated to look other than Black, to look more 'desirable'. I still have to deal with people who go to touch my 'soft' or 'loose' or 'wavy' hair as if in the touching something (what I don't know) will be confirmed. Back then in the 60s it seems to me that my options regarding the look of my hair were to keep it short and thereby less visible, or to have the living curl dragged out of it:

'Maybe then you'd look Italian...or something.'

Derrick manages to hold in a fine tension the particularities of personal history, and the broader, generalising history of recent social movements. He writes of his parents, 'Apart from their hopes, anxieties and dreams for the future they brought with them two different colonial histories.' His central interest, though, is not so much in the ramifications of the two colonial histories, converging in the formation of the 'light-brown subject', but rather misrepresentation in the photographic discourse of the post-war decades. At one point his theoretical (deconstructive) analysis of signification threatens to displace altogether the human subject, with its complex psychology and its capacity for intention and action. The mixed-race child appears to be conceptualised solely as a site of discursive struggle: 'with our arrival there is a shift away from the binary opposition of black/white, masculine/feminine, the threat/the threatened, to a position where the single brown body might hold all of these tensions simultaneously'. But then, in what follows, lived experience is reintroduced in a penetrating and moving way when he writes,

> 'Maybe then you'd look Italian...or something.'

Parental fears and the wish to protect the light-brown child from the hurtful realities of growing up in the 'miscegenated society' are suggested, though never made explicit. The reader is not invited beyond the threshold of a family's history. A voice is heard but not attributed. A parent's desire for, at least, outward assimilation, attempts to remove the child from history, and it is this history which Derrick seeks to reintroduce as part of his analysis of the shifts in the representation.

The complexity of the processes by which children forge their identities permits no simple description. Behind my account of moments in the learning histories of Tony, Ahmed and Derrick lies a view of English elaborated by Tony Burgess (1988) as centrally about difference. Difference, Burgess argues, is constructed historically. More than individuality lies behind it. I have suggested that the individual stories, as they enter school, may be seen within the broader currents of social movements. In addition, I have tried to show that the various cultural traditions and social practices present in classrooms are not frozen, but are continually being made and remade, as part of a wider process. Anthropological accounts of difference, which fail to attend to questions of conflict and history and to the point where communities interact, fail significantly to attend to social realities.

For Tony, his story marked a beginning in his effort to engage with his own and his family's complicated movements and separations. Ahmed wrote about what it meant to be one of the first generation of Pakistani children in his school, and of the difficulties of entering the mainstream classroom activities. His life was shaped by Pakistani perspectives, but, from within the tensions of classroom relations, a new identity began to take shape. Derrick, as we have seen, continued his studies beyond school. By taking on the analytic discourses of media studies and in rejecting representations of the 'light-brown subject' afforded by the wider culture, he achieved a more sharply differentiated sense of self.

The specificity of these three stories stands in contrast to the abstract universal learner upon which progressive and child-centred versions of English depend. It was Ahmed's recognition of the stubborn particularity of his own position which he found 'necessary to explain'.

Brathwaite, Edward Kamau (1968), *Masks*, Oxford University Press

Brathwaite, Edward Kamau (1970), 'Timehri' in *Savacou 2*, September

Burgess, Tony (1988), 'On difference: cultural and linguistic diversity and English teaching' in M. Lightfoot and N. Martin (eds), *The Word for Teaching is Learning*, essays for James Britton, Heinemann

Brice-Heath, S. (1983), *Ways with Words*, Cambridge University Press

Hewitt, Roger (1989), 'The new oracy: another critical glance', paper presented to BAAL annual conference, September

Lamming, George (1953), *In the Castle of My Skin*, Longman

McClintock, Derrick, 'Colour', *Ten 8*, no. 26

Minns, Hilary (1988), 'Jaspal's story: learning to read at home and at school', *English in Education*, vol. 22, no. 3

Steedman, Carolyn (1982), *The Tidy House*, Virago

PART THREE

The Deep Play of Literature

Behind all the essays in this book lie the reading histories of the writers. Here these autobiographical shadows are more distinct, more explicit, because the topics are poetry and fiction, the production and reproduction of what adults call literature, a category which young people discover, just as they begin to change it by what they choose to read and write.

Throughout his life as a teacher–philosopher James Britton has emphasised the seriously exploratory nature of children's play. Now, from his long-pondered readings of Vygotsky, he re-examines both children's and his own 'use of language in creative and constructive modes'. As he penetrates further into the nature of inner speech – that underground dialogue we have with ourselves – he shows its working in the making of a poem. This 'anatomy of human experience' is explored also by Aidan Chambers, first in his examination of the multiconsciousness implicit in children's picture books, and then in his own practices as a creator of 'writerly' texts for adolescents. More directly, Philippa Pearce explains the complications of writing for the young, including her instinct for 'what will work'. She hopes no teacher will dismantle the world she has created for her readers. In contrast, Margaret Mallett shows how a children's author, who aligns herself with current concerns to make children responsible for the environment, can make a fictional world which encourages children to speculate 'on issues that might not normally have been accessible to them'.

The strong influence of feminist criticism on the many women who read literature has emphatically entered the discourse of classrooms where the teachers are female. There too the aims are political and ethical as well as literary. Gemma Moss shows how, by stressing the gender differences of readers, 'contrasts can be made between different forms of meaning'. Her analysis of reading in a particular English lesson shows girls becoming conscious of their own experience as members of a group, a distinctive critical readership. From this aspect of reading literature and making things with words there can be no going back.

JAMES BRITTON

The Anatomy of Human Experience: the role of inner speech

In play, children move from the world of objects to the inner world of ideas. In playful ways, bounded with cultural overtones and meanings, language seems to go too. This segment of Vygotsky's visionary theory is the beginning of James Britton's reinterpretation of the developmental link between make-believe play in infancy and the practice of the arts, at all stages, from the kindergarten to old age. Here he brings together, with new insight and relevance, D.W. Winnicott's notion of the 'potential space' of play as the intersection of nature and culture, and Jacques Lacan's sterner idea that the unconscious is 'structured like a language', to underpin his description of the birth of the imagination and social and individual growth of products of a literary nature. The ideas and operations are exemplified in a discussion of how a poem came into being. These insights can be re-threaded through the essays that follow in this section and looped back to Alex McLeod's poem and the complementary ideas of Carol Fox and Myra Barrs.

Waking in the morning, throwing back the bed-clothes, already assailed by an unfocused sense of the day's responsibilities; parting the curtains and looking up at the sky – to approve or disapprove. Emerging into the silent house – moving in a way that will preserve its silence as a kind of freedom, yet at the same time submitting to the routine activities that respond to the needs and expectations of others – the acts of an automaton fulfilling inbuilt neuro-muscular instructions. But look far enough into the past, and it will be clear that the patterns were probably first recognised in other people and imitated – clumsily perhaps, playfully perhaps – certainly with deliberation. Experience grows for me as I take over these discovered behaviours, adapted to my biological self and the social environment in which I operate.

'Recognising', 'discovering', 'observing' – these indicate too passive a process for what appears in fact to take place. If we begin at the earliest stages of infancy the active world starts to impinge on the infant as a kind of invitation to miming – routines or formats of interactive behaviour that are instituted by an adult (most often the mother) – by becoming recognisable – that is to say 'familiar' – emerge as distinct from the meaningless flux of other, unfamiliar, events. They are likely to be accompanied by talk on the mother's part – that puts into words the activities she initiates, but at the same time embeds them in a more general, if fragmentary, representation of the life of the family. While the infant at this stage can respond only to the emotional intonations of the talk and not to its encoded meanings, it will not be long before such talk begins to fulfil the crucial role of providing her/him with the key to linguistic meaning. What had become meaningful from enacted routines may then be matched with what is communicated by the mother's verbal behaviour; and we must assume that it is that matching process that leads to a gradual mastery of the spoken language. Thereafter, talk becomes a principal means of interacting with other people and it is this continued interaction that constitutes the recognition/production of meaningful behaviour.

So the interacting, responding, observing provide the indispensable key to the origins of those patterns of behaviour and then to their subsequent modification on my part as they constitute my accumulating experience. And on this aforementioned morning, glancing at the weather, contemplating the day's activities, interacting with members of the household, making some demands and responding to the demands of others, it is still the alert and sensitive interacting that holds the key. Should that become something I am no longer capable of, I might as well go back to bed and stay there!

If I were to complete a detailed account of the morning's activities – describing the food and the utensils, the drink and the layout of the table, I should be likely to create an increasing certainty that my home belonged to a particular geographical and social area – and not any other. There might, of course, be anomalies – reflections of activities observed and imitated during periods of my life when I lived in other surroundings – foreign countries, perhaps, or came under alien influences. Patterns of behaviour will distinguish not only my individual self, but also my family, and beyond that my social groups, local, regional, national.

A closer look at adult/child interaction will make quite clear how important is the role played by exchange of talk. Here is a brief interaction between Laurie, my grandchild, at 3 years 8 months, and myself. She is paying a visit to our home and we are in the garden, talking, first, about a thrushes' nest, now empty.

Laurie:	Where's the birds' nest?
Me:	It's still there, darling, but...they're not...
Laurie:	Are the birds coming?
Me:	No, they're not coming, darling, because
Laurie:	Why?
Me:	Because they've left the nest.
Laurie:	When will they be little babies?
Me:	They were little babies – they're not now – they're big birds now.
Laurie:	When were they little babies?
Me:	Oh – about six months ago.
Laurie:	's a long while ago.
Me:	Yes.
Laurie:	And I was BIG!
Me:	Were you?
Laurie:	Yes – big.
Me:	How big were you?
Laurie:	Not like Mummy and Daddy.
Me:	Mm?

Laurie: Not like Mummy and Daddy...
         [a distraction] Fluff!
Me: That's fluff from the tree – that's seeds that fall
         down from that tree. Do you see where it's
         coming down?...Do you see that coming down?
         That's where all that comes from.
Laurie: How are they coming down here?
Me: Well – that's – see, lots of it – some more there –
         everywhere there's fluff – come down from that
         tree – that's called a...an aspen.
Laurie: Why is no more birds going in there – in the nest?
Me: Eh, I don't know love – I think – they've gone
         somewhere else, perhaps.
Laurie: Why are they leaving all the nest there?
Me: Well, praps they'll come back to it next year when
         the birds have another family, – praps they'll
         come back.
Laurie: Why?
Me: Well, they built it there, didn't they?

Other members of the family arrive on the scene and that
conversation is over.

It will certainly not be true of all children everywhere, but with a great many of
the children I have known, or learned of from records, by far the greater number
of exploratory, interactive meaning-making occasions have been in the context of
make-believe rather than in daily real-life activities. In co-operative make-
believe the child is likely to be the one who calls up the scene and directs the
action: and in doing so, Vygotsky points out, 'the child learns to act in a cognitive, rather than an externally visual, realm, by relying on internal tendencies
and motives and not on incentives supplied by external things' (1978, p. 96). In
this way the number and variety of activated concerns is vastly increased, but –
even more significant – these concerns are inherently representative of the
child's stage of experience. There is no shortage of recordings to illustrate this
aspect of interaction. Here Laurie and I take part in a game of shops earlier on
the same day that the garden encounter was recorded above. In one form or
another, playing shops had become a favourite make-believe scenario with the
three-and-a-half-year-old:

A shop space is marked out by a tea-trolley (a pretend
cooking stove) and a gate-legged coffee-table.
Laurie: Switch. I turn 'em all on – they're cooking – Switch.
         What cake do you like?
Me: Have you got chocolate cake? I like chocolate cake.

Laurie: Yes...Why does this fall over? It's — Why does this
          tip over – this one doesn't tip over – it's got wheels!
          Why?...
          [*The coffee table versus the tea-trolley*]...Look there:
          Are you coming? There! I turn the cakes off: they're
          READY!

Me: Oh, good – are they cooked?

Laurie: I'm going to pass these – I'm walking did you see –
          Come here! Come in my shop and I'll give you one.
          What kind?

Me: I'd like chocolate cake please.

Laurie: O.K. How much money?

Me: Two shillings – twenty pence – twenty pence.

Laurie: Here 'tis then.

Me: Do I give it to you, then? O.K. There's twenty
          pence for the cake...What's that cake?

Laurie: A shallow cake?

Me: Yes.

Laurie: A brown one or a yellow one or a pink one.

Me: Chocolate – a brown one. Do you say these are
          shallow cakes – do you call them? What are these
          then?

Laurie: Those are chocolate cakes with banana.

Me: Oh, that sounds lovely. How much are they?

Laurie: Fifty pence.

Me: How much?

Laurie: These will be...

Me: Fifteen pence?

Laurie: Thank you.

Me: Thank you...Lovely...What kind of cakes are those?

Laurie: China cakes.

Me: Chung cakes...? What's the word?

Laurie: Chi-i-i-na cakes.

Me: China cakes – oh – I'll have one of those.

Laurie: [*abashed*] Well – there are only these many...*Please
          can you go to another shop?*

Me: Oh – yea – O.K., O.K.

Laurie: Ask Alison for one.

Me: Bye-bye, thank you.

Laurie: Bye!

Spoken dialogue is at this stage the principal means by which a child's linguistic
resources are recruited and experiences internalised. Some children will, as early
as this, attempt spoken monologue, but when they do their utterances are likely
to be of the somewhat dream-like, loose, illogical kind that I have called *spiels*
(1972, p. 83) – word-spinning performances, jigsaw collections of remembered
phrases – offered as entertainment to admiring listeners – not as conversation.

Utterance as celebration would designate some of such performances, as for example the following, spoken in a sing-song voice by Clare at 3 years 0 months:

> Angels at head, fairies at foot
> The stars are shining with golden light –
> Hit on the ball with golden light
> Loo-ing, loo-ing. Darling child
> The children in bed
> – *it's the big one that's saying it, you see* –
> Lighting up the candles so early
> Holy night – silent night.

I should add that the sources of the language of most *spiels* would be more diverse and less easily recognised than those of this example.

Genuine monologic speech is another matter, and a later development, though, as might be expected, the transition may not be at all clearly marked: that is to say, expressive performance-directed speech may play some part in utterances that would otherwise be recognised as communicative monologue carrying cognitive messages.

The transition from dialogic to monologic speech in young children has been helpfully described by A.R. Luria (1981). He traced the development of a child's problem-solving speech from its beginnings as expanded – fully verbalised – vocal speech, through speech for oneself, where it becomes abbreviated in the process of being internalised, becoming – that is to say – inner speech.

> Only when external speech has become abbreviated and
> converted into inner speech does it become possible to carry
> out the opposite process: the expansion of this inner speech
> into an external, connected text with its characteristic
> semantic coherence...We would argue that once a child has
> mastered these operational components of expanded speech,
> he/she goes through an equally complex path to develop real
> speech activity. This activity is guided by a motive, is
> subject to a specific goal, and constitutes a constantly
> regulated, closed semantic system. (p. 158)

These are developments he would have expected to occur 'as a child approaches school age': and the earliest monologues, he suggested, are likely to take a narrative form. An early example of what I take to be essentially monologic speech is provided by Laurie at 4 years 1 month in a make-believe situation in which she is the mother and I play the part of her small child. The situation she implies is fictional (she has in reality one younger sister only), although it clearly represents some aspect of her own real experience. The tape-recording shows hesitations that suggest she is improvising as she speaks; that is to say, in Luria's terms, that her utterance is an expanded version of her inner speech. I think it is a fair description to call the piece as a whole *enacted* (rather than *related*) *narrative*. Finally, if we accept Vygotsky's (1978, p. 102) view that in make-believe play a young child is able to act some months – or even years – ahead of her chronological age, it may well be that true monologue is likely, in the case of many children, to make its earliest appearance in make-believe play.

Laurie: Now it's time for little darlings to go to sleep.

Me: Yes.

Laurie: You've got to go to sleep now. Your blanket –
pillow. Lie down! Now you're going to have a
little – if you don't want to go to sleep – you *must*
go to sleep, 'cos – or you will be afraid of night, 'cos
the owls come at night...Yes, they go to-whoo! They
don't frighten *you* – they don't eat you, only rats or
mice – that's good, isn't it?

Me: Yes.

Laurie: Now I've got to sort your cover, 'cos you messed it
up last night, didn't you?

Me: Yes, I wriggled about so much, didn't I?

Laurie: Yes, 'cos you're afraid of the *owl*, aren't you.

Me: Yes.

Laurie: *To-night* I have to sleep in my own room which is
downstairs and Dad sleeps downstairs too and you
only sleep *up*stairs. And the baby sleeps (*pause*)
downstairs too and the big girls – and your two
sisters sleep down too and you only sleep up, don't
you? So you have to be very quiet. If you hear – if
you – um – hear a *monster*, I'll come running up. I
hope – if you dream about one, just cry and come
down and say 'Oo-oo, Mummy, I had a bad dream'.
Yes. Now you're going to go to sleep, aren't you?
Close your eyes!

It seems to me that the play of imagination illustrated in transcripts of this kind
provides a key to the continuing role of creative language in human existence –
whether manifested in the verbal arts or in the probing curiosity that empowers
scientific inquiry. Vygotksy (1978, p. 93) has spelt out his account of the transition from make-believe behaviour to the birth of the imagination:

> Imagination is a new psychological process for the child; it
> is not present in the consciousness of the very young child,
> is totally absent in animals, and represents a specifically
> human form of conscious activity. Like all functions of
> consciousness, it originally arises from action. The old adage
> that child's play is imagination in action must be reversed:
> we can say that imagination in adolescents and school
> children is play without action.

It will raise no eyebrows to acknowledge here the existence of a close developmental link between make-believe play in infancy and the practice of the arts at
all stages from kindergarten to the grave. The link has been widely and variously
formulated. In *Play, Dreams and Imitation* for example, Piaget (1951, p. 155) characterises make-believe play as *symbolic assimilation* and concludes that it is 'rein-
tegrated in thought in the form of creative imagination' or 'spontaneous constructive
activity'. Freud (see Vygotsky, 1971, p. 73) claims that 'The poet does the same
things as the child at play: he creates a world, which he takes very seriously, with a lot

of enthusiasm and animation, and at the same time very sharply sets it apart from reality'. Vygotsky (1971, p. 258) goes on to state his own view that art functions for the child in ways that differ from its role for an adult, and he explains this by referring to the work of Chukovsky (1963) on the young child's use of nursery rhymes: the way their topsy-turvy nonsense appeals to a child at a time when he is consolidating his mastery of the actual. 'By dragging a child into a topsy-turvy world,' Vygotsky writes, 'we help his intellect work, because the child becomes interested in creating such a topsy-turvy world for himself in order to become more effectively the master of the laws governing the real world.' If rhymes and stories – seen as works of literature – have this effect, they will clearly be serving a purpose that diminishes as the child grows older: as what T.S. Eliot – in his poem *Animula* – called 'the imperatives of is and seems' grow less insistent. Vygotsky goes on to suggest that, while adults have no such predominance of 'seems' over 'is' to contend with, there is also for them in art something of the same dualism – that art serves to present modified, even somewhat distorted, views of reality – and thus has the effect of strengthening in the viewer his grasp of the nature of reality; while at the same time, let me add, exploring the structures of *what it might become*. In short, art by this view is 'a method for building life'. It is an interesting feature of Vygotsky's book that while it bears the title *The Psychology of Art*, its subject matter and its exemplification throughout is, in one form or another, *literature*, the verbal arts.

It is my purpose in the rest of this essay to ask how central a function in human development is the use of language in creative, constructive modes; how important to us, in other words, are social products of a literary nature and what do we achieve by ourselves experimenting in the production of such works? In pursuing this inquiry there are two ideas put forward by early Soviet students of language – contemporaries and probably professional associates of Vygotsky, that we need to consider at this stage:

(1)   The notion that meaning is, in the first instance, inter-personal, constantly created, adapted, modified in the course of person-to-person verbal exchange. The same idea has been elegantly put by Georges Gusdorf, the French philosopher (1965, p. 48):

> In essence, language is not of one but of many; it is *between*.
> It expresses the relational being of man...The self does not by
> itself alone have to carve out for itself an access to being –
> because the self exists only in reciprocity with the other. An
> isolated self can truly be said to be only an abstraction.

(2)   That human experience in its organised and recoverable form is a network of verbal meanings. Volosinov (1973, p. 118) spells out this view in the course of answering the question 'How, in fact, is another's speech received?' 'Everything vital to the evaluative reception of another's utterance', he writes,

> everything of ideological value is expressed in the material
> of inner speech. After all, it is not a mute, wordless creature
> that receives such an utterance, but a human being full of
> inner words. All his experiences...exist encoded in his inner
> speech, and only to that extent do they come into contact
> with speech received from outside. Word comes into contact
> with word.

However, it does seem to me that the encoding process is a selective one, and that the selection will entail an element of individual responsibility. What I encode will reflect to some degree the biological, psychological and social aspects of my life, and what is encoded will shrink or expand or suffer other transformation in the light of my changing conception of the world I inhabit. Verbal interaction will be the means by which what I encode will be shaped and stored, and my choice will come to influence what counts as experience in the social group to which I belong. Volosinov uses the term 'behavioral ideology' to distinguish this level of activity from the *established ideology* represented by institutions – the press, literature, science, etc. – a more stable system, yet one that relies for its vitality upon the support of behavioural ideologies.

Volosinov introduces this notion of individual initiative early in the first chapter of his book, *Marxism and the Philosophy of Language* (1973):

> Although the reality of a word, as is true of any sign, resides
> between individuals, a word, at the same time, is produced
> by the individual organism's own means without recourse to
> any equipment or any other kind of extracorporeal material.
> This has determined the role of word as *the semiotic material
> of inner life – of consciousness* (inner speech).

Finally, Volosinov tackles what he regards as 'one of the most important problems in the science of meanings, the problem of the *interrelationship between meaning and evaluation*'. He stresses that the overriding purpose in speaking is an *evaluative* purpose (p. 103). 'All referential contents produced in living speech are said or written with a specific *evaluative* accent. There is no such thing as word without evaluative accent.'.

Having embarked on an attempt to specify the purposes of literature, I must now go on to raise a question that Volosinov does not at this point consider. What are the consequences of an evaluative utterance upon the choice of subsequent action on the part of the speaker? If, for example, an experimental enquiry fails to yield any evidence upon the hypothesis that underlies it, what effect may that be expected to have on the enquirer? Will she merely reframe the hypothesis in alternative terms and try again? Or may the failure matter so much that life no longer seems worth living? And of course there have been cases of such disillusionment. I believe we would have to conclude that what is evaluated in any broadly speaking scientific activity is likely to be within limits prescribed by professional practice and epistemological levels, or the current state of knowledge in a field.

Consider, in contrast, the evaluative scope of such a document as the suicide note discovered and reported by Aldous Huxley in *Texts and Pretexts*: 'No wish to die. One of the best of sports, the boys will tell you. This b, at Palmers Green has sneaked my wife, one of the best in the world; my wife, the first love in the world.' Not that I wish to call that heartfelt cry *literature* – but I would claim that it represents a type of discourse that is in every way responsive to human evaluative needs and a type of discourse that is also capable of the highly sophisticated and influential expression we cannot fail to recognise as literature.

Such discourse, across such a range, must be seen to occupy a key place in the functions of language, and to be of vital importance not simply to addicts, scholars, writers and critics, but to every man, woman and child alive in a literate society.

As a postscript to this section of my account, and as a truce in the handling of abstractions, let me offer a brief autobiographical fragment, something I produced – by chance – a few days ago. The final product, thirteen lines of verse, is clearly a personal evaluation on my part. Arriving at it was a complex process – the one-line opening cadence came quickly to the pen – but what followed was more of a check than a spur: in transition from inner speech to verbal speech two words surfaced which proved to be unacceptable, and for an interesting reason. Here is the whole story.

It was early evening on a September day: I had fallen asleep on the sofa and when I woke I had, momentarily, some glimpse from a fading dream – or perhaps some image germane to the half-waking state. I wrote a line which seemed a way of approaching what I wanted to say:

> *Opening my eyes on the half-light of an autumn evening*

– and I needed to find a way of suggesting that the world I awoke to seemed one which I could appropriately share with the recent dead – the family and companions whom I had outlived. The logic – if logic could be found – lay in the idea that the difference between us was one of time-scale rather than total severance – and the evidence for that lay in the extent to which aspects of what they were survived as legacy that made up a great part of my environment.

I struggled with the second line that should approach that idea: one attempt began, *Here were...* But as I worked on that construction (which above all involved *listening to it* – 'word speaking to word') I became aware that it already carried *somebody else's meaning*; that is to say, it was another of those powerful remembered cadences that I have discussed on previous occasions. I tried to fill out that recalled fragment. I surmised that what followed the words *Here were* in the original were words that described features of some landscape long familiar to the writer – but that the recollection would be short-lived, some other image supervening. By now I had Dylan Thomas clearly in mind – thence to 'Poem in October' – and recall of the line that made the break – *But the weather turned around.* So I went to the source and found what I wanted:

> A springful of larks in a rolling
> Cloud and the roadside bushes brimming with whistling
> Blackbirds and the sun of October
> Summery
> On the hill's shoulder,
> Here were fond climates and sweet singers suddenly
> Come in the morning where I wandered and listened
> To the rain wringing
> Wind blow cold
> In the wood faraway under me.

– and then – at the beginning of the final stanza –

> ...there could I marvel my birthday
> Away but the weather turned around.

Had the recollected fragment been such words as *A springful of larks* I should probably have known the source at once. What is interesting is that so semantically neutral a phrase – so simply structural a signal – as *Here were* should have that evocative power. I wondered whether it was the tautness of the whole construction – *Here were such and such suddenly come* – that made it memorable. But as I realised this I remembered some of the other fragments that had shown the same characteristics – the same memorableness: *but not this* from Auden's poem 'Taller today we remember similar evenings'; from Wallace Stevens' poem 'The Idea of Order at Key West', the skeletal fragment *and knew that we should...?...often for...?...*, and a similar algebraic formula from Auden's *Age of Anxiety:* 'Whether by A or by B, in X or in Y' (*English in Education*, vol. 19, no. 2, 1987, pp. 83–4). What I must conclude is that the structural framework, the grammatical forms that enter such expressions, are a more powerful part of the total literary experience than we usually reckon.

This, no doubt, is something I should do well to bear in mind in returning to the production of the second and subsequent lines of my poem on waking. However, as I did so, it seemed evident that my original opening – *here were* – beckoned too strongly in the direction of Dylan Thomas's poem to suit my purposes.

And here is the outcome:

> Opening my eyes on the half-light of an autumn evening
> I was newly aware that the world I inhabit
> Is a world I can share with the recent dead –
> The family and friends whom I dared to outlive.
>
> I knew that their presence survives, alive in the words
> And the tones of their voices; in their sudden appearances –
> Claiming a thought, a step in the argument,
> A move in the game...And it seemed
>
> That what holds us apart is no more than a time-warp,
> A trick of the clock that time will correct:
> Then those who outlive me – family and friends –
> Will join in the dialogue,
> And mine will be one of the voices they hear.

A first draft and, as such, still open to the kinds of complication that refinement of the forms – lexical and syntactic – might produce: though, to tell the truth, my mode of writing does rely more on 'shaping at the point of utterance' than it does on refinement by revision.

It is the nature of inner speech as bearer of experience that concerns me in offering this example: the persistence of that remembered phrase from Dylan Thomas, despite its seeming paucity of meaning, and the way fresh experience – the dream-like recognition of a conviviality with the recent dead – is realised in terms of the resources inner speech provides.

This essay was written as part of work in progress, November 1989.

Britton, James (1972), *Language and Learning*, Pelican
Britton, James (1987), 'Call it an experiment' in *English in Education*, vol. 19, no. 2
Chukovsky, K. (1963), *From Two to Five*, University of California Press
Eliot, T.S. (1936), *Collected Poems, 1909-35*, Faber & Faber
Gusdorf, Georges (1965), *Speaking*, Northwestern University Press
Huxley, Aldous (1986), *Texts and Pretexts*, Grafton Books
Luria, A.R. (1981), *Language and Cognition*, Wiley
Piaget, Jean (1951), *Play, Dreams and Imitation in Childhood*, Heinemann
Thomas, Dylan (1952), *Collected Poems*, Dent
Volosinov, V.S. (1973), *Marxism and the Philosophy of Language*, Seminar Press
Vygotsky, L.S. (1971), *The Psychology of Art*, M.I.T. Press
Vygotsky, L.S. (1978), *Mind in Society*, Harvard University Press

And They Lived Badly Ever After

In the novels he writes for young adults Aidan Chambers experiments with narrations which invite readers to explore how authors write and how reading is not always the same process. As an anthologist he emphasises the evaluative function of literature by bringing together writers who exploit a common theme or genre. Here we see him moving from an appreciation of a child's story to a more general description of authorial practice. He illustrates the negotiations, which are often struggles – between readers and writers, and the same kind of struggle within language itself – to reflect what is, responsibly, meant. Although no author can be objective about readers (nor constrain them to *re-read*), this author knows and shows how words go from him (ignoring, perhaps, what they repress). Here we see autobiography becoming fictive text, a process that is as constantly fascinating as it is elusive.

I've chosen three aspects of literature that I think, taken together, possess enough value – never mind all the other good things it offers – to justify placing literature at the centre of the curriculum.

I'll begin with some thoughts about the potential of children's literature – of all literature – in the profoundly important task of developing interpretive awareness in the reader. Then I'll look at how literature helps us, in Jerome Bruner's words, to 'subjunctivize life' (1986, p. 159). Finally, I'll consider literature as an object of reflection, how it enables us to become more than we thought we could be.

To come at what I want to say about interpretive awareness I'd like to read you a story. This is how it goes:

The Little Goblin
and the ghost
by Stephen

Once upon
A time there
was A Goblin
who was always
naughty.
One day a ghost
came to visit
the naughty
Goblin.

and the ghost
was naughty
to so they
were
naughty all their
Lives. and they Lived
Badly ever
after
the End

I wonder what you made of that. Did it engage your attention? If so, would you say it's a story for children, and how do you know that? Would you say it was written by an adult? We're told its author is called Stephen. Do you assume this is a first name for a male, or a family name for someone who is perhaps female? Do you wonder how and why it came to be told? Was it written for a particular audience? What kind of sense does it make? And do any of these questions matter?

Let me repeat some statements we all accept. Reading is always an act of translation: translating, for instance, marks on a page into patterns we recognise and understand. Reading is always an act of interpretation: the marks on the page have to 'make sense' to us. All this we know to be a complicated business that involves what Jonathan Culler calls 'literary competence' (1976, chap. 6), which is something we learn in a number of ways, principally by doing it. Margaret Meek has recently and succinctly shown us how texts teach what readers learn (1988). We also learn to read, as we learn so much else in life, by working alongside people who know how to do it. Liz Waterland (1985) and others have called this the apprenticeship approach to reading. But equally we learn how to do it by telling other readers about what we have read, and how we constructed meaning as we went along.

One of the trade secrets apprentices soon learn about interpretation is that it is always done by highlighting. All stories involve selection, whether they are of the originating kind, like Stephen's, or of the interpretive kind, like the story of our reading of 'The Little Goblin and the ghost'. When we are originating a story, we have to pick and choose from all the possible events that might be included. When interpreting, we have to pick and choose from all the elements that caught our attention while reading, and while we thought afterwards about what we had read.

Let me show this happening by telling you the interpretive story of my own reading of Stephen's fictional story. A few months ago, my wife Nancy and I were visited at the Thimble Press by Liz Waterland, who had come to see Nancy about the revision of *Read with Me*. Afterwards Liz said she was sure I'd like to see a story written by one of her pupils, and handed me a sheet of A4 paper folded to make a little book of four A5 pages.

On the front, written in a childish hand, the letters large and separate, was the title, 'The Little Goblin and the ghost', and the author's name, Stephen. I noticed that the words 'and the ghost' had been squeezed in as an afterthought. At the bottom of the page was a drawing of what I took to be the goblin, a human figure with large fingers like talons, and of the ghost, which resembled a ski-helmet joined to a ragged shoulder-cape. The inside pages contained the story. On the back page was another drawing of the ski-helmet ghost who was saying 'bye-bye' in bubbletalk.

When I came to the ending, 'and they lived badly ever after', my first thought was what a good title that would make, and what a good opening to talk about how children use their reading to sharpen their wits and how, once they have learned the rules of stories, they love to play with them to their own satisfaction. So here was a good example of some of the more obvious potential to be found in literature.

I read the story again.

'The Little Goblin and the ghost by Stephen. Once upon a time there was a goblin who was always naughty. One day a ghost came to visit the naughty Goblin. And the ghost was naughty, too, so they were naughty all their lives. And they lived badly ever after. The end.'

This time I noticed a number of things. First of all, it's a story which is all beginning and end with very little in between. The middle, where you would expect to find the guts of the thing, is contained in a précis: 'And the ghost was naughty, too, so they were naughty all their lives.' We're not told what they did, why they were naughty, or where or when.

What else? I counted the substantive words and found 'naughty' the most used: four times, as against twice for goblin and for ghost. I saw that Goblin is always given a capital G, whereas ghost is accorded only a lower case g. But then Lives, Badly and End are all given capitals, as is the indefinite article in two places. Was this arbitrary or did it mean something? I began to wonder who Stephen was, what significance his story might have, how it had come about, and how old he'd been when he wrote it. No matter that critics of a structuralist stripe say we ought to stick to the text alone, we all know that once readers are captivated by a story, more often than not they want to know who made it and why. This isn't surprising. Literature, as we all know, is a high form of gossip. And gossip – the story of our everyday lives told in daily episodes – is our most popular form of talk.

I telephoned Liz; this is what she told me. Stephen wrote about the naughty Goblin when he was not quite five years old. A year later he is a stocky little boy, very bright, with a beautiful singing voice. His favourite song at the moment is 'When a knight won his spurs'. He comes from a single-parent family, living with his mother, who rules him very firmly because she knows he can be a little devil when he wants to be and is extremely clever at seeing through the devices adults use to keep children of his age in check. He is always on the go, to the point of being hyperactive, and always wants to be the centre of attention.

'The Little Goblin and the ghost' was the first story he had ever written. He was lying in bed one night waiting for his mother to come and switch off his light, when he picked up a pencil and scrawled the story down in one go. Of course, not yet knowing the secrets of authorship, he did not appreciate that writing stories is an agonising business, requiring much thought and research and hard work, not to mention numerous closely edited drafts before publication. Not knowing this, he proudly gave his story to his mother to read as soon as she came in to settle him down for the night. After she had praised him and behaved as mothers do, she asked what gave him the idea. To which Stephen replied, 'I think it was my head.'

Is it too fanciful of me to bring Stephen's world into his fictional text? Am I wrong to read the capitalised little goblin, who is drawn like a human being with large talonish hands, as himself, the goblin's naughtiness as his own, and the ghost as his newly imagined friend who, being naughty too, lends literary if not literal support to Stephen's own compulsive behaviour that so often gets on grown-up nerves? Are these the secrets embedded in this narrative, which begins in the way of fairytales, and ends with a witty twist to the usual ending, because fairytales are the literary form he's most familiar with? And aren't those unspecific endings of fairytales most appropriate for a writer like Stephen, because they declare a non-specific future, for what do you know about possible futures when you're only just five and starting school?

I don't think it was entirely arbitrary that Stephen's head gave him the idea of writing about a naughty goblin who acquires a naughty spooky friend to be naughty with for ever. Stephen's story clearly demonstrates a truth I think I know, that the principal drive to read and write is the desire, as Jerome Bruner put it, 'to distance oneself in some way from what one knows by being able to reflect on one's knowledge'. The knowledge that interests us the most is the knowledge of our own selves. The questions, 'Who am I, and what am I, and why am I, and what have I been and what might I become?' are what keep us reading and writing with the most fervour. Perhaps to five-year-old Stephen his apparently light-hearted fiction was not so insignificant. Perhaps he wrote it as a way of interpreting to himself what he thinks of fairy stories, and of telling himself what they mean to him. And perhaps he shows his story to his mother as an achievement that also helps him say to her something important about himself.

Thinking of Stephen's story like that seems to me to show Stephen telling himself and then his mother that:

Anything can happen in a story.

He can do anything he wants in a story, including assert himself and his future, whether other people want him that way or not.

He has discovered that storying is a serious kind of play, and that all stories are variations on other stories that already exist and you re-create in your own way by changing and remodelling them within the rules of the game.

He has discovered that in a story – in the making of it – he can *objectify* his own wishes, his dilemmas, anxieties, imaginings, and thus gain control over them, by holding them up to his own and other people's view.

He has discovered that a story interprets the world, and that in a story he can reinterpret the world, because by gaining command of a story he commands himself and the powers that have so far ruled his behaviour, and thus he is able to act differently.

Stephen's story, therefore, may not be about living badly ever after but about gaining power over badness so as to live well ever after. By *objectifying* his naughtiness, and holding it up for his own and his mother's reflective thought, he may in fact be re-creating his world on new terms.

And finally, he has discovered that a story can be a disguise that codes secrets about himself in such a way that only those who know how to read the secret can penetrate the disguise and view the real Stephen who hides behind it. In a story, he now knows, you can both hide yourself and reveal yourself.

This aspect of literature, which Frank Kermode has described in *The Genesis of Secrecy*, is to me the most fascinating of all the values offered by the reading and writing of it. Such is the nature of storying that infants as young as Stephen can benefit from its potentialities quite as much as can experienced adult writers and readers.

What is also true about Stephen, however, is that he is not yet explicitly conscious of what he has discovered. He depends on adults – mainly his mother and his teacher – to provide an awareness for him so that he can act on his story-making instincts. This is Vygotsky's 'zone of proximal development' (1978. p. 86).

One essential point about interpretation. In putting down my thoughts about Stephen's story, I am aware that some of my ideas came from intuitive feelings and that I had to formulate these in words and read the words to you in order to test their validity. I think we all do this all the time when we're trying to make sense of things.

The fact is that in making sense of any text one's own mind is never enough. Nor are two minds enough, not where the interpretation of complex texts like those we find in literature are concerned – even literature as apparently simple as Stephen's. What all of us know is that meaning is not made in isolation but by negotiation with other people. We share what we think, we listen to what others have to say, we add to and modify each other's perceptions, and move towards agreement. Jerome Bruner puts it this way in his book *Actual Minds, Possible Worlds*:

> ...if one asks the question, where is the meaning of social concepts – in the world, in the meaner's head, or in interpersonal negotiation – one is compelled to answer that it is the last of these. Meaning is what we can agree upon or at least accept as a working basis for seeking agreement about the concept at hand. If one is arguing about social 'realities' like democracy or equity or even gross national product, the reality is not the thing, not in the head, but in the act of arguing and negotiating about the meaning of such concepts. (p. 122)

That we cannot read anything without engaging in an act of interpretation is a first truth. A second, co-equal truth is that our interpretation finally depends upon our negotiating with other members of the society in which we live in order to construct a meaning we can act upon.

Therefore, whenever we talk seriously about what some call 'the reading process' we should always include the art and skill of interpretation as an essential part of the process. Then it becomes clear that reading isn't a silent, anti-social activity at all, as some people often say it is. Rather, it is one of the most social and sociable activities we engage in.

In talking about interpretation I haven't mentioned books much, and it may appear that I'm like those reading specialists who don't think texts matter. They certainly do, and it is true that any text needs interpretation, even when it is as bald as the word 'Exit'. Above one kind of door it can mean 'this is the way out' but above another door it can mean 'this is the way in to the office of the organisation for euthanasia'. There is, too, the famous notice in London's Underground, which reads 'Dogs must be carried on the escalator'. Both these examples show that meaning always depends on readers knowing the context of what they're reading.

So, yes, texts demand interpretation, but not all texts subjunctivise reality. Those that do, make the most demands on us as interpreters and also, by the way, give us the greatest pleasure.

I've borrowed the phrase *subjunctivise reality* from Jerome Bruner (pp. 32-37). A narrative engages the reader in 'the performance of meaning under the guidance of the text'. Bruner selects three features which are crucial to this activity.

The first is *presupposition*, by which he means the creation of implicit rather than explicit meanings in the text. Explicit meanings leave little doubt in the reader's mind, by eliminating indeterminacy. We know, for example, that the word 'Exit' is being used as explicitly as possible. So is the notice about dogs on escalators. And we don't think twice about their meaning when we meet them in their home contexts. In Stephen's story, however, we're left entirely free to decide for ourselves what the goblin and the ghost did when they were naughty. There isn't even a hint. This is a thoroughly implicit text. But of course we all have ideas about what goblins do and what ghosts get up to when they want to annoy other people. There is a narrative tradition which offers plenty of examples, and we read whichever of these possibilities we want into Stephen's story. We don't have to make it up; we bring to Stephen's story our knowledge of other stories about similar characters. But was this what Stephen had in mind, or was he working from a learner's instinct? We can't tell, because no one thought to ask him. Knowing what and how to ask young readers and writers is one of the discoveries teachers are now making.

An example of presupposition put into sophisticated play is the double-page spread that forms the narrative hinge in John Burningham's masterly picture book *Granpa*, where the two characters, Granpa and the little girl, stand with their backs to each other, widely separated by the gutter of the book and what feels like a room full of cold white space. The dialogue caption reads: 'That was not a nice thing to say to Granpa'. I know a class of eight-year-olds who were quite put out when they came to that moment in the story. 'Why doesn't it tell us what she said?' they asked indignantly. Their astute teacher replied with a question that required them to become the author. 'What's the worst thing you can think of to say to your grandfather?' she asked. The class took it in turns: 'You smell,' 'I hate you,' 'Silly old goat,' were some of the replies. 'Drop dead!' was another. They giggled at the time. Only when they reached the penultimate page and saw Granpa's empty chair and the little girl staring bleakly at it did the enormity of that not-very-nice-thing-to-say cause them to gasp.

Afterwards, when the book had been read again, the teacher reminded the children of their question and asked if they still thought they should have been told what the little girl said. Of course, they didn't. Now they knew it would have spoilt the story. Guessing what might have been said was part of the narrative game. The indeterminacy, the implicit nature of the text at this point, caused them to presuppose, to begin interpreting the narrative in a way they hadn't until that moment in the telling.

Literary texts, as distinct from all other kinds, use the potential of presupposition in the creation of the text itself, and in the relationship the text builds between the writer and the reader. That is one of the reasons we enjoy them so much. Literature is an end in itself, but reading it also prepares us better than anything else can to handle every other form of communication. For those who question the practical value of literature in schools, this is one of the answers.

Narrative texts which trade too little in presupposition, or do it ineptly, end up by boring us with their banality, which is precisely what is wrong with most of the books included in reading schemes. On the other hand, texts which strain our ability to handle complicated presupposition end up uncompleted because they defeat us. *Finnigans Wake* is like that for most readers.

Bruner's second feature is *subjectification*, by which he means the depiction of reality through 'the filter of the consciousness of protagonists in the story' rather than 'through an omniscient eye that views a timeless reality'. If we go on thinking of *Granpa* as an example, we see how the pictures show us, on one side of the spread and in full colour, the scene we understand to be taking place in the present time of the story, and on the opposite page, in sepia, pictures which depict images that might be memories or imaginings or flashbacks or flashes-forward. And the implicit question is, 'Who is seeing these images? Granpa, the little girl, the narrator?'

As we try to answer, we find ourselves thinking about how the world created in the book looks to the characters in it, seeing it through their eyes but also, at the same time, seeing it through our own. So that as we contemplate their world, we set against it, also, the world we live in, and think about that too. What are granpas to us, and us to them, and what does it mean to us that they disappear from the pages of our lives' own narrative? We are all subjects, limited by our always too narrowly subjective vision. To know ourselves more fully we need to know others, see with their eyes, think their thoughts. Literature works at the heart of that engagement.

This potential embodied in the very nature of literary writing – that it can present experience to us seen through other people's consciousness – helps create the third of the features Bruner analyses. This he calls *multiple perspective*: by which he means 'beholding the world through a set of prisms each of which catches some part of it'.

In *Granpa* there is a complex multiple perspective achieved by Burningham's handling of time. For example, there are the four seasons of the year, and the natural and symbolic meanings these suggest in relation to the characters and the human experience the plot deals with. There is the multipresentness of the story's present time, laid side by side with time as we know it in memory. There is the way the first picture contains within it images of the future, the second spread images of the past, and so on.

Added together, Bruner suggests, these three features of narrative discourse – presupposition, subjectification, and multiple perspectives – succeed in subjunctivising reality. They help produce narratives that, as he puts it, 'traffic in human possibilities rather than in settled certainties'. He sums it up like this:

> I have tried to make the case that the function of literature
> as art is to open us to dilemmas, to the hypothetical, to the
> range of possible worlds that a text can refer to. I have used
> the term 'to subjunctivize', [meaning] to render the world
> less fixed, less banal, more susceptible to recreation.
> Literature subjunctivizes, makes strange, renders the
> obvious less so, the unknowable less so as well, matters of
> value more open to reason and intuition. Literature, in this
> spirit, is an instrument of freedom, lightness, imagination,
> and, yes, reason, (p. 159).

What is more important, what has more value, than something that does this for us?

I'd like to change perspective here from that of the reader and teacher to that of the author. My daily life is mainly spent writing novels and stories, and the letters and notebooks and diaries and essays and lectures that, so to speak, feed them and feed on them. That is, I make objects out of words. I don't find it a very easy job, and there are people who tell me I don't do it very well either. So why do I go on?

I can give you two answers from many. First, I write because writing stories is the best way I've found of sorting myself out. And second, I write in order to read what I've written, because it is only by reflecting on what I've written that I can make myself into what I want to become. In other words it is my experience that writing and reading literature have a self-creating and re-creating power. I think Stephen wrote his story for those reasons as well. Let me try to explain by taking one of my books as an example.

I spent very nearly five years, from the first impulse to delivery of the final proof, in writing my novel *Now I Know*. One reviewer described it as an unorthodox detective story about belief. The plot concerns a seventeen-year-old boy, Nik, who sets out to discover what he can about religious belief, during which he comes across a true-believing girl, Julie, whom he falls for. In the process of finding out what religion means to her, Nik gets involved in a bomb explosion, spends some time afterwards conducting further research while convalescing in a monastery, and finally tries to crucify himself in a kind of experiment that goes wrong. This, at least, is one thread of the plot; another concerns Julie, a third has to do with a young policeman who is trying to solve the riddle of the crucified boy.

The story is told, or so I'm informed by the blurb on the American edition, as three simultaneous plots presented through a combination of prose and poetry, journal entries, letters, jotted notes, flashbacks and puzzles. As you may guess it is also quite a long book, 237 pages in the British edition. I write for re-readers rather than for those who are looking for ephemeral entertainment.

Why? Because for me a story is an object made for contemplation. It is not a pastime. Literature is there to transcend the passing of time. It dwells upon time timelessly. A story can capture a moment of time, and carry that moment across time. The moment when the story was written, and the moment the story tells about are both contained in the work – the book – that can be held in the hand and carried about from place to place and even from one era to another. And this object, this book, can be read and read and read again, each time revealing to anyone who knows how to penetrate it more of the secret text that is held in the language represented by the marks printed on the page.

But why a story about a seventeen-year-old boy who wants to know about belief and who ends up crucifying himself? Here we enter that dangerously blurred territory of an author's motives. Half the time he doesn't know the answer himself. All I can tell you is that I became interested in religion when I was in my mid teens. At twenty-four I became a church-going Anglican Christian; two years later I entered a newly-founded monastery; seven years later I left it. For fifteen years thereafter I paid very little attention to religion, except in the way an ex-professional remains interested in his former occupation. When people asked me why I had become a monk I tended to evade the question.

Early in 1982 I finished a novel, *Dance on My Grave*, and didn't know what to write next. Perhaps this was the moment, I thought, to try to make some sense of belief, one form of which, religious belief, had determined the course of my young manhood. I was reading Milan Kundera's *Book of Laughter and Forgetting* at the time. Towards the end there is a passage where the narrator describes how his father, after years of studying a difficult piece of music, finally pointed at the score in great excitement and said, 'Now I know'. The narrator then goes on to use this incident to explain the nature of the novel he's writing.

As I read this, it became charged with a significance of the kind you can't quite grasp but which you feel intensely. Something is being said to you, and though you can't say *what* it is, you know *that* it is. And even though after a while the excitement dies away, there remains an undeniable impulse to do something about it, to find out what is being said.

The first thing I did on this occasion was to tell Nancy about it and read her the passage. When I'd finished, all she said was, 'Now I know. What a marvellous title.' If a story can be talked of biologically, this was the moment of conception. I felt it at the time. So I did what I always do when this happens, I started a notebook into which is written anything that might help in the writing of the story. That's how I know the date: Saturday 27th February 1982.

The next entry is dated Saturday 6th March. It records an image of a boy who is, as the note puts it, '"crucified" by being tied to some surrogate form of cross'. I didn't know what it meant or why it was important, only that it was somehow essential to the narrative. So begins the search to discover what sort of story this is, who is telling it, who it is about, what happens in it, and where and when. It is not until a year and nine months later, on Tuesday 15th November 1983, that I attempt to write an opening passage. It turns out to be useless, a false start. There are several more before I write the one used in the published text. The first complete, much revised, much groaned-over draft is finished two years and nine months after that, on Thursday 14th August 1986.

So much for the outline. What I can't show you is the stuff that really matters – the 200 pages of notes that come between first entry and last, in which I brood upon belief, and on religion, and on my own experience and on other people's experiences of them. And how this contemplative wool-gathering begins to shape itself into a metaphor, a story which can satisfy me by, on the one hand, helping me discover what I now think I know, and, on the other hand, disguising what I know in the story of a loquacious, slightly arrogant, often confused, somewhat disturbed, now and then witty adolescent, who is desperately trying to understand a force, a power in human life that words seem quite inadequate to capture or communicate.

Only by *object*ifying this complicated, slippery personal material in writing was I able to sort out my own stance, my own understanding, of the life I had lived twenty-five years before. Only in the process of *object*ifying what I thought in the patterns of story images could I turn and face that period of my life with any hope of under-standing it and thereby gaining control over it and of using it to help me go on with a clearer head from where I'd left off all those years before.

Bruner reminds us that language is our most powerful tool for organising experi-ence and that narrative deals with the vicissitudes of human intentions. By writing into a story what I could discover of belief as it affected myself and others, I made an object that allowed me to stand back and view a complicated experience with the detachment of an observer, while yet at the same time experiencing it with the deeply-felt involvement of a participant. That dual condition, of being in and out of the story, of observing it while living it, is one of the inestimable values of narrative literature.

Furthermore, only by making this object – this story written in language printed in a book – can a compelling human plight become accessible to others. And only a story can, to use Bruner's word, subjunctivise the experience, bringing it to life – a life into which the reader can enter because its implicit meanings, its invitations to presuppose and to view the story through the subjective eyes of various other people, and from multiple perspectives, all enable the reader to 'rewrite' the story, making a strange text her/his own.

Which brings me back to the educational value of the writing and reading of literature and Bruner's words that I quoted earlier. 'Much of the process of education consists of being able to distance oneself in some way from what one knows by being able to reflect on one's own knowledge' (p. 127).

This enabling of the reader to be inside and to be outside, active and contemplative, at one and the same moment, seems to me to be a feature of all art. Indeed, I'd go so far as to say it is why we make art in the first place. But an especial quality of literary art is that it deals in ethics – in the nature of human action and in the motivations of people when they engage in action. Literature deals in the 'Why?' of life. How often, reading a novel, living with the characters, does the reader think, 'Well, I wouldn't do it that way', or 'Yes, that's exactly how I felt' or 'There but for the grace of God...'.

And we do this from a very early age. Here is six-year-old Katie telling me about her reading of Charles Keeping's picture book *Railway Passage* and providing a perfect example of a reader engaging in reflective objectification, being in and out of the story and matching the world of the text with the world of her own life:

> There were two people who were kind at the beginning of
> the book and they were still kind at the end. The money
> didn't make much difference to the people. The miserable
> people got even more miserable after they had won the
> money. I think if I won a lot of money I would buy new
> clothes but I don't think I would be happy because I would
> wear them and then they would get worn out and I would
> be miserable again. (1980)

I don't want you to think I'm saying that literature is only a kind of gymnasium where we make ourselves fit to face the world, but I'll risk it. The better we see through stories, the better we see through life. The better we are at interpreting the ins and outs of fictional narrative, the better we'll be at interpreting the narrative of our own lives.

The role of the teacher is to enable this interpreting to happen every school day, which means providing books that subjunctivise life richly. It means ensuring that children have time to hear stories being read and to read them for themselves. It means providing time for interpretive talk, and the teacher knowing what to ask children to talk about. It means that teachers must be readers captivated by the work of literature. Being captivated by the work of literature will enable them and their children to live their lives more freely.

This essay, reprinted by permission of Aidan Chambers, originated in a lecture to a conference of the Victorian Reading Association in Melbourne, Australia, 1988. © 1988 Aidan Chambers and Victorian Reading Association.

Burningham, John (1984), *Granpa*, Jonathan Cape

Bruner, Jerome (1986), *Actual Minds, Possible Worlds*, Harvard University Press

Chambers, Aidan (1987), *Now I Know*, The Bodley Head

Culler, Jonathan (1976), *Structuralist Poetics*, Routledge & Kegan Paul

Katie, in *A Book All About Books*, unpublished children's comments on their reading, written for Aidan Chambers in 1980

Kermode, Frank (1979), *The Genesis of Secrecy: on the interpretation of narrative*, Harvard University Press

Kundera, Milan (1982), *The Book of Laughter and Forgetting*, Faber & Faber

Meek, Margaret (1988), *How Texts Teach What Readers Learn*, Thimble Press

Vygotsky, Lev (1978), *Mind in Society*, Harvard University Press

Waterland, Liz (1985), *Read With Me: an apprenticeship approach to reading*, Thimble Press

The Writer, the Children and Box B

Throughout her distinguished career as a writer for the young, Philippa Pearce has kept in close contact with her potential readers by reading to them. Her stories are subtly crafted in voice and pace. But their most remarkable feature is the rounded quality of feeling, recognised, if unnamed, which pervades them all. There is no representation of a child's disappointment to match *A Dog So Small*. To tamper with the wholeness of the network of conflicting emotions so carefully drawn out in *The Battle of Bubble and Squeak* by introducing contingent classroom activities, however well-meant, seems to the author to miss the point at issue in the world she has worked to create. By gently rebuking those (but she does call them a *force*) who thrust their interpretations between the readers and the text, Philippa Pearce makes a claim for the nature of reading that goes beyond unexamined notions of relevance. In this she is making a plea for the future competences of her readers.

I stand in front of a class in a primary school. The teacher stands beside me, smiling at the class and smiling sideways at me, to encourage me. She introduces me. I am the one who wrote the story they have had read to them this term – the story they enjoyed. They have written class-letters to me about the story (one, I now remember, rather gave the game away: across the very top of the page my correspondent wrote, '*How to sat* (sic) *out a letter*.') The children in their letters – and the teacher in a covering letter – have invited me to visit their school. I have accepted the invitation, and here I am. I am here to talk to the children – to talk *with* them.

The children stare and stare and stare at me.

So far, so ordinary. But, because I have got into a habit over many years of conveying ideas in story-form, I shall make things happen differently this time.

I sit down at the teacher's desk and invite the children to come close to me – as close as they like. They can touch me, if they like. In a rush, they are round me; and I feel their fingers touching me, poking me, even – a little giggling here! – pinching me gently.

Flesh and blood, no less!

I draw towards me over the surface of the desk a sheet of blank paper. I take a pencil from my pocket and hold it over the paper.

At once the children have become still and quiet, watching intently. I lower pencil to paper and begin to write a sequence of words. Perhaps: 'One stormy night a stranger walked down the village street...' Or perhaps: 'The bell had stopped ringing when the girl reached the school gates. She was never late for school, but to-day she was...' Or perhaps just: 'Once upon a time...'

The children stare at the words appearing on the paper as the pencil presses down and moves on. They whisper – I can hear them: 'She's writing a story – she's writing it *now*!'

And then, round my skull above my ears, I feel the touch of inquisitive but careful fingers – this is a school that grows seedlings and keeps pets and does quite tricky little experiments that are halfway to real chemistry. Delicately the fingers search for the suture they are sure must be there – more than a suture: a continuous and deliberate fissure round the cranium. Somewhere along it there is a tiny latch to be found and unfastened. They've got it! Taking great care, they raise on its hinge the whole of the top of my skull – raise it high enough for them all to peer inside as I write.

'So that's it! *That's how she thinks a story*!'

This more or less (as the fancy or the scepticism takes you) is what I experience of young children's critical response to the children's stories I write. Not much criticism, you may say – and children younger than these want *only* the story. Nothing more.

At first I used to be surprised, touched, even flattered that children marvelled at my being able to write stories. But then I considered: myself, I am always ready to marvel at something skilfully done, from a serviceable wooden box to the pyramids of Egypt. I have my own skills, and I am not ashamed of them, nor (I think) vain.

How is the thing – the story – done? Pencil? Pen? Typewriter? And how long does the whole thing take? Children fumble forward in their inquiries; adults tend to ask the same questions, but more sophisticatedly. Any age at all may ask the final baffler: 'Where do you get your ideas from?'

(To which Agatha Christie used briskly to answer: 'From Harrods.')

There is seldom much deeper critical analysis from the children I meet. But their *response* to the story I have to tell can be intense. If I am telling a short story of mine (I prefer story-telling to reading aloud, when possible), its success (or failure) appears instantly and physically in the children listening. They are immobile, except for some unconscious movement; their faces rapt. But then, perhaps they may begin to fidget, their eyes flicker from my face, they yawn openly. (That's what I like so much in this age of children: they're not polite, they don't conceal boredom with irony). These are warning signals, and I am glad of them. Somehow I must regain and re-grip the attention of my audience. It's up to me to use all my varied skills to achieve that. If I succeed, all is harmony again.

This kind of experience is one of the happiest aspects of a children's writer's relationship with his or her reading public. It is also one of the most direct. Why, then, do many children's writers deny – quite angrily, sometimes – that they write *for children* at all?

How odd of them! But consider.

In the classroom I have just been imagining, there were a number of children and myself – and a teacher. She (or, it might have been, he) was a teacher I liked. This teacher had the ability to make the children listen to stories, read stories, *love* stories. She (or he) stood smiling beside me as I faced the class; she (or he) was *on my side* – as well, of course, as on the children's side. In fact, there were no sides: we found ourselves in a harmonious circle of mutual interest.

There is always a teacher in the classroom, of course; and, in the wider world, the space between the children's writers and the child-readers is taken up by a whole occupying force of parents, teachers, librarians, critics, publisher's editors, child-psychologists, educationists and child-experts of all kinds. Some of these I respect and like, both professionally and personally; others I don't. Most children's writers that I have known view them with suspicion.

Nowadays the status of a children's writer is higher than it used to be. People whose opinions matter tend to accept that children's writers really are *writers*. What they write can be considered – possibly rejected, too, of course – as literature. Even so, a children's writer is expected not only to write well but also with responsibility. There is a responsibility (besides an artistic one to the story itself) to the children as readers. The responsibility is not defined by the children but by concerned adults. They may go so far, for instance, as to wish the writer to promote certain good causes – multiculturalism, anti-racism, anti-sexism, environmentalism, the brushing of one's teeth after breakfast, and so on, and so on.

This is the point at which some children's writers decide to say that they don't write for children, anyway. They don't write to please children; they write to please themselves. This sounds a little mad; so they elaborate. They write to please the children they once were themselves – the children time-buried deep within them. Thus a defensive circle is completed, which successfully excludes the possibility of outside interference.

Writing to please the children we once were (I'm almost sure I've used the tactic myself in the past) is an explanation that begins as a desperate evasion and ends by being a useful cliché. Like all hard-working clichés, it has a good deal of truth in it.

The truth is that, in confronting (in imagination or in physical fact) children who expect a story, a writer usually has an instinct for *what will work*. This instinct is only indirectly rooted in the skills of literature. More importantly, there is an instinctive understanding of children's tastes – their longings, fantasies, fears, delights; what stirs their minds and hearts and strongest imaginings. This understanding must come from a continuous and more or less unconscious recall: the writer, too, was a child and remembers that. He or she knows something of the expectations and hopes of the children waiting for a story. Expectations are more likely to be satisfied, hopes fulfilled.

If we writers write to please the children we were, then what kind of children were we? Hopelessly varied; but, almost inevitably, story-readers. So we have in our minds the image of a child huddled in a chair with a book, reading; or prone on the grass, oblivious of any enchantments of Nature, reading; or very late at night, in bed with a torch under the duvet, still reading.

There must still be children who read in solitary absorption. But it seems to me likely that more children experience more books in classrooms than anywhere else. So I return to my happy experience in the classroom described earlier.

It's important to note that my experience in the classroom was isolated in time, with very little Before and After. Before, it's true, the teacher had suggested the letter-writing; and she (or he) had also got the class to make pictures. I know that, because the walls of the classroom were bright with children's paintings, and some of them I could identify as re-creations of scenes in my story. (After, might there be other pictures – perhaps of *me*?) That was really all I knew for certain of this hinterland of education.

Then, at quite another time, I heard about the use in schools – the possible use, with preparation beforehand and follow-up after – of a particular story of mine, *The Battle of Bubble and Squeak*. (Very briefly, the story is of a family divided: the children and their affable step-father want to keep two gerbils, called Bubble and Squeak; their mother passionately doesn't. Hence the Battle.)

The paperback publisher of my story wrote congratulating me on the book's having been chosen by a reputable educational publisher as the subject of one of their *Book Study Guides*. If teachers used the *Guide*, then classes would need multiple copies of the story in paperback. Publisher and author would both benefit financially.

Note, by the way, that no permission was needed for the publication of the *Guide*. It used the minimium of actual quotation from the book studied – no question of copyright infringement, therefore. A *Book Study Guide* was simply a book about a book, which anyone is free to write.

A complimentary copy of this particular *Book Study Guide* was sent to me, and I read it from cover to cover.

The Study was divided into six Units, each focusing on a section of my story; and there was a seventh Unit of Review and Evaluation. The first page of each Unit started with two boxed passages of *Guide-text*, set side by side. For convenience I call them Box A and Box B. Box A contained a synopsis of that section of my story. Box B contained – well, what exactly was it? An interpretation of that section of the story? A commentary upon it? I suddenly felt that I must leave Box B to be thought about later, coolly and calmly if possible.

The two Boxes were followed by a '*Read* to the end of the chapter (page so-and-so)' and by a '*Discuss*'. Some of these discussion topics were really just tricky questions, such as: 'Would you have been able to give anti-biotics to the sick gerbil?'

After these came *Development Work*, printed against a grey background. There were sometimes as many as two pages of print-on-grey for any one Unit. The Development activities suggested were varied. I thought the jolliest was the cooking of bubble-and-squeak: 'This can be prepared in the classroom on a camping-stove or small cooker.' (There was also a recipe for sugar mice, which are mentioned at the end of my story.)

So many possible activities! Wall-friezes, of course, with speech-bubbles wafting from characters' mouths; research on pet-keeping, leading possibly to an informative visit from a guide-dog owner or an RSPCA officer; compilation of a 'Gerbil word-bank', a gathering together, Unit by Unit, of all the words I had ever used to describe gerbils and their movements; and this led on to something more ambitious: 'Gerbil movements can then be tried under, over and between a variety of gym equipment (to simulate the newspaper rolls). Finally, pupils can put together a sequence of "gerbil movements", perhaps to a percussion accompaniment or suitable passage of music.'

While reading the *Guide*, I never felt that it bore a grudge against my story. Quite the contrary. Only once, when suggesting the pupils' construction of a 'time-line' was there a hint of criticism, and that in an Appendix: 'The author is not always specific about the lengths of various episodes, and occasionally the amounts of time said to elapse between particular episodes do not seem consistent within the story.'

As I have said, the *Guide* seemed really to like my story. Why, then, can I not courteously and gratefully reciprocate?

The answer is a child. Not the supposed child-within-me; not the solitary child-reader; not even the child, one among many, in the classroom. The answer is by metaphor: the story is a child – my brain-child, my heart-child, the child of my imagination and of all the literary skills at my command. I cared deeply about my story as I wrote it; and I believe I have a kind of parental right to care what happens to it. Its needs are so simple: it needs to be read. That is the most important thing that can happen to it. Classroom cookery and visits from guide-dogs are only extras, just as my own classroom visits to have my head examined was an extra, a curiosity.

The story is only what readers perceive it to be. According to contemporary literary-critical theory, the original intentions of myself, as author, are irrelevant. I am not allowed to tell readers – but I don't *want* to tell readers, anyway – what the story is about. The story – only the story – can tell them that.

But remember Box B, about which I decided to think later. This is the moment to do so. Box B is doing what I would not be allowed to do, even if I wanted. Unit by Unit, the Boxes B in the *Guide* tell the teacher what to think about the story, with the evident intention that, directly or indirectly, the teacher should pass on to the children the Box B interpretations. Some of these interpretations seem to me wrong-headed or misleading; but, even if they had all delighted me with their perceptiveness, I should not want my story to be so hung about with commentary. It should speak for itself.

With increasing unease I had read the *Book Study Guide* from cover to cover, and so came at last to the back of the back cover. There I found a list of titles that were – or were to become – the subject of other *Book Study Guides*. In the ordinary way of things I should be proud that my *Battle of Bubble and Squeak* was in the same company as *Charlotte's Web*, *The Little House on the Prairie*, *The Borrowers* and *Carrie's War*. But what will the *Guides* – in particular the Boxes B – be doing to these stories? Some of the authors are by now forever beyond the reach of exasperation; others are not. Have they, perhaps, ever looked into a Box B?

I am forced to admit that the *Book Study Guide* I read was put together with a high degree of a certain kind of skill. I marvel at it, therefore, but without any sense of exhilaration. And that's a sad thing to say, even about a book about a book.

But I cheer myself by thinking yet again about the classroom I visited. I cannot positively swear that the teacher had never read a Book Study Guide, but intuition tells me that she had not. There was such an easiness of manner, a brightness to the eye; the smile was so unforced. And the children? Ah, there I am positive. No shadow of a Box B had fallen across those intent and eager faces.

MARGARET MALLETT

How Long does a Pig Live? Learning together from story and non-story genres

Following Philippa Pearce's claim that 'study guide' activities are inappropriate as ways of reading *The Battle of Bubble and Squeak*, here is Margaret Mallett showing how a novel can provoke acute, necessary questions about the ways of the world, that are relevant kinds of classroom enquiry. In *The Sheep Pig*, by Dick King-Smith, they have the author's 'what if' as a starting-point from which their teacher draws both imaginative and nature-related speculations, followed by scholarly checking and research. (Edmund Leach does the same thing when he asks why the English don't eat dogs.) The children learn to reflect on their experiences of what the text reveals. The teacher-writer shows what difference the information that emerged made to her understandings and displays two different ways of 'taking from the culture'. There is a growing interest in the function and nature of non-narrative texts in the context of school learning to which this sustained enquiry is highly relevant. Also, it might meet with Philippa Pearce's approval.

'How long does a pig live?' asked Tara. We had reached the end of Chapter 2 in our shared reading of Dick King-Smith's *The Sheep Pig*. Ben supplied the obvious answer, 'Not very long because we kill and eat them', but of course Tara was really wondering about the likely length of a pig's natural life. Earlier these nine-year-olds had shown great interest in Fly, the sheepdog's comment to her puppies: 'People only eat stupid animals like sheep and cows and ducks and chickens. They don't eat clever ones like dogs.'

The children quickly noted the tension between what Fly says and one of the main messages of the book: that even though we eat them, pigs are intelligent creatures. It is through such tensions and subtleties that fiction yields its meanings. Narrative has a special power to engage the reader and involve them in the world of the possible: what might happen if a pig wanted to herd sheep as a sheepdog does? The story provided a context in which the children began speculating on issues that might not normally have been accessible to them. They were reminded of other stories – E.B. White's *Charlotte's Web* and Nina Bawden's *The Peppermint Pig* which, like *The Sheep Pig*, cut across the usual boundaries, making us perceive pigs in a way we normally reserve for pet cats and dogs. Pigs – these creatures of fable and fantasy, symbols of greed and dirtiness (and we must be sensitive to religious sensibilities here) – are intriguing! No wonder the children wanted to know more. Many other questions like Tara's were asked. Are pigs social animals? Should they be reared in family groups rather than in pens? If they are really as intelligent as Babe in the story is it cruel to eat them? The keen interest awakened was a tribute to the vitality of Dick King-Smith's narrative. As an ex-farmer he writes about what he knows well and we learn much about farms and animals whilst enjoying the story.

However, the children sensed that we needed to consult a quite different kind of text to find the answers to some of our 'wonderings'.

National Curriculum Attainment Target 2 tells us that reading requires us to help children 'to respond to all types of writing'. Becoming a mature reader is partly to do with recognising how far particular texts can help with particular purposes. The children's questions provided an ideal context for discovering some of the differences between story and non-story genres.

There are a number of studies exploring how children become increasingly sensitive readers of narrative. It is accepted that its time sequence structure, echoing the unfolding of real life experience, is a particularly accessible form for young readers. Less is known about how children can be helped to learn from non-narrative texts. These make quite different demands on the reader. The personal voice of the narrator tends to be lacking. Vocabulary is sometimes technical and syntax tends to be unlike the patterns of spoken language. Instead of a chronological ordering, the topic dictates the organisation of the text. Information tends to be arranged hierarchically, and in the more difficult types of this genre we need to follow through and assess an argument.

There are strategies which writers can adopt to help make children's early experience of this genre less intimidating: life cycles of creatures can retain a very broad chronological framework, although of course such texts do not read like a conventional story. One of the information books in the case study to be described later, *Understanding Farm Animals*, is arranged in sections, some of which very broadly parallel the progress of a pig's life: 'making a nest', 'giving birth', 'young piglets', 'feeding and playing' and 'weaning'. I believe this makes the information more accessible to the young readers.

A more personal tone can be achieved by the use of pronouns – 'if you can visit a farm where there are pigs you could make a chart like this to show how fast a pig grows'. This extract also shows that the writer has retained some of the rhythms of spoken language, and this too is helpful. Too many technical terms are avoided, and where they do appear their meaning is either clear from the context, or they are explained: 'Young female pigs (called 'gilts') are first mated at the age of eight months'. Thus there are ways of easing children gently into the demands of what may be a new genre for them. But, as the next section shows, the reading materials available are not always appropriate.

Those who have recently considered the quality of information books for the primary age range, including Paice (1984) and Von Schweinitz (1989), find much room for improvement. They deplore the banality of the text in books which may be superficially bright and attractive. The writing is often incoherent, lacking overall cohesion, so that the text fails to hang together. Pictures and text do not always interact, and retrieval devices are deficient. Institutional buyers such as schools and libraries are often pressed to order series of books, having only had the opportunity to scrutinise one example. Clearly we need to be much more selective when choosing reading materials. Since schools and public libraries make up 80% of the information book market, teachers are in a strong position to insist on the very best for their pupils. Part of the problem is the way in which information books are commissioned: authors are contracted to write about a topic even though they may have no previous knowledge or special interest in it. No good writer of fiction would dream of writing where commitment and experience were lacking.

Children appear to benefit most from books which do something specific really well: *How to Observe Owls* rather than books with general titles like *Birds*. Reading and thinking about observing owls gives children a way of observing birds in general. The superficial glimpses in more general books do not show children how to observe anything at all. What we know about learning suggests that children move from the specific to the general. It is time we applied this insight to choosing and using information materials. There are, of course, some good information texts for children; and the publishers of these deserve encouragement. Why is it that while there are many awards for excellent fiction there are only to my knowledge two major prizes for achievement in the informational area – *The Times Educational Supplement* junior information book award and Friends of the Earth's Bookworm award.

We cannot produce a blueprint for a good information book any more than we can for a successful story. It all depends on how the book is to be used. Good clear contents pages, indexes and glossaries are helpful to children researching topics, but these features are not always appropriate.

In *Dinosaur Bones*, an original book, bringing a sense of excitement and discovery as we follow a child's research into the history of fossils, Aliki Brandenburg manages well with just a detailed glossary of dinosaurs, together with the dates when the fossils were found. What seems to characterise the successful information book, whether it is to support children's research or for browsing, is the authors' ability to communicate their own excitement and commitment. *Squirrels* by Jessica Holm shows what can emerge when an expert is invited to write about her special subject for young readers. In a humorous yet scholarly way a great deal of information is imparted, anticipating the most obscure questions the reader may be asking. She does not avoid the less savoury aspects of squirrel diseases and problems about their relationships with human beings. There are hundreds of squirrel books, often featuring delightful photography but usually giving the same well-known facts, sometimes with a good deal of misinformation. Holm's book takes the young reader much further, offering, for example, the latest insight on the subtle role of the grey squirrel in the dwindling population of red squirrels.

How did the children wanting to find out about the nature of pigs and how we treat them fare in their search for helpful texts? We found it very difficult to gather together suitable books and materials. Either they were of the 'Pigs live on a farm' variety or they were complicated manuals for pig breeders. (Statement of Attainment 3C, Attainment Target 2 English in the National Curriculum assumes appropriate materials will be available to answer children's questions!) We could certainly find nothing as lively and interesting as Jessica Holm's book on squirrels. The claims on the back of *Understanding Farm Animals* attracted us. The book promised to explore 'how far domestication has affected animals' instinctive behaviour'. The information is clearly expressed, and text and illustrations integrate nicely. The idea that some ways of treating pigs may be controversial is not made explicit, however. Jane Miller's *Birth of Piglets* also reads clearly, and the fifty-five photographs take us from the birth of piglets reared out of doors until they are three-week-old weaners. Reasons are given for all that happens – 'then he (the stockman) snips off part of each piglet's tail. This is necessary because they sometimes chew each others' tails!' – but again none of the practices is described as controversial.

We turned also to an adult book written in clear prose but entirely from the point of view of the pig breeder, *Pigs*. Interestingly, the NFU (National Farmers Union) pamphlet representing the views of British farmers, which someone added to our collection, did mention that there were different views about humane ways of breeding pigs. But for the wholeheartedly pro-animal view we turned to booklets from 'The Farm and Food Society' and from 'Compassion in World Farming'. Our collection of texts was not ideal. We lacked a truly inviting book at just the right level. But it did provide a selection of viewpoints for our consideration.

The children brought their own questions to their research. It cannot be emphasised enough that our starting-point was a novel. An interest in the destiny of one pig in particular had led to a concern about the fate of pigs in general. Just as our reading of the novel had been a shared activity, our work with the informational materials was also collaborative. A small group – Ben, Tara, Wendy and Stuart – agreed to research the questions, with some help from me, and to report back to the class.

Using information books has too often been a solitary task. Children have been left to struggle with difficult texts in the belief that they were 'engaging in independent research'. The paradox is that we are more likely to become critical and independent readers if we have benefited from the special kind of adult support Bruner calls 'scaffolding' and the 'thinking aloud' of our peers. Much has been written about Vygotsky's 'zone of proximal development', and certainly the gap between what a child can currently do and what she can manage with help is something we need to consider when children are grappling with difficult reading materials. For a child who is becoming a reader of non-narrative texts, it is helpful to watch a mature reader using such texts in order to observe the scanning of contents pages and indexes for particular pieces of information. But the abilities we are trying to help young readers acquire go well beyond what we usually mean by 'study skills' and bring us into the area of how we learn in general. It has to do with children becoming able to hold the information they already have in their heads, while taking something new from the book and assimilating it. We want them to be active readers, reflecting on the information they encounter, understanding its implications and, in the light of this, evaluating it. I am becoming increasingly convinced that these abilities are learnt collaboratively, sometimes in small teacherless groups, sometimes in groups of which the teacher is a member.

The nine-year-olds whose researches we have been following helped each other reflect on the texts. They had to think beyond what was actually made explicit to answer their questions, bringing their knowledge of the world to their reading. Two members of our group had special experience and knowledge on which to draw. Ben watches nature and wildlife programmes on television, and had fairly recently seen a documentary about farming. Wendy's father's friend has a pig farm which she visits, and she has been allowed to 'adopt' a small pig she has named Jessie.

One of our main purposes was to discover if there were humane and less humane ways of keeping pigs, and if particular practices could be described as 'cruel'. Thus the children were asking questions in an area where readers looking at similar evidence might draw different conclusions. They were not simply looking up the answers to specific questions such as, for example, how long is a sow's pregnancy? We did, however, need to bring our general area of concern to a more specific level to make it manageable. After much talk, and quite a lot of help from me, we agreed to bear in mind the following questions, as we grappled with the materials. First, does anything here suggest that pigs are intelligent? Second, does anything here indicate that a particular practice causes them stress and might be 'cruel'? Tara thought a specific example of the latter might be the practice of inserting rings through pigs' nostrils.

Let us trace the journey a reader might make from a simple statement of a fact to a consideration of the full implications of a practice.

1 Pigs sometimes have metal rings inserted in their noses.
2 Farmers do this to stop the creatures from churning up the soil and spoiling the ground.
3 Pigs have a natural instinct to 'root' in the ground for food. The ring hurts the nostril if the pig tries to root.
4 The interests of farmers and pigs may be at odds here:
    (a) because of the possible pain or discomfort during the actual insertion of the ring;
    (b) because it makes instinctive, and therefore presumably deeply satisfying, behaviour (i.e. rooting) impossible.

Of course, the reality was much less tidy than the pattern above suggests. I realise that I should have brought in the 'Compassion in World Farming' material about rooting much sooner, so that the children could understand just what it might mean to deny a creature indulgence in such natural behaviour. At stage 1 we saw pictures of ringed pigs in some of the reading materials and pictures we had gathered together for our research. Wendy mentioned that she had 'The Owl and the Pussycat' at home which showed Piggywig 'with a ring through the end of his nose'. The interplay between learning from stories and learning from informational materials penetrated our work. Stage 2 was reached when Tara read the following sentence to us from *Understanding Farm Animals*, 'If the farmer does not want the soil churned up... he will put a metal ring through the pig's nose to stop it rooting.' As soon as Tara had uttered the sentence Wendy broke in with 'My little pig had it done and it cried. The man said I could pick it up if I wanted and then it was quiet.'

Our conversation continued as follows:

MM:	Did he say why he put the ring through?
Ben:	It's to stop them disturbing the soil.
MM:	Yes, it is to stop them messing up the soil. But that little piece that Tara read to us tells us just the facts, doesn't it...what happens. But it doesn't tell us if it is right or wrong to do that to a pig. What do you think? Is it all right for a farmer to do that to a pig...when rooting is its natural behaviour?
Wendy:	I don't think they cry because of the pain...more because they don't know what's happening and they're frightened. It don't hurt much but they think it might.
MM:	Does it bleed?
Wendy:	Sometimes it does a little bit...
Ben:	They do kick out when it is first done.
MM:	You've seen this happen, Ben?
Ben:	I saw it on tv – a farming programme.

The impact of Wendy's actual experience is greater for her than pictures and writing in a book. My questions are genuine requests for information. For Ben the images in the television programme dominate.

It is clear that at this point Wendy's first-hand experience on a pig farm has not really caused her to consider the ethical problems involved in different kinds of pig rearing, and particular practices such as ringing pigs' snouts. Nor has Ben's viewing of television programmes directed his thinking this way, although he has observed pigs 'kick out' when ringed. We might guess that the programme was heavily weighted towards the pig breeder's interests, because Ben sees things from the farmer's point of view. He comments that farmers need to ring pigs early if they want to preserve their ground.

Of course, the children are still only in the second year of the junior school, and we would not expect them to have thought through all the subtleties of humane treatment of animals. But it does seem, as Vygotsky, Donaldson and others claim, that it is grappling with written texts that brings about a certain quality of reflection, which is itself linked to a growing awareness of one's own thinking processes. Most children need considerable support if their encounter with the written word is to move them forward. I have to say that my points about rooting made little impact. A change of perception came when material from 'Compassion in World Farming' arrived. This provided a striking comparison, which helped the children and me towards point 4b. This was that a pig's rooting disc, at the end of the snout, contains as many nerve endings as a human hand! This kind of information helps us to make the imaginative leap towards understanding what mutilation of such a sensitive area might mean for the creature. Imagine the sensory deprivation if our hands were partially bound so that we could not use them properly!

At this stage two things were becoming clear to the children. First, we are unlikely to find the answers to all our questions in one text. Second, you have to be conscious of the likely perspective of the particular writer: members of 'Compassion in World Farming' will tend to say something different about methods and practices in rearing pigs from members of the Association of Agriculture. Interestingly, we found a group with a midway position, 'The Farm and Food Society', whose slogan, 'Farming Humane to Animals, Wholesome for Consumers, Fair to Farmers', neatly encapsulated the three viewpoints. Here the children are moving towards National Curriculum Level 5(iii), Attainment Target 2, which requires them to 'recognise, in discussion, whether subject matter in non-literary and media texts is presented as fact or as opinion'. Of course, however the material is presented, as fact or as opinion, all texts are unavoidably biased to some extent. It is partly a matter of which 'facts' you choose to include and which to leave out which weights a text towards one viewpoint or another. (I did not come across Miles Barton's *Why Do People Harm Animals?* (Aladdin Books 1988) in time to use it in this work. It introduces controversial issues in a way children can understand and discuss.)

In the course of trying to answer the question – are there humane and less humane ways of keeping pigs? – we had to extend our reading beyond texts like *Understanding Farm Animals*. I read out, and paraphrased, this extract:

> Existing scientific knowledge is unclear on the extent to which pigs actually *need* space, or whether close confinement causes distress. Given this state of affairs, pig farmers see animal welfare in practical terms. (From *Looking after Pigs*, NFU representing British Farmers)

It all depends of course on how you define 'stress'. The children felt more convinced by the evidence offered in the extract from a letter which follows:

> Piglets reared on range are extremely lively and behave like puppies, playing, running and exploring, eating herbage which contains iron...At Edinburgh School of Agriculture, a research project has been under way in which pigs have been kept in family groups, sow, boar and piglets, in natural surroundings, and this has proved very successful...the great majority of pigs are still kept in conditions which are unacceptable to humanitarians. (Letter to the children and myself from 'The Farm and Food Society', 29 June 1988).

All readers bring their knowledge of the world to the texts they read as well as their knowledge about the conventions of the particular genre. Sometimes the act of reflection reveals a mismatch between our common-sense knowledge and what we read. I asked the children if reading the books and pamphlets had changed any of their views.

Stuart:	...that pigs are very clean animals!
MM:	You had had the impression before that they were dirty? Why do people think that?
Ben:	Because they roll in mud and things like that.
Stuart:	...and they smell a little bit.
MM:	...if they are kept indoors. Do they smell if they are kept out of doors, Wendy?

[Wendy's special experience makes her the 'expert' in the group.]

Wendy:	They still smell a little bit outdoors but the little ones don't.
MM:	It's in our language isn't it – this idea of 'dirty pigs'?

One of the things being learnt here is that our common-sense knowledge is sometimes modified by what we read. It is this dissonance which can stimulate reflection.

MM: What does it say here that makes Stuart now say the pig is a clean animal? What does it do that makes us think it is clean?

Stuart: It says they roll in the mud and then they clean themselves off and they go to the toilet in a separate place. [Looking at the text and paraphrasing]

Wendy: Yes, they don't sit in the part of the field where they go to the toilet. [Wendy brings in her first-hand knowledge appropriately.]

MM: What I did not know was that pigs cannot sweat. Did you know that? [This is mentioned in the text]

Wendy: Their skin is more dry and they haven't got as much salt in their body as us.

MM: How do you know that, Wendy?

Wendy: Because I asked the farmer about their skin and he said they do not sweat as they have less salt than us.

MM: That's interesting.

Wendy: Yes – because when you sweat salt comes out, doesn't it?

[Here the text has helped Wendy to reflect and make sense of her first-hand observations. The metabolism of a pig is different from that of a human being.]

Finally, let us draw together what I think has emerged about the benefits of collaborative scrutiny of reading materials. Three main activities seemed of particular value: asking questions, sharing anecdotes and offering and challenging hypotheses. Let us consider each briefly in turn. They came to the texts with the questions that had arisen during the reading of *The Sheep Pig*. The reading material generated more questions. In looking at a picture showing pigs in a field bounded by an electric fence Stuart asks, 'What exactly happens if they get electrocuted by the electric fence?' Wendy is able to explain, because she knows about farms, that the current would only be strong enough to make them feel dizzy. Asking questions out loud in a group like this reveals the sorts of things that occur to other readers and reinforces the idea that we are active in grappling with the text.

When it comes to sharing experience both Ben and Wendy have much to contribute. Ben constantly refers to wildlife programmes and Wendy has actually been present when pigs were ringed. She has observed how sows outside make nests and she knows about the realities of taking pigs to market. But the others are able to tell helpful anecdotes as well. Stuart read about the young pigs playing and having 'mock fights'. He has noticed his young budgerigars play together. At that point the anecdotes about other creatures that play together (or, like guinea pigs, do not) seemed to be taking us away from the pig topic in a relentless chain. Then Ben said his next door neighbour's two dogs played together and that they were 'intelligent'. This brought them to a 'zone of proximal development' which enabled me to nudge them towards the general point that the young of more intelligent creatures tend to play. Thus far from becoming increasingly remote from the topic the children were coming close to answering one of the original questions that inspired our research. Is the pig intelligent? The fact that the young play together suggests that indeed they are. We have to be wary of anthropomorphism here, but it seems likely that such a creature would be 'happier' free on the range than in a battery.

With just a little nudging the children sometimes shared their insights and knowledge about language, noticing conventions in the non-story genre and discussing the meanings of particular words and phrases – for example 'nimble,' 'gilts,' 'farrowing pens' and 'excreting in dunging alleys'.

In a group context suggestions and ideas can be offered and tested. Tara suggests at one point that it might be kinder to keep pigs and sell them for meat only when they die naturally.

Ben rejects this with:

> 'But if they die they might have a disease and we can't eat
> them then... You couldn't butcher them if they had a
> disease!'

The group came round to feeling that, given people want to eat port and bacon, the humane thing to do was to provide as natural and happy a life as possible for the pigs *before* they were slaughtered. Perhaps how long a pig lives is less important than the quality of its life before slaughter. Just as a matter of interest, in researching one of the questions we initially brought to the research – and it appears as this chapter's title – we discovered that a pig kept for breeding and not slaughtered would live about as long as a dog.

This proffering of theories, which are then challenged or modified by others, helps us to take into account more factors in reflecting on the issues than if our reading were solitary. In this case-study one of the collaborators is the teacher, who mediates between pupils and text by reformulating children's offered experiences, helping them to evaluate what they read and helping to make explicit their intuitive knowledge about language. I believe most importantly that, as mature readers, we can offer this kind of intellectual companionship to young readers.

When offering anecdotes inspired by shared reading, children do not always make explicit the link between the ideas in the text and the related experience. Wendy, for instance, often breaks in with lively anecdotes about what she has seen and done on the farm. As Shirley Brice Heath (1983) argues so powerfully the teacher's role is to help children to see how their experience of the world and as language users can be made to serve their school learning. Wendy expresses what happens on a pig farm with great accuracy and vitality, but she was less inclined to say whether her observations supported or challenged what the text said. She needed to be helped by my questions to make the link explicit and to move her own thinking forward. Perhaps the most powerful example of my role as 'reformulator' of experience occurred when I was able to suggest to the children that their anecdotes were heading towards the insight that it is the 'intelligent' creatures whose young play together.

Another version of this essay was published in *English in Education*, vol. 26, no. 1, Spring 1992.

I appreciate the help of Dennis Pratt, Jill Hawkins and the pupils of Rowdown Junior School in carrying out this project. I am also grateful to Usborne Publishing for permission to quote from *Understanding Farm Animals*.

Bawden, Nina, *The Peppermint Pig*, Puffin
Brandenburg, Aliki (1989), *Dinosaur Bones*, in the First Sight Series, A. & C. Black
Brice-Heath, S. (1983), *Ways with Words*, Cambridge University Press
Bruner, J. and Haste, H. (eds.) (1987), *Making Sense*, Methuen
English in the National Curriculum, Cox Report, June 1989
Holm, Jessica (1983), *Squirrels*, Whittock Books
King-Smith, Dick (1983), *The Sheep-Pig*, Puffin
Looking after pigs: some facts and figures, NFU representing British farmers
Miller, Jane (1984), *The Birth of Piglets*, Dent
Paice, Shirley (1984), 'Reading to learning' in *English in Education*, vol. 18, no. 1
Thompson, Ruth (1978), *Understanding Farm Animals*, Usborne
Von Schweinitz, Eleanor (1989), 'Facing the facts' in *Books for Keeps*, March
Wheeler, H.L.H. (1978), *Pigs*, published by the Association of Agriculture
White, E.B., *Charlotte's Web*, Puffin

Rewriting Reading

The majority of English teachers in secondary schools are women. Until recently, their role in teaching literature, and the position of the girls who learn to read it, has been a particular case of 'learned androgyny', as Jane Miller discusses it in *Women Writing About Men*. By describing a particular lesson Gemma Moss analyses the means and results of persuading boys to adopt the perspectives of the girls in their class, thus 'diverting attention back to what the boys were trying to exclude'. By taking away the boys' position of privilege she shows that feminist teaching practices cannot be separated from the content of the curriculum. We also see how, as a teacher, Gemma Moss becomes a model for the girls, who are then encouraged to take up challenges to their meaning making: a viable feminist pedagogy of transformation.

The relationship between English teaching and feminism is not always an easy one to tease out. Feminism has traditionally operated in non-hierarchical ways. English teaching takes place within stratified institutions where structural distinctions are always drawn between teachers and the taught. Feminism depends upon identifying oppression through the sharing of women's experience and so turns the personal into the political. English teachers may encourage personal expression, but how and where that translates into political action is a moot point. Different things happen to the category 'personal' in these two different contexts. Given these kinds of contradictions it is perhaps not surprising that English classes have seldom looked like consciousness-raising groups, even when gender issues are being most strenuously addressed. Most of the attention on sexism in English has focused on what teachers can do with books, a comparatively clear-cut issue, which seems relatively straightforward to address. Yet there has to be more to the relationship between the two areas than the kind of uneasy compromise I have sketched out above. Indeed, as I hope to explore below, it is high time for a radical reappraisal of the contribution feminism can make to English teaching.

Of course, English teaching itself is not homogenous. There are at least four major strands. One prioritises the teaching of literature, another the teaching of basic skills. One sees the prime aim of English teaching as being the encouragement of personal growth, another as helping pupils develop the ability to question the social world. At the level of rhetoric these remain distinct positions; in practice, most English teachers use all of these approaches some of the time. Despite the fierceness of the debate, there are hidden continuities and overlaps. Those seeking to improve language skills are unlikely to rely solely on the use of decontextualised drills, no matter how hard the Secretary of State for Education may seem to be pushing teachers in that direction. (The compromise effected by Cox has been to itemise some skills but to insist on placing them in a context where meaning is stressed.) Those who emphasise the place of literature in the classroom often see reading as a morally-uplifting activity, not just the means to knowledge of a cultural heritage. Those committed to either child-centred or radical pedagogies seek to build from what children already know and so privilege autobiography, though for very different reasons; yet neither tradition excludes reference to other forms of literature, nor seeks to dispense with basic skills. If disputes between such diverse traditions can be so easily reconciled in practice, does feminism have anything to offer in the way of a radical critique of English teaching? Or can it, too, be appropriated readily, becoming just another strategy alongside the rest?.

Of course, in one sense feminism may already be said to be represented in the English classroom, in the form of anti-sexist strategies. But anti-sexism is not synonymous with feminism. At best it remains one particular strand in feminist thinking, one which in the context of English teaching, I would want to argue, has been appropriated to fit existing approaches rather than constituting a challenge to them. This is not to say that the appropriation is altogether a bad thing. It has led to some very real achievements. Many English Departments have reviewed the kinds of literature they offer in the main school. There has been a sustained effort to include more books with female central characters and to exclude some of the existing stock. Anti-sexism can be a powerful weapon in the hands of female teachers wanting a better deal for their pupils in this respect, one which has been very effectively used against colleagues.

Other gains are less clear-cut. I have said that anti-sexism has been appropriated within existing approaches in English teaching. What I am getting at here is that it leaves intact many of the existing assumptions that English teachers already make, most notably about the relationships between texts and pupils. Anti-sexism joins in a rather odd alliance with Leavisism and the kind of vanguardist Left perspective associated with media studies in treating particular kinds of texts as potentially powerful in their effect. Linked to the notion of powerful texts is a notion of vulnerable readers. As a consequence of these views the teachers' role becomes one of regulatory control: without teacherly intervention, the assumption is, pupils may go astray. This kind of argument is most strongly played out around the sorts of text which are represented as being of dubious quality. Whilst opinions differ on which are the preferred texts, there is a fairly broad consensus in terms of what constitutes trash, and formulaic writing of the kind epitomised by the romance genre is pretty high on the list of dislikes. The effect of such a broad consensus is to close down debate about the model of reading which is involved here. Yet it is precisely this model of reading which I want to go on to examine, not least because it poses some problems for feminists when it comes to considering the girls in our classrooms. After all, many of the latter are avid consumers of precisely those kinds of texts which this argument views with suspicion: romances and photo-love stories. Accept this model of reading, and what do we make of the girl readers of such texts? That they are passive victims of a set of values which work against their own best interests? That they are learning a set of behaviours they would be better off without?

The view that texts are powerful and can fundamentally influence their readers, whether for good or bad, works from the assumption that particular textual features have particular fixed meanings, and that consequently the mes-

sage any one text holds is quite easy to determine: by exercising skill and judgement teachers can identify what kind of text they have in front of them, and
whether its effects will be good or bad, an image positive or negative. But there
are difficulties here. For instance, a recent issue of *My Guy* included a photo-love
story whose central character was an unmarried mother/teenage single parent. She
meets the potential new man in her life when she's out with her child. Is this a
positive image or not? How do we judge? Do we assume that any story in which girl
meets boy is negative, reinforcing heterosexual desire (in which case do we pass the
same judgement on a text such as *Pride and Prejudice*)? Or does the inclusion of the
child in the story disrupt the romanticised representation of girls' sexuality more
ordinarily associated with girls' teen magazines? Should the fact that the young
mother appears neither upset, ashamed or embarrassed about her lot be welcomed as
a change from the stereotype, or is the association of women with children reinforcing women's reproductive role? In which case should we reject all stories which
include women as mothers as being dangerous texts? Of course, without the original
in front of you it is hard to judge. But even if it were reproduced here I'm not sure on
what grounds we would settle the argument. The image is contradictory, capable of
being read in several ways.

Even seemingly more straightforward positive images are not without their
difficulties. *The Turbulent Term of Tyke Tyler* is a case in point. If we imagine that all
stories about girls show them as passive and resourceless individuals, involved in
soppy plot-lines revolving round flowers and cuddly toys, then *Tyke Tyler* provides
a useful corrective. But in turning Tyke into an active and resourceful individual
with a strong role to play, the book also effectively transforms her into a boy. Indeed,
this is part of the point the book has been designed to make. By disguising Tyke's
identity until the final chapter the idea is that expectations about gender role can be
challenged – the message can be put across that girls can behave like boys. But is this
the only way that girls' behaviour can be valued, if they can pass as male? Interestingly enough, Tyke's elder sister, clearly identified as female throughout the story,
gets the same kind of disparaging treatment normally reserved for girls in more
obviously conventional texts. So just what has been changed? At least some of the
subtext still seems to be that girls being girls in some way don't count, their interests
and concerns only matter when they look like boys. Specific textual features *are*
contradictory. Yet within the current terms of debate, it is not always easy to see how
to respond. On the one hand, it is tempting to persist in denying that there is any
difficulty. Some teachers, faced with a difference of view, insist that their interpretation is right and just try harder to persuade their pupils to subscribe to the teacher's
tastes. In this way, battle lines get drawn and opinion is sharply polarised. Either
pupils concur with the teacher's view or they don't. If children get the point the
teacher is driving at and come into line by dropping their reading of second-rate teen
comics, for instance, all well and good. They win the teacher's approval. If they don't
it is hard to know what to do next. It is the classic vanguardist dilemma. What do you
do when the followers refuse to be led? The alternative is to accept that the meaning
of any text is ambiguous, and open to more than one interpretation, but then to make
the adoption of one interpretation rather than another a matter of purely individual
choice. Consequently, the teacher ends up advocating an entirely hands off
approach, in which anybody is entitled to think anything they like: the classic
laissez-faire liberal tactic, which obscures any political dimension to debate.

I have suggested some difficulties in holding to a view of powerful texts. If texts contain contradictory images, it is hard to see how we could imagine that they exert a simple effect. On the other hand, admitting some of the difficulties involved in getting pupils to agree with teachers about the meaning of what gets read doesn't in itself provide much of an alternative. Within the existing consensus in English teaching, the choice of response seems to come down to old-fashioned liberalism or the kind of policing of children's reading which smacks of hard-Left vanguardism. Meanwhile, a specifically feminist contribution to this debate is missing.

What way out of this impasse does feminism suggest? The single most important point which has got lost in feminism's appropriation as anti-sexism is the pro-woman line, by which I mean the assumption on feminists' part that women are not to blame for the inequalities of patriarchy, and that on the contrary, what they do is a legitimate response to the realities of male power. An example of what this means in practice can be provided by looking at the debate about promotion prospects for women teachers. One explanation of why so few women hold senior posts goes something like this: women themselves are under-confident. They have been handicapped by not being brought up to behave like men. What they need is assertiveness training. Once they have gained their confidence, then they will be able to compete equally with male colleagues and take their rightful place in the hierarchy. The pro-woman perspective would start from the assumption that it is not women's confidence or lack of it which is at fault. The fact that women don't apply for senior posts is due to a realistic assessment on their part of what would be involved in climbing the career ladder. They are not prepared single-mindedly to pursue promotion in a system which makes unacceptable demands on those who compete within it. In contrast, the men who are prepared to make that sacrifice can do so only because much of the work has been taken out of their personal lives by the women they live with. In this analysis it is accepted that women don't fit the system, but the conclusion is that it is the system which needs changing, not the women themselves. The point of a pro-woman line is not to show that women are always right but, by starting from the premise that women's behaviour makes sense, to challenge what men are up to. If we accept the analysis that the current set-up works in the interests of men not women, that is surely what we need to do.

In the classroom, taking a pro-woman line would get us out of the vanguardist perspective so often associated with anti-sexism, whereby teachers assume all the responsibility for telling students what they need to know. Such an approach consistently underestimates girls' experience. They do not arrive in our classrooms as blank slates, waiting for teachers to tell them the score. Of course, girls know that they get a rough deal. How could they avoid being aware of what is only too clearly spelt out to them by boys' behaviour every day of their lives? The confusion arises simply because they are not taking stridently militant action. Well, is that the only legitimate way of dealing with male power? Hanging around a neglected area of the playground with your friends to chat about the kinds of things that boys aren't interested in may be just as profitable as having the hassle of competing with them for space to play football. Why does the latter seem to win all the approbation? What is actually being decided in this way?

Taking a pro-woman line would also get us away from the kind of contempt that often trails in the wake of anti-sexism. In attempting to resolve the differences between girls' and boys' behaviour anti-sexism puts a high priority on getting them both to behave in the same way. But often in practice this means encouraging girls to behave like boys, in which case no radical re-evaluation of girls' activities takes place, and no real challenge is made to boys' behaviour. Instead, girls become the problem. 'Since girls in general are so severely conditioned and repressed and so turned in upon themselves, they fall victim to fantasies in consequence,' Bob Dixon (1977) has written. Girls are assumed to be lacking in a way in which boys are not. Where there is an attempt to encourage boys to behave like girls the assumption is that the former are oppressed by gender stereotyping in exactly the same way as the latter. But how can this be the case? Asking girls to take on boys' behaviour means asking the powerless to appropriate the strategies of the powerful; asking boys to take on girls' behaviour means expecting the powerful to appropriate the strategies of the powerless. The invitations are not equivalent.

Unless we revalue what girls are up to in the way that a pro-woman line suggests, it remains possible to use the discourse of anti-sexism to put women in their place. Judith Williamson (1981) in a piece entitled 'How does girl number twenty understand ideology?' writes about an incident where exactly this happens. A boy making a presentation in a media studies class on Images of Women has chosen girls' comics as his topic.

> 'I can see why Mark has chosen this topic: it's easy work, in a way, we can all see how stupidly girls are shown and that's what this course is all about, isn't it? He thinks I'm going to approve. But as we go through his careful presentation – packed with gems of teaching material – my flesh creeps at the note of scorn in his voice. After all, girls read this rubbish, don't they? It just goes to show how stupid they are. The problem arises openly in class. *Why* do girls read these? *We* can see at a glance how unrealistic the stories are, how trashy the images. So why do girls read them? It just confirms, for the boys at least, that girls *are* somehow silly or dumb.'

Taking a pro-woman line and starting from the assumption that girls' behaviour makes sense, mean re-evaluating male behaviour. It can no longer be treated as neutral, the norm against which other ways of operating can be judged. Instead it becomes visible as a strategy for taking and holding on to power.

Positively valuing girls' activity and raising questions about boys' provide new and much more useful approaches to questions about reading (and writing). For it also suggests a different way of thinking about the relationship between pupils and texts, both the texts they read and the texts they produce. Rather than trying to establish once and for all what a text means and then trying to police children's reading of that text, or alternatively endorsing any and every response, the pro-woman line shifts attention to the context in which any one reading takes place. In this way there is no difficulty in understanding how a boy can use teenage girls' comics to denigrate female pupils. It is precisely the kind of power play one might expect. For what matters about texts is not the content alone, but the way that content can be mobilised and used by readers. And feminists would expect differences here to be governed, not by randomly individual choice, but by social and collective histories. In other words, we would expect there to be conflicting readings, which could not be settled by reference to the text alone. Rather than attempting to close things down by fixing once and for all what the text means, feminism would fore-ground the social strategies readers bring to the text.

This means putting to one side the kind of rudimentary content analysis which has been used to establish whether a book contains positive or negative gender representations. Such analysis will not tell us very much about the reading strategies pupils use, nor, consequently, what the books 'mean'. Anybody in any doubt about this should try applying this sort of checklist analysis to texts which aren't reading schemes or school textbooks. The results look decidedly odd. Jane Austen would appear to be unacceptable because her female characters occupy an unhealthily limited range of social roles. Shakespeare would have to be rejected on the grounds that he dangerously under-represents women. *Hamlet* would have to be considered a deeply unsatisfactory text because women readers can only identify with either Gertrude or Ophelia, neither of them positive role models. As Jane Miller (1986) has already pointed out, this would hardly sum up the possibilities for women readers. If we allow that women readers may have other options when reading these texts, why shouldn't the same be true when they pick up a magazine? The categorisation of content should not lead to assumptions about how a text gets read. Instead of extrapolating back from content to reading strategies, we should start the other way round, with the readers themselves and the social contexts within which texts are produced and circulated.

Adopting this perspective means reconsidering some of the other assumptions on which current practice is based. It would certainly raise doubts about the value of stressing a personal response to texts. If we accept that response to texts is socially constructed then the search for the individual and unique experience is rendered illusory. Perhaps we should replace the personal response principle with an ethnography of reading? An ethnography of reading would stress the role which diverse social and cultural practices play in shaping how texts get read. This would enable contrasts to be made between different forms of reading, associated with different kinds of texts and different groups of readers. Such an approach suggests a new study of comics, magazines and generic fiction. The latter are hard to accommodate whilst the stress is on the uniqueness of the reading experience, for such texts are deliberately constructed to make the most of familiarity with the conventions of the form. They play on repetition (Neale 1983). An ethnography of reading would expect such literature to be read differently from, rather than in the same manner as, other kinds of texts. At the same time, because they are aimed at gender-differentiated markets, they provide a focus for exploring the different ways in which boys and girls read. We could begin by asking some of the following kinds of questions. What is the significance of the fact that the magazines teenage boys purchase appear to be aimed at an adult readership, when girls seem to choose magazines explicitly targeted at a teenage audience? What is the appeal of the stress on technical language, or the apparent need for expertise on the part of male readers, which boys' magazines cultivate? What range of images of masculinity are to be found in girls' magazines? What is the function of the 'pretty boy' version of masculinity associated with many of the pin-ups? What effect does the selection of this image (rather than any other) have? What makes it so difficult to persuade boy readers to cope with genres which they consider to be primarily aimed at girls? What is at stake here? This kind of approach, expecting difference and asking questions about it, could usefully be extended and applied to children's writing too. Do the genres of romance and science fiction have a different function in children's writing? What are the implications of the virtual absence of female characters in the genres boys use in their writing? What function does the double perspective of the romance (the boy's view of the girl, the girl's view of the boy) have in girls' writing? In asking these kinds of question we would be re-casting writing as primarily a social, not a private and personal, activity.

So far I have been indicating the role a feminist perspective could have in re-shaping the ways in which English teachers think about reading and writing. Turning our attention to the function texts have for their readers or writers means concentrating first of all on differences and beginning to account for the patterns which emerge (Moss 1989). At the same time this has implications for the way in which gender is addressed in the classroom as an explicit topic, not least because it emphasises finding ways of exploiting potentially conflicting points of view. Making the most of such conflicts depends on taking a pro-woman line. In what follows I want to give a clearer indication of how this perspective might work out in practice, by looking in detail at a particular lesson I had with a fourth-year English group.

I had set the class a writing task which was gender-specific by asking them to write as realistic an account as they could manage of the sort of talk that went on in small groups during registration, with this proviso: they were to restrict themselves to the sort of talk that went on in single-sex groups and were to begin with their own sex. Once they had done this they were to go on and write down what they imagined the conversation would be like between members of the opposite sex in the same circumstances. So each individual wrote two pieces, one entitled 'Girls' Talk', one entitled 'Boys' Talk': one piece drawing on what they knew from first hand, the other speculative. When the tasks had been completed, I divided the blackboard into four columns, two headed girls' talk, two headed boys' talk. We began to write down all the subjects that had been mentioned by the class in their writing. In this way we established an impression both of what the girls and the boys had actually been talking about and what they thought the other sex would have been talking about. What emerged was as follows: the girls thought the boys would have been talking about sex and violence. The boys described themselves as talking about sex and violence, although they had also talked about hobbies (something the girls hadn't thought of).

> 'Geoff,' Neil and I shouted in unison as Geoff walked
> through the door. 'Ah,' as Geoff heaved his bag off his back,
> '...caught three chub yesterday, down Keynsham.'
> 'Oh yea,' said Neil.
> 'Yea,' said Geoff, 'I've frozen them. You can see 'em tonight
> if you want.'
> 'You're on. Coming tonight, Rich?'
> 'Might as well. Nothing else to do.'
> 'Call about 5,' said Geoff. 'After, I'll get my radio-
> controlled car out.'

The boys thought the girls would have been talking about boyfriends, pop groups and records.

> 'Hello Sarah,' said Catherine as she walked in.
> 'Right. Hey I got my Wham fan club letter back today,' said Debby. 'Hey, what did it say?'
> 'Well it said all about their coming tour and...'
> 'Hey, guess what,' said Louise running in, 'Jeremy is going out with that new girl. You know, the one with spots all over her neck and the fat legs.'
> 'How could he stand it?' said Sarah.
> 'How could she stand it?' said Debby. 'How could they stand it?' said Louise.

None of the girls had described herself as talking about pop groups. They had described themselves as talking about boyfriends, but they had also covered a much wider array of topics: clothes, friends, teachers, homework, parents, watching television, buying presents. The list went on. But at the same time there was a common thread running through much of what they wrote about. Almost regardless of the subject matter, the conversation would be used to define relationships.

> 'Me and Christine went up Kingswood on Saturday, right?' Sharon said to me. 'I bought a chip-fryer for my Mum and a big doll for my sister and I made Christine carry it all the way home.'
> 'Yeh, they were really heavy and I couldn't see where I was going and I hit my head,' said Christine. 'And Sharon just stood there laughing.'
> Alison then came into the room and told a dirty joke.
> 'My Mum nearly hit me when I told her it,' she said after.
> 'I should think she did,' Christine replied.

It was once we'd established these broader headings that the conversation became interesting. At first the boys were quite happy to have the subjects of their discussion listed as sex, violence and hobbies. The mention of sex and violence produced loud laughter and a variety of other noises from the boys in the class. But as the conversation developed around the differences between the boys' treatment of these subjects and the complexity of the girls' writing, other things began to happen. The girls became increasingly restless, both impatient with the way the boys had underestimated what they were up to and critical of the topics the boys had chosen. This culminated in Angelique turning round to the boys and saying: 'The trouble with you lot is you just haven't got any feelings.' In the rather stunned silence that followed I picked on the one boy in the class who I thought would be prepared to give me a straight answer and said: 'That's a very serious charge. What have you got to say about it?' Suddenly the whole tenor of the conversation changed. The boy began to talk about how difficult it was to express your feelings as a boy talking to other boys, how the pressure was on to disguise the feelings you have, or if you couldn't do that, show them through violence. The whole basis for the boys' pride in their ability to talk about sex and violence had been undercut.

That is the brief outline of the lesson. Now let me consider in more detail just what was going on here. When the boys wrote about what they imagined the girls' talk to be, they wrote about it with contempt. Richard, whose piece of girls' talk I quoted from above, had this comment to make when, following the lesson, I asked the class to summarise the discussion that had gone on under the heading 'The differences between boys' and girls' talk':

> Girls talk about boyfriends and how well they get on with
> them. Also they talk about more trivial things than boys and
> things which are less important. Girls always seem to talk
> about clothes right down to the last detail. Boys like being
> fashionable but girls are more fussy.

The topics that the boys chose for the girls were ones they considered trivial and not serious. At the same time they also misrepresented how the girls actually talked about boyfriends. They imagined that such talk was either about status (so Jeremy can be mocked for going out with an unglamorous girl) or revealed the girls as being fixated on the boys (given over to their power?) or showed them to be soppy (given over to feelings) unlike the 'hard' boys. Here is Richard again:

> The main difference in boys' and girls' talk is that boys
> think about the rougher side of life and girls think about
> appearance and relationships more.

So in other words, in their account of girls' talk the boys were attempting to 'do power' over the girls. When it came to discussing what they had written in the lesson, the boys' initial concern was both to show that they were different from the girls and to show that the girls' concerns weren't up to much. However, in the process of discussion the girls became increasingly vociferous in refusing the boys' valuation of them. They were trying to get out of the position in which the boys were trying to place them and to defend their own interests against the boys. I went along with what was going on and supported the girls by encouraging them to look at what they themselves had written, and to find ways of validating it. I did this both by asking them to reflect directly on their own work – 'How is what you've written about different?' – and by giving them the space in the discussion to do so – in other words, shutting up the boys.

The key to the radical shift in the conversation came when Angelique directly challenged the boys about what they were up to by applying the criteria the girls had established in their own work to the boys. By saying that this was a very serious charge and insisting that a particular individual answered it rather than dismissing it, I changed the whole grounds of the discussion. Now the boys had to reconsider what they had been talking about from another perspective, one which had been identified as the girls'. The outcome was that the girls got their own power back and refused the boys' definition of them, whilst the boys had the opportunity to rethink their own position in different terms.

What was the gap in the discourse which allowed this to happen? In the version of their own talk that they had given in their writing the boys had been pushing away feelings so that they could rehearse a strong objective masculinity, dealing in the impersonal. In so doing they were claiming adult male status. Their version of boys talking about girls was to talk about girls as sex objects, rather than who they were interested in going out with and how they might manage that: 'Angela's a bit of all right. Cor, what a pair of knockers.' In writing about violence they were most interested in establishing the status of the participants according to who was most prepared to throw punches:

> 'Did you see that scrap last week? Terry really gave it to
> him. You should have seen the blood. Paul got it right on
> the nose.'

But in saying this they were not giving the complete truth about themselves. They were covering over certain areas of their lives in an attempt to give a strong public performance which could establish their status in relation to the other boys. At times their writing showed another side to the way things were even if only by implication. Richard's piece of conversation, which had been summed up under the heading 'Hobbies', is also in an oblique way about friendship. Even if the tone is casual – 'Coming tonight, Rich?' 'Might as well. Nothing else to do.' – it's also about being friends and the relationships between boys. In a way the boys' biggest mistake, which was ultimately to lead to them failing to 'do power' over the girls, was in accepting the summary of their agenda as sex, violence and hobbies. They accepted it because it looked impersonal and also made them look big. In their own terms handling these subjects in rather racy conversation was proof of the masculinity to which they aspired. It was what made them different from the girls:

> If someone notices boys have feelings and consideration for
> girls they will call them soppy and other stuff. So just to
> prove to their mates, when the girl isn't around he will talk
> about her with his mates saying 'Oh, she's all right, but a bit
> of a cow at times'...Boys don't involve girls in their
> conversations because they think she wouldn't know what
> she was talking about. If it was a girls' conversation he
> wouldn't be interested because if he was his mates would
> call him sissy.

> Boys think about the rougher side of life and girls think
> about appearance and relationships more. The rougher side
> of life is horror films, rough sports and fighting, etc. Also
> things like cars and bikes, etc., are often talked about.

But it was also their undoing, because this impersonal agenda is not a complete representation of who the boys are, and once questions had been raised by the girls about feelings, the boys' bluff had been called. So the terms of the conversation were switched by directing attention back to what the boys were trying to exclude. Instead of trying to argue with what was there in the boys' talk – this sex and violence is repulsive – the girls won back the agenda by pointing to what was absent in the boys' talk: feelings. They identified the absence by establishing the difference between what was present in their own work and what was present in the boys', but also by taking their own work as the norm against which the boys' could be judged. It was this sort of positive comparison between the two that pushed the discourse over into something new.

Of course, that doesn't mean to say that the particular strategy the girls used here will always work, nor that it is the only one. But it does indicate that a useful starting-point can be made by exploiting the differences between perspectives in the classroom. If we are serious about our politics, it is not so much a matter of coming to the classroom with a fixed position, a set of ready-made answers, as setting the agenda for the discussion and, through our support of the girls, setting out how that discussion will take place.

Feminism has much to offer English teaching. The kind of pro-woman perspective I have been outlining suggests new ways of taking up gender issues in the classroom. At the same time it raises questions about many of the kinds of practices which English teachers take for granted in their classrooms by stressing the place of social and cultural histories rather than privileging personal and individual expression.

A version of this essay appeared in *The English Magazine* 22, Summer 1989.

Dixon, Bob (1977), *Catching Them Young 1: Sex, Race and Class in Children's Fiction*, Pluto Press
Miller, Jane (1986), *Women Writing About Men*, Virago
Moss, Gemma (1989), *Un/Popular Fictions*, Virago
Neale, Stephen (1983), *Genre*, BFI
Williamson, Judith (1981), 'How Does Girl Number Twenty Understand Ideology?' in *Screen Education*, no. 40, 2

PART FOUR

Building the Future.
Teaching as Science and Art

The central paradox of education is the profession of teaching. Learned scholars consorting with clever students see it differently from the thousands of practitioners on whom fall the social and intellectual responsibilities for the future of an educated society. The current nature of teaching and the education of teachers need fundamental reappraisal, in terms of both theory and practice. If teachers are to make all children literate and learned in terms of the National Curriculum and encourage them to have a vision of their future, then the education of teachers is bound to be a reflexive process, a continuum that runs alongside that of the learning processes of the children in their care. It also means that pedagogies are not techniques for transmission, but sets of critical practices with regard to what counts as knowing.

The five essays in this section review the development of critical pedagogies. Josie Levine considers how teaching, to be active, collaborative learning for teachers and students, must reject the meagre apprenticeship model of transmission. The 'everyday imperative of the classroom' makes rigorous claims on teachers' active theory-making and confident knowing. Coming from a different tradition where *didactics* and *pedagogies* are current terms of reference, in the 'sciences of education', Anne-Marie Goguel appreciates a personal construct psychology and the pragmatic instances of literature teaching which she sees in England. A specific example of a small child learning to read gives Judith Graham the opportunity to examine why it is so difficult for adults to believe that children learn to read by reading a text written by someone who wants it to be read.

The taken-for-granteds of our culture emerge from each of these essays as the place for necessary reconsideration. Phillida Salmon questions the narratives the young may demand of the old, not in ordinary social exchanges, but suddenly as part of school 'projects'. Are the 'possibilities of human enlargement' part of the educational process? If so, what kinds of pedagogy bring them about? In an era when education begins earlier and lasts longer than at any time in the past, when we all expect to live longer, 'the whole standpoint, from which life was viewed, and meaning given, is altered'. Margaret Meek draws together in the final essay of the book many of the threads woven through it. Her panoramic vision encompasses change in what counts and will count as literacy. It is an apt and optimistic place to pause.

JOSIE LEVINE

Pedagogy: the case of the missing concept

No one can deny the weight, constant and continuing, of teachers' responsibilities. These must be fulfilled in a social and intellectual context that also demands recurrent inventive interactions with growing minds and bodies. Josie Levine spells them out as the 'acquired and continuously honed qualities of individual good teachers'. Why, if their work is so important for the learning that enables successive generations to become full members of a complex, literate, democratic society are teachers publicly discredited and regarded as lowly servants in the educational processes entrusted to schools? The answers to these and similar questions are embedded in the structures of our society. Persuaded that the time has come to make some answers more explicit, Josie Levine redefines *pedagogy* as the art and science of education. She analyses the exploratory, reflexive, critical work that characterises good practice in schools. The 'reflexive developmental' interaction of teachers and teacher educators has been the dominant characteristic of her innovative work in the domain of bilingual teachers and learners, where her own pedagogy is both skilfully practised and imaginatively theorised.

Many years ago, when I was looking for a concept-framing word to stand for what I like to think of as the greatest of the plastic arts: the on-going practice of teaching, I decided to ignore its negative connotations and adopt the word 'pedagogy' into my professional vocabulary.

I was looking for a word which I could use in my work in teacher-training and which, with some appropriate explanation, would stand for that complex of thinking, feeling, information, knowledge, theory, experience, wisdom and creativity which are the inherent, acquired and continuously-honed qualities of individual good teachers. I needed also a word, the same word if possible, to carry within it the sense of teaching as a theorising profession offering scope for the building of theory and practice out of its essential elements via processes of reflection, analysis and synthesis – a profession capable of development, renewal and rigorous intellectual activity in its own right.

My choice of word was deemed somewhat pedantic then, perhaps even unnecessary. After all, were there not words already in use in teacher-training which did the job perfectly well? Words such as 'theory', 'practice', 'methodology'? Surely, these were good enough labels to describe what it was we knew about and taught when we said we worked in teacher-training?

But, in fact, they were not good enough descriptions; unless, that is, the prevailing conditions and attitudes reflected one's own position. My appropriation of the word 'pedagogy' was not intended as just a straight swap for 'tuition', 'method' or 'practice'. Rather, it was to try to encapsulate *unacknowledged* concepts of what teaching was about and what can and should constitute its professional subject matter.

I chose the word 'pedagogy' to name these things because, despite its narrow usage in English, elsewhere in Europe the word has more positive meaning. 'Pedagogy' – meaning the *science* of teaching – lent the activity a certain cachet absolutely in contrast to our own system of thinking about it. In this society, we certainly did not, and still do not, grant the study of teaching either the standing of a science, or the practice of it the standing of an art form. Indeed, historically, we have defined the study and practice of teaching narrowly and, even if unconsciously, we have arranged things so that the profession and its practitioners have every possible kind of low status conferred upon them. When teaching is so complex a set of practices, when it is so important to the development of individuals and of society, when it is culturally and economically of such importance, how is it that it can be so negatively positioned?

The fundamental answer to this question is to be found in a class analysis of the relationship of teaching to education. As a teacher colleague put it, 'Teaching is for the masses, educating for the classes – upper, of course.'

I want now to draw out some of the strands of the legacy bequeathed us by the hierarchical class reality that lies behind the low status perception so often accorded to the teaching profession and to show how, having entered the collective unconscious, such perceptions in turn contribute to the construction of a system which inhibits and limits both teaching and learning.

One strand of this legacy of what constitutes teaching is nicely reflected in *Roget's Thesaurus* (1853; Penguin abridged edition, 1953), which, being what it is – a classification of words 'according to their signification...', 'arranged so as to facilitate the expression of ideas and to assist literary composition' – mirrors and preserves, through its inclusions and omissions, its groupings and collocations, the received attitudes and cultural meanings of 'teaching'.

Although there is an extensive entry in the *Thesaurus* under 'teaching', our profession is narrowly defined. The lists we are offered are heavy on didacticism and light-to-invisible on teaching/learning as science, art, process. For example, we have 'instruction', 'edification', 'education'; 'pedagogy' – in the narrow English sense of having equivalence with – 'tuition', 'tutelage', 'direction', 'guidance'; 'exercising', 'drilling', 'practising', 'persuading'; 'propaganda', 'indoctrination', 'inculcation'; 'lessons', 'lectures', 'sermons', 'homilies', 'parables', 'discourse'; 'discipline'; 'educate', 'form', 'habituate'. But what is minimal, if indeed it exists at all in the entries, is any reflection of teaching as an understanding of and ability to support pupils through stages of development and achievement. Where are the concept-framing words which indicate that teaching is an integrated set of practices based on understandings of pupils' actual lived experience and modes of learning? Where are the words to indicate teaching as an extensive understanding of educational theory interrelated, in practice, with a wide range of classroom management skills? References in the *Thesaurus* like 'prepare', 'familiarise with', 'nurture', 'initiate', 'direct attention to' and 'guide' would seem the entries approximating most closely to this complex of meanings, to this construction of a facilitative and developmental meaning for teaching, except that they collocate so unfortunately closely with 'break in' and 'tame'.

As for the persons themselves, a teacher is a 'trainer', 'instructor', 'initiator', 'master', 'tutor', 'don', 'director', 'coach', 'crammer', 'governess', 'disciplinarian', 'professor', 'lecturer', 'preacher', 'missionary'. We find that s/he is also a 'guide', 'mentor', 'pioneer', 'example', but again, there is no word or set of words which describes a teacher as one who, as an informed and intellectually rigorous partner to her pupils or students in a context of mutual responsibility, provides for active learning processes which both promote development, skills, knowledge and achievement and also support learners' confidence and independence. Interestingly, 'pedagogue' appears in a subset with 'schoolmaster', 'dominie' and 'usher', while 'schoolmistress' appears in a subset with 'monitor', 'proctor' and 'pupil- teacher'!

With such a long history of 'teaching's' popular association with notions more akin to training and habituation than with active meaning-making or intention on the part of the learners, it is small wonder that today it is such a battle to redefine 'teaching' as something which legitimately includes facilitative practice. Moreover, it is easy to see how, if teaching is constructed in the collective consciousness as training and habituation, it is only 'natural' that becoming a teacher will involve teacher-trainees in going through, not professional education but something designated, still, as teacher-training, an activity narrowly conceived *and*, in this culture, disparagingly perceived in comparison with academic study. In relation to the low status of the teaching profession, we should not forget that 'training' is the word reserved for the 'education' people are offered if they have not chosen – and for 'have not chosen' read 'are not perceived as up to' – academic work.

This 'normal' construction of teaching as training – and, inescapably, of learning as being trained – has had ideological and methodological consequences. The 'normal', traditional paradigm, which to this day leaves its mark, was overwhelmingly didactic, with pupils positioned minus a truly active role in their learning, and teachers in a reciprocal transmission mode. Teachers' own training followed the same pattern. Thus, not only does the training paradigm fail pupils, but 'trained' teachers contribute to this failure.

To mitigate this, we needed to detach ourselves from notions that preparation for teaching, in-service and further professional development in teaching means *merely* a matter of becoming acquainted with a body of already extant knowledge (theory) and an agreed set of skills and strategies (practice) to which all sensible people subscribe. And we needed to deny that all a person has to do to be a teacher is to learn how to do the set pieces; and that these can be learned like movements in a traditional dance under supervised practice – capable of some manipulation and re-alignment by the trainee, but staying, nevertheless, within a set frame – choreographed by an expert trainer.

This is as true for those undertaking further professional development as it is for initial teacher trainees. Counteraction was necessary because knowledge of teaching (whether for or about it) is neither finite nor capable of being so directly transmitted; neither is the content of the theories chosen for transmission universally recognised as apt for the building of a broad theory of education. Furthermore, the application of skills and strategies just cannot be independent of learning contexts. There may be agreement about general educational principles – if derived from theories of learning development – but there is no good or best practice derivable from the principles without its being grounded in specific contexts.

As for the *concept* of practice: that also needed, and still needs, to be reinterpreted in the light of the differences in outcome between a training mode of learning and an educational mode. Teaching is 'practice' in the sense that what we learn to do is a set of 'practices'. It is also true that teaching is 'practice', in the sense that we learn to do it by 'practising'. But both the 'practices' and the 'practising' are only part of the whole. They do not adequately describe what real teaching is any more than the wordstrings in the *Thesaurus*. For teachers to be able to help pupils achieve and be self-respecting, confident and independent learners, they themselves must surely have courses that provide them with the broadest educational knowledge, skills and understanding of learning development. They must have courses that give them the experience that will enable them to educate, not merely train, their pupils. These things have been impossible to achieve within the practices associated with 'normal' teacher-training.

'Normal' teacher-training was offered in the mode Freire called 'banking'. Characteristically, it was a componential approach, which maintains strong boundaries between the subjects on the timetable. Typically, such courses had three main strands, Education, Curriculum and Methodology, and Teaching Practice. The first comprised further separate areas, History of Education, Sociology of Education, Psychology of Education and Philosophy of Education, each taught separately by experts in each field. The second, usually taught by someone different again from any of the others so far mentioned, was about the content of the curriculum and about methods of teaching it. Teaching Practice might also have been supervised by an 'unknown' tutor. Certainly, except in a minority of training institutions, it was not supervised by a student's main subject or 'methods' tutor. In this traditional pattern of preparation for teaching, the relationship between the components was not studied. Students were expected to relate in their own minds the range of extant theory to a selected body of knowledge about practice. As a result, theory and practice came to be seen as being in opposition rather than in a complementary and developing relationship. Moreover, theory was not seen to be as relevant as 'practice', a view which has left us with an interminable, damaging and misplaced debate about whether theory is at all relevant to the preparation of teachers.

Although questions about which and what kind of theory and which and what kind of practice certainly arise, the real issue does not lie in this opposition between theory and practice. Rather, it lies in the debilitating consequences for a profession, which should rightfully be based on rigorous thinking, analysis and the development of practice, of raising this false polarity. In recent years, programmes of study of this kind have been designed for teachers' professional education so that links are made between theories, practices, actual teaching contexts and the art of teaching; and it is on these that teacher education should be based.

'Splitting' is not the only limiting factor in 'normal' teacher-training. Other factors, too, reflect back to potential and practising teachers a limited perception of what they can be and do as teachers. For example, critical analysis is experienced by student teachers as a tool of external assessment which emphasises dominance and unequal power relationships, rather than as a tool of ongoing, self-motivated enquiry. Yet teachers need to use critical analysis in this second, educational and developmental way if they are to become the practitioners and theory-makers who are needed to create real achievement for all pupils in the educational settings in which they will do their work.

Yet, what they need could still not be what they get. The 'normal' framework does not legitimate students in this way. It merely positions them as jobbing apprentices: a construction of learning which is no more appropriate to craft apprentices than it is to student teachers.

If teaching has suffered in status from being denied many of its essential features in both popular descriptions *and* professional constructions of it, the final irony is that teaching's low status can also be ascribed to what it must intrinsically be if it is to be successful.

Teaching is an eclectic undertaking, and complexly so, its character frequently arising from putting together often very disparate, even unlikely, concerns related to theory, knowledge, understanding and experience. Yet, while eclecticism *can be* construed as wise and informed choice among relevant concerns or the reconciliation of principles and opinions belonging to different schools of thought and bodies of knowledge, it is just as often construed as a 'butterfly' activity, a picking up of gleanings from here and there. In the academic world it is this second construction which is placed on the activity and which contributes to the positioning of teaching as a low-level intellectual undertaking, inferior in status to 'pure' and 'applied' fields of knowledge and research.

Was Shaw creating or reflecting this view when he reputedly said of teachers, 'Those who can, do; those who can't, teach'? What ignorant nonsense! Only the gate-keeping born of our élitist class system would need to evaluate teachers as failed writers, artists, historians, scientists, mathematicians, athletes, musicians, whatever; or want to rank forms of thinking. Such dominant assumptions obscure the truth that teaching contains within it all the same necessities for on-going, successful outcomes of theory-making and the development of practice as any of the more narrowly and more statically defined fields. Such assumptions also obscure recognition of one of the most rigorous of testing grounds imaginable for any profession: the everyday imperative of the classroom.

Absolutely unacknowledged in these assumptions is the fact that teachers are, in consequence, uniquely positioned to make a rigorous contribution from within the context of their own teaching to important areas of knowledge about teaching and learning. From this point of view, and to paraphrase one of the titles of James Baldwin's essays: If teaching isn't doing, then tell me, what is?

At present, we work in an inadequate and self-fulfilling system, which builds on the preconditions of under-achievement for pupils, student teachers, teachers and teacher-training establishments. There are well-founded fears that the new National Curriculum, with its hierarchical levels of attainment and its rigid, age-related arrangements for assessment – alongside the reorganisation of funding for initial and in-service courses for teachers – constitutes a reactionary retrenchment which will do all too little to support real achievement either for pupils or teachers. It is not difficult to foresee who will be blamed when failure within the system is perceived yet again.

It is always difficult to work against dominant assumptions, especially when these are held by many within the profession as well as more widely in society. However, if pedagogy, as an area of reflective study, practice, analysis and action research seems still to be a missing concept within the dominant construction of education, the pedagogy principle itself is not missing. It exists, developed over some considerable time by a minority of teachers and educationalists, who have the intel-greater equality of outcomes in education. The pedagogic medium for the growth and nurture of this praxis within teacher-education has been a continuing *developmental* interaction, with teachers as theory-makers in their own right in reflexive partnership with teacher educators. The product of this dialectic relationship between teachers and teacher educators, and between theory and practice, is an increasingly recognisable area of practical and theoretical knowledge, at once integrative and autonomous.

There is no doubt that the key to improving the state of education at every level – teacher education and teachers' professional status included – is situated within the practices and orientations for which I have reappropriated the word 'pedagogy'.

At a time when the government – with the ostensible purpose of raising standards – enacts decisions which misguidedly emphasise the training paradigm, it would be reprehensible on the part of teacher educators to continue or return to an uncritical maintenance of the same paradigm. What is needed are the reflections and actions that legitimise pedagogy as an area of study and practice.

In teacher education, as in other areas of teaching, what we *do* is what we teach.

Baldwin, James (1985), *The Price of the Ticket: collected non-fiction 1948-1985*, Michael Joseph
Freire, Paulo (1972), *Pedagogy of the Oppressed*, Penguin

ANNE-MARIE GOGUEL

Teacher Education for the Europe of Tomorrow

The continental European intellectual tradition, in which the philosopher ranks as the appraiser of what counts as knowledge, lies behind Anne-Marie Goguel's view of the more pragmatic world of British classrooms and the teaching of English. In France, psychology, which she teaches, is one of the 'sciences of education'. Her ethnographic experiences in developing countries influence her analyses of the continuing tensions between rational education planning and the transforming values of teaching and learning. The technological changes, the result of 'new literacies' and the didactic application of packaged classroom materials, increase her concern for creative pedagogy.

This essay demonstrates how complex are the cultural issues in studies of comparative education. Research and teaching, definitions of 'the curriculum' and what school is for will need continuous redescription following the changes that are envisaged in Europe in 1992. The education of teachers in Britain will be drawn into the European circle, with its professional challenges and opportunities.

If there is a problem in education which is common to all European countries at this time, it must be how to revalue teaching as a profession. For the work they do teachers need social recognition even more than financial reward if more of them, men especially, are not to leave the profession, and it becomes ever more difficult to find enough candidates for the available jobs. At present, many teachers are disheartened. They believe that they are the target for unfair criticism, because they haven't been able to bring about the 'democratisation' of society on their own, a process which depends on factors other than those related only to schools.

On all sides demands are being made on education which can be summed up in the idea that the systems should be accountable to the taxpayer: that it isn't enough that standards and objectives set by the local and national authorities should be successfully met, these aims must be reached by means which are both efficient and cheap. Given this common situation, many of us in Europe are interested in the work of the University of London's Institute of Education. In our view it is an exact example of a high-level university school which, in an original way, combines fundamental research, without which educators would be confined to empirical methods of trial and error and short-term pragmatic routines, and reflective consideration of teaching practices.

It seems to us that in London, more than elsewhere, teachers and students have gone beyond the damaging convention – still prevalent in France – whereby the most highly qualified teachers teach the most successful students in the top classes. In France, the notorious example is the class which prepares pupils for the *Grandes Ecoles*, while the least experienced teachers, whose training has also been shorter, have to cope with the most difficult pupils. Yet everyone knows that it is from situations of this kind that the most original pedagogic innovations may emerge. But for this to happen classroom teachers at the chalk face must not be abandoned, left to work things out for themselves, and consequently be worn down by the wearing routine that goes with the kind of work they are expected to do. This doesn't happen where the teacher-researchers of the English Department in the Institute of Education work together with teachers in schools, and we in continental Europe admire them for this form of collaboration.

While we might be inclined to associate this mode of teacher education with 'action research', which may rest on certain confusions (the same person cannot, at one and the same time, be involved in a project and look objectively and scientifically at its results), we might do better to speak of 'innovation-evaluation', which takes into account the circularity of the process and the way these two procedures are linked together. In fact, many educational innovations are not the result of the direct application of theoretical discoveries; instead, they may be ideas born of tentative muddling through and then worked out by trial and error. But only subsequent reflection, thinking about which new practices 'work', makes possible the emergence of more general concepts and propositions, which allow new ideas to be developed and become more generally applicable.

For that to happen, the 'theoriser' – the teacher-researcher – has to give up all preconceptions, both prescriptive and normative, and to establish instead an effective collaborative relationship with classroom teachers. In this connection we think of the exemplary relations which Margaret Spencer has had with hundreds of teachers in the course of her career, especially in the context of the professional associations for the teaching of English in Britain, Canada, the United States and Australia.

We have to realise that teaching as a profession has changed and will change even more fundamentally in the future. No longer will it be possible for every teacher to be a kind of jobbing all-rounder (*artisan polyvalent*), capable of fashioning her or his own tools and being trained in the handy knack of what to do in classrooms by imitating those who taught them. We seem to have arrived at a time when education has become a kind of industry which has to be rationalised in order to yield 'results' and to become 'performance'. Every teacher will be expected to know about, and to use, the resources that are systematically banked reservoirs of evaluation exercises, remediation techniques, 'packages' specially prepared by the new specialists, the authors of new computer programs for teaching, *didacticiels*. Before long we can expect to see the emergence of pedagogic *engineers* who are capable of constructing pedagogic devices for use in all kinds of situations.

But an evolution such as we are now aware of brings its own kinds of risk, especially if we apply to the teaching industry the Taylorian model, which would produce the fragmentation of teaching operations and the hierarchic division of educational labour. This would make the individual teacher in a class with pupils a simple, specialised worker, a simple executant at the end of the line, whose job is to carry out the directions that come from above.

We also have to realise that, in France and Britain, there are different conceptions of the role of engineers and of their relations with technicians and skilled workers. It seems that in Britain the traditional view of an engineer is of a specialist in machines, constructing them, making them work, repairing the devices even before the theoretical physicists are able to work out the reasons for their efficacy. In

France, however, engineers are trained in the Cartesian tradition in the selective *Grandes Ecoles*, which were founded in the eighteenth century to provide the *Grand Corps* of civil servants. Now, as then, their education is, above all, mathematical and hypothetico-deductive, a specialised training, which prepares them for positions of authority. The difference between this situation and those of Britain and Germany is that, until very recently, there was no possibility of promotion to this high level for manual workers, no way for them to qualify as titled 'engineers', (this status in France is protected and guaranteed by the state).

Now this élitism (the experts separated from the practitioners) might well find its equivalent in education if we were to make the mistake of underestimating the competences, intuitive and practical, of classroom teachers, and of leaving the control of teaching (programmes of study and classroom interactions) in the hands of specialists in cognitive psychology and of those who concern themselves with the psychology of 'acquisitions'. Hence the importance for educational research of empirical enquiries, which are detailed and precise, of all that goes on in classrooms: the verbal and non-verbal exchanges between pupils and teachers and those that occur amongst pupils themselves; everything, in fact, that they encounter as formative experiences.

It is undoubtedly significant that in French there is no exact equivalent of what in Britain and the United States is called 'curriculum research'. This isn't because we haven't moved on from the period (well known and much mocked) when any one of Napoleon's ministers of public instruction could look at his watch and tell at what hour precisely all the pupils in French lycées were busy with Latin prose. Instead, nowadays we are too preoccupied with maintaining what is called the level or standard of learning by concentrating our concern almost exclusively on the content of subject matter to be transmitted rather than on the effective ways by which pupils of a given age can learn. As a result the introduction of 'modern' mathematics and 'linguistics' has resulted in monumental mistakes during the last thirty years. Fortunately, we are now reconsidering these errors, particularly as the result of what is happening in other European countries. We have begun to be interested in the problem of 'didactic transposition', that is, how school subjects can be presented to pupils in ways in which they can be learned. But that isn't enough. Perhaps the most important move now is to avoid separations, gaps, between the *didactic* (the act of organising subject matter to be assimilated) and the *pedagogic* (the art of organising human interactions in classrooms and institutions) as if it were possible to separate these, when clearly it isn't.

The most recent research in social psychology has demonstrated the conditions in which the socio-cognitive 'clashes' between children, or even between adults and children, may not hinder new understandings but may even promote the grasp of new mental operations (in the Piagetian sense of the term). This is why the many British research projects which take into account the 'micro-sociology' of schools and classes show us how enquiries of this kind may be carried out.

Before making rules about what *has* to be done in class, we first have to become aware and take account of the diversity and richness of the skills of practising teachers in thousands of classrooms, including those in education systems which appear to be centralised, but even more so where the educational institutions are seen to recognise explicitly the teachers' autonomy in their choice of objectives and methods. It is to be hoped that in Britain the introduction of the National Curriculum and the procedures for control that come with it do not effectively diminish or impoverish in any way some remarkable creative pedagogy. In this connection we know how Margaret Spencer and her colleagues in the English Department in the Institute of Education have worked in partnership with classroom teachers to ensure a collaborative definition of objectives and criteria of evaluation.

It may come as something of a surprise that, at the very moment when the centralised system of French education is being loosened, the British Parliament has passed a law which, amongst other innovations, includes a national curriculum. We ought not to exaggerate the apparent contrast between these two forms of evolution. France still hasn't given up national programmes of study, even if by now a certain number of school hours in a year are left to the discretion of individual institutions. 'Pédagogie par objectifs', that is, teaching targets that define the intellectual abilities to be developed in pupils, rather than those which list detailed 'subjects', seep in more slowly than in Britain because of the resistance of university teachers, who cling to their specialised disciplines.

In both countries, the current reforms result in an increase of power and responsibility for the heads of educational institutions, who have to make adjustments to both the school population and the local employment situation.

Perhaps the most important thing is to recognise the challenge which not only France and Britain but all communities in the European Community face in the competition set up by the United States and Japan. European industrialists (after a Round Table conference in Brussels in February 1989) insisted that to defeat unemployment and to encourage economic growth it would be necessary to develop the basic abilities of all young people: that they should read, write and count and use the languages of mathematics and information technology in order to base their later professional development on these competences. The difficult problem, one which presents itself differently in France and Britain and which may produce a variety of answers in our institutions, is to know how to spell out those things which depend on early development in the form of school learning, and those which are the responsibility of business enterprises. We also have to decide what the long-term role of government should be in supporting objectives, financing training programmes and making sure that the diversification of local educational institutions does not result in the maintenance and aggravation of social inequality.

To bring these considerations back to teachers and children in classrooms we are bound to acknowledge the central role of teaching the mother tongue. By definition, there can never be any question of *transmission* of informed understanding in the case of mother tongues from those who know it to children who don't. What is to be known is integrated with the means of learning. Teachers and pupils are straightaway taken into the language and carried away by it in as much as they are also the carriers of it. 'Honneur des hommes, Saint Langage!' exclaimed Paul Valéry. Teaching one's own language can never be, must never be, reduced to the business of acquiring a certain number of automatic repetitive routines. Piaget and Chomsky, on the occasion of their famous debate, were entirely in accord (whatever else they disagreed about) that neither of them, nor anyone else, knew *exactly* how children learn to speak their own language, that is, how they acquire the competences that allow them to produce an indefinite number of original utterances which are intelligible to others. Margaret Spencer and her colleagues in the teaching of English have always maintained that speech, talk, is never the reproduction of ready-made expressions. For example, to learn a poem by heart, to interpret it, is to be able to write one, to 'play' in Donald Winnicott's 'third area', the zone between the 'me' and the 'not me', which he shows us is the recreative matrix of what we know as 'culture'.

It is sometimes surprising for French scholars to discover that in the graduate school, the Institute of Education, in the University of London where Basil Bernstein conducted his pioneering studies into the social differences and the language differences that schools risk turning into inequalities, the members of the English Department have devoted themselves to enquiries into the development of reading and writing abilities amongst adolescents, the teaching of reading, the different languages and language varieties of London school children, and the teaching of literature, especially in relation to culture, class and gender, in conditions which in France would be called disadvantaged. In France, sadly, there is a much greater disparity between Pierre Bourdieu teaching at the Collège de France and the research carried out by lecturers in the Ecoles Normales. This gulf results in the disaffection of a certain number of teachers, who submit to a kind of sociological fatalism, ('There's not much you can do for the disadvantaged,') which is based on a series of misinterpretations.

Reflecting on the difference between the logic of computers and of human reasoning J. Weizenbaum, the M.I.T. specialist in artificial intelligence, shows that computers are not capable of performing metacognitive functions and cannot cope with humour. At the very time when computers, indispensable as they are for scientific thinking – as their calculating power far outstrips that of human brains – are being developed even farther, what could be more important than to think about what can, and what ought to be 'the human use of human beings'. Weisenbaum's appeal is that we should link our distinctively human capacity for creative imagination with the effective performance of machines and think about 'outcomes' and values which the machines can be designed to promote.

In this connection, the exploratory experiences which come to us from literature allow us to develop these possibilities. Margaret Spencer has shown how this kind of literary experience (of what *could* happen) begins in early childhood and is encouraged by books specially written for children. These are in no sense a minor genre, as they are designed for the most demanding of readers: those who are discovering what reading is good for. As soon as this becomes a matter of schooled 'reading and writing' we see the inadequacy of behaviourist psychology, and even of psychology which appropriates to itself the study of 'acquisitions'. What is important for a teacher is not only to observe the behaviour and the 'responses' of the pupils, but also to understand the significance of the responses as these reveal the pupils' empathy with what they are reading, their view of the tasks they have been set and what their teachers expect of them. To help pupils to overcome their difficulties the teacher has to understand the epistemological obstacles which they encounter and how they incorporate into their vision of the world as a whole what comes to them from their dialogues with poets and storytellers. [In this connection we can see how the personal construct theory of George Kelly joins with the 'dialogic imagination' of Bakhtin in the thinking of Margaret Spencer and her colleagues.]

We should also note in this connection the relationship, and the difference, between the personal construct theory of George Kelly and that of social representation, which Serge Moscovici borrowed from Durkheim. But where Durkheim speculated almost exclusively about myths, religious representations and the belief systems of those he called 'primitives', Moscovici invites us to a more demanding reconsideration: to grasp consciously all that 'goes without saying', the 'common sense' of our day and age which is the current equivalent of these earlier myths and primitive beliefs. This system of interpretations, which is also Tajfel's 'social categorization', is a way of coding, which sorts out, organises and interprets whatever counts as the facts of dominant social norms. In this connection M. Gilly wonders about the social perceptions that teachers have of their pupils, and those that pupils have of their teachers: perceptions which derive from the school as an institution. The risk for the teacher is to see the children only as pupils and to be interested in them only in ways which seem pertinent to their accomplishing classroom tasks, to their willingness and their capacity for assimilation of what they are told. From this comes the need to pinpoint a fair number of misunderstandings which come from the discordant expectations that pupils and teachers have of each other.

Here we have the difference from the notion of 'personal constructs'. To speak of 'social representations' is to insist on modes of thinking which are socially determined and which act as ways of legitimising institutional practices. To consider personal constructs is to underline the nature of each individual original world view. In both instances, however, we have to point out what it is that influences us; not only objective situations in their material form, but also the way we represent these to ourselves, and the verbal descriptions we give them.

In this context, are not the poet and the writer those whose very role it is to help us to go beyond our worn-out ways of saying things and to 'purify the dialect of the tribe'? This would transform a commonplace, worn-out social perception into a highly particular way of looking at the world, one which is shared by an increasing number of readers, so that the utterances, new-minted by the writer in the original, finally enter the treasury of the speech which is common to all. But the teacher, in so far as she or he succeeds in introducing a new generation to reading, succeeds also in giving back to old texts the immediacy of their youth, despite their coatings of chill pedantic commentaries with which scholars have overlaid them. And it is for this reason that the friends and colleagues of Margaret Spencer will always be grateful to her, because she has given them the golden key which lets each in turn into the secret garden of *Alice's Adventures in Wonderland*.

Bakhtin, M.M. (ed. Michael Holquist) (1981), *The Dialogic Imagination: Four Essays*, University of Texas Press

Doise, Willem and Mugny, Gabriel (1984), *The Social Development of the Intellect*, International Series of Experimental Social Psychology, Pergamon Press

Durkheim, Emil (1956), *Education and Sociology*, Collier-Macmillan

Eliot, T.S., 'Four Quartets', Faber and Faber

Farr, Robert and Moscovici, Serge (eds.) (1984), *Social Representations*, Cambridge University Press

Gilly, Michel (1969), *Bon Elève, Mauvais Elève*, Colin

Gilly, Michel (1980), *Maître Elève: rôles institutionels et représentations*, P.U.F.

Kelly, George A. (1955), *The Psychology of Personal Constructs*, Vol. 1, W.W. Norton

Moscovici, Serge (1976), *Social Influence and Social Change*, Academic Press

Piatelli-Palmorin, Massimo (ed.) (1979), 'Théories du langage; théories de l'apprentissage: le débat entre Jean Piaget et Noam Chomsky', Centre Royaumont pour une science de l'homme

Tajfel, Henri (1978), *Differentiations Between Social Groups*, Academic Press

Taylor, F.W. (1967), *The Principles of Scientific Management*, Norton

Weizenbaum, J. (1976), *Computer Power and Human Reason: from Judgement to Calculation*, W.H. Freeman & Co.

Winnicott, D.W. (1971), *Playing and Reality*, Tavistock Publications

JUDITH GRAHAM

Teachers Learning about Literacy

In the current debates about reading, the missing evidence is, what do competent readers actually *do* when they read, and how do children turn instruction
– of whatever kind – into successful meaning-making. Judith Graham
explores how student teachers, encouraged to reflect on what they take for
granted about their own reading histories and textual practices, come to a
greater understanding of what children are doing as they learn. She then
shows how children, encouraged to relate the structured meanings of a complete text to its constituent features, the words and the pictures, begin to make
patterns of their learning in a subtle toing and froing which the adult encourages and supports. This kind of pedagogy (an examplar of the kind discussed
by Josie Levine) also indicates how the author and the reader come together in
a series of re-readings that are never 'just' memorising or guessing. The text,
as it stands, is all important. Here we have distinctive evidence of reading
teaching in stark contrast to the imposition of a closed system of coded rules
for word recognition.

Margaret Spencer had an effective and dramatic way of starting the literacy
courses for students in initial training at the University of London Institute of
Education. She would begin by asking for ideas from the assembled group about
what they thought children had to do to read a page. Back came the answers,
more or less the same every year. Readers had to know the alphabet, to know
what sounds the letters make, to process print from left to right, to read every
word, to know about syllables, to recognise some words on sight. Margaret
would gather these contributions in without comment and when all was done she
would distribute a sheet of the toughest bit of William Faulkner that she could
find (the opening page of *The Unvanquished*) and ask everyone to read it. In the
silence that followed one could observe alarmed, darting eyes as students confronted
Faulkner's thickly embedded language, 'swarming with syllables and letters'.

When Margaret considered that the students had struggled enough, she would
re-open discussion by asking what everyone had to do to read that page. 'I kept on
reading even though I didn't understand much.' 'I let my eyes race ahead to where
the dialogue came in; I came back to the long descriptive paragraph afterwards.' 'I
scanned it, got an impression, selected odd bits to try to get a sense of what it was
about.' 'I created a picture in my mind's eye of these children playing.' 'I had to keep
re-reading, going back to see what on earth was going on.' 'I decided it didn't matter
that I didn't know what Vicksburg was, or "ponderable though passive recalcitrance
of topography" or "recapitulate mimic furious victory" as long as I held onto the
idea of these two children's games being spoilt by someone.' 'I read the end first.' 'I
had no difficulty with the words on the page – just with the meanings!'

Steadily the group shared understandings of the passage, adding knowledge gleaned from film, TV, school history lessons and other books to the clues in the text (smokehouse, Negro, Philadelphy, *that* summer) to conclude that we were in the time of the American Civil War. Drawing on memories of playing, perhaps with sand and water, perhaps with toy soldiers, perhaps with any old thing being used to represent something else, we knew the boys (why did we assume the narrator was a boy?) were preparing a pretend battle, yet 'doom' was not the language of children's games and we knew a real tension existed between the narrator (whom we now felt must be white) and the triumphant Loosh.

At some stage, Margaret would read aloud the passage and 'put the tune into it'. This always gave us a purchase on those centipede sentences (there is one with over 100 words in it) and enabled us to hear repeated notes ('living' is echoed by 'lived') and we begin to see that the battle of Vicksburg is taking place at the same time as the children's game.

By the end of the session, a different model of what we have to do to read a page had emerged. It had much more to do with recognising that words on the page depend for their life on how much we already know; that the meaning we bring to the page derives from our accumulated experiences of life, from our understanding of the way words are used, from other books read and from media images and many other sources. It was clear that holding data in our heads, revising it in the light of new data, re-reading, leaping forward to gain clues more quickly, to reduce uncertainty, visualising the scene, 'hearing' the voices, knowing about tension – that all these play a part.

What had happened to the earlier list? It looked a little threadbare by comparison, not to say irrelevant. The rest of the one-year course would be spent persuading students that the model of reading that we had jointly constructed – one whereby we read by entering into dialogue with an author – was a model that beginning readers need to operate also.

People find this very hard to believe. If you ask intending teachers (or perhaps any adults) if they can remember learning to read, most will have no clearer memory of learning to read than they have of learning to talk. Those who do remember speak of flash cards, reading schemes, sounding out, blending. The memories are always of the bits and pieces of literacy. Even those with no clear memories conclude that someone must have taught them 'the basics' to enable them to decode print. It is the assumption that we owe our literacy to methodical teaching of 'basics' that is one of the hardest to shift when we are asking student teachers to consider where their full literacy has come from. They in their turn will have their persuasion skills taxed when they meet their pupils' parents, who have similar assumptions.

So our next task, with our intending literacy teachers, is to dig into their memories again and unearth the literacy events which they have discounted and yet which seem to us now to have a far more critical role than any decoding skills. Jean-Paul Sartre's account in *Les Mots* may be something to share with students. Sartre was used to hearing stories told by his mother, often at bath-time. Although he had insisted upon owning books of his own, he had been unable to make them work for him, despite kissing them, beating them and making them creak. He put them in his mother's lap and to his bewilderment the mother of the halting, haphazard bath-time stories becomes a fluent, confident stranger emitting sentences too polished and perfect for Sartre to relate to. Eventually, however, he begins to prefer 'prefabricated tales' to his mother's impoverished inventions and finally he sees no reason why he should not usurp the reader's role and so he gives himself private lessons. 'I climbed on to my folding bedstead with Hector Malot's *Sans Famille*, which I knew by heart and, half-reciting, half- deciphering it, I went through every page, one after another; when the last was turned, I knew how to read'.

Given this sort of prompting, students demonstrate almost as sharp a recall as Sartre, and we begin to give value to their early literacy biographies. One student remembers pretending to read aloud to her cat because no one else would listen; another feigned illness so that a string of adults would come to read to her. One loved the gold letters on her parents' books and another pored over *Alice*, long before she could read, because she liked the type 'with its curly bits'. Another demanded, again and again, the fairy stories she was frightened of, especially *The Snow Queen*. *Hiawatha*, with its frightening pictures, was hidden (and unearthed) again and again. Memories of early writing surface, too. One student had hypothesised that difficult words had xs and zs in them, so she always wrote her name with lots of them. (Her name was Thomasina.) Another was hospitalised and wrote a letter home, a page covered with loops which let her mother know that she hated the porridge. And all the time, with luck, books were being read, stories told and writing demonstrated. Huey, as early as 1908, knew what Sartre describes and what our students come to believe about themselves. 'Many a child cannot remember when reading began, having pored over books and nursery jingles and fairy tales that were read to him until he could read them for himself' (*The Psychology and Pedagogy of Reading*).

Feeling more interested in where their own literacy is rooted, students are ready to look more closely at a representative early literacy exchange. Many of those with children of their own are encouraged to monitor their shared book experiences and bring back to the group valuable evidence of how children become readers.

I might tell how Jessica, my neighbour's child, is becoming a reader. Jessica is just three. For a few days before her birthday, I'd been sharing *Where the Wild Things Are* with her. Unlike Sartre's mother, I cannot let Sendak's sentences 'roll nobly towards their end without sparing [Jessica] a comma'. Sartre's little volumes cannot have had illustrations. Sendak's illustrations, in common with many modern picture books, *are* the story as much as the text is and Jessica needs time to look. I try to show students how Jessica lets the book teach her how to read. The notion of 'texts that teach', which has been such a fruitful concept over the past half dozen years and which Margaret Spencer has done much to illuminate, is difficult for students to accept initially, so I monitor each reading Jessica and I share and allow students to see how Sendak is as much a teacher as I am.

At the very first reading Jessica looks carefully at the pictures. She comments on the size of the bare feet of the monster on the book's cover and the hammer with which Max is making mischief. Subsequently, she does not refer to these details, having learnt that the story hinges on different things. Similarly, at first reading, she worries that Max had no chair in his bedroom. 'He'll have to sit on the bed' (to eat the supper his forgiving mother has brought him). Later, in the final illustration, she notices the more significant detail that Max's wolf-suit is slipping off his head, revealing the tame child inside. She is not yet picking up that his dazed smile, hand to head, probably indicates that he has been dreaming. I will let students know when this understanding occurs; in the meantime it serves to demonstrate the multi-layered nature of this text.

If it's 'texts that do the teaching', what, students ask, is my role or the teacher's role. In fact it is a full one and essential in both global and particular ways. I tell them that Jessica had nightmares after the last monster book I shared with her (Russell Hoban and Quentin Blake's *Monsters*), so, if I am not to be mighty unpopular with her mother I will have to tread carefully with this one. Students often know *Where the Wild Things Are* well, but they may not know that the book took some time to be accepted in this country and many adults feel rather doubtful about it still. On the other hand, children are seldom frightened by it, almost certainly because Max is so totally in charge of the wild things and because his mother's enduring love is symbolised by the still-hot supper.

My role, in introducing this book to Jessica, is to ensure that she identifies with Max, feeling some of his power. She reads the expression on Max's face promptly on the turning of each page, noting that, even when his bedroom turns into a forest, 'he's happy'. But before he is clearly happy again, there are several pages of Max looking tough or superior and even one opening, when he meets a wild thing for the first time, where he looks distinctly dismayed. My role here is to keep Jessica aware of how strong Max is. So we 'become ' Max. We prop the book up against the sofa, face the monsters stoutly and conjure them to 'Be still!'. We authorise the wild rumpus and then join in. As our gallumphing takes us past the sofa I flick over those magical textless pages until we jointly command the monster to 'Stop!'. Having tamed the monsters, Jessica is free to inspect them, and by a third reading I am sure she knows them individually. I would wager that the monster whom Margaret Spencer's son called Granny twenty-five years ago is the very same one whom Jessica calls the sister monster.

My role is also to encourage Jessica to make personal connections. Max's hammering reminds her of her grandfather who is making a staircase up to the loft in Jessica's flat. 'My mummy doesn't like the noise,' says Jessica. 'Maybe Max's mummy didn't like Max's banging noise either,' I reply, acknowledging the relevance and bringing her back to the book. Every child will make different links; what is important is that students understand that this drawing on first-hand experience is part of the reading process. Probably only a fraction of this connecting process can ever be made explicit. What is clear is that it is essential and is the same for three-year-old Jessica as it is for adults reading Faulkner.

On the third or fourth reading of *Where the Wild Things Are*, Jessica starts to read along with me. She already knows whole phrases of Sendak's distinctive text off by heart. What is my role here? Clearly I must not alter a single word of his carefully-constructed text. I am always distressed by a phenomenon that is probably widespread in teacher-training establishments. Look through a handful of picture books in our resource library and pencilled in above the author's words are anonymous students' ideas of what is more appropriate. There must be a research project in examining what assumptions lie behind the alterations and simplifications made. No, I keep the text the same, Jessica murmurs in unison and soon she will be in a position to give herself 'private lessons', just as Sartre did. Sendak's text must remain the one constant. At our first sharing of the book there was so much incidental talk that Jessica would not have known what was text. With each subsequent reading, there may still be much running commentary, but it never takes the same form and so throws Sendak's unchanging text into relief.

'Do you run your finger under the print?' the students ask. 'Not quite,' I reply and try to catch what is an 'approach' governed by what the child herself shows me she is interested in. As is common with many children of this age, she already knows how the print is different from the illustrations and that it 'tells' me what to say. (Does this understanding of the symbolic nature of writing come gradually or is it, as Sartre suggests, a sudden realisation? Frank Smith calls it the 'great intellectual leap'.) I can reinforce this in many ways. When I open the book at the first sentence and wait, Jessica says 'One day Max weared his wolf-suit' (Text: The night Max wore his wolf-suit and made mischief of one kind...or another). I ask her where it says that, and she runs her finger backwards and forwards over the line of writing. I say 'That's right,' and we turn over. Sometimes Jessica turns over before I have finished reading and I say, 'Wait for me to finish reading' and I point to where I am. We come to words made distinctive by Sendak, either because they are alone on the page or printed in upper-case letters. We both stab our fingers on the 'BE STILL!'. Perhaps Sendak's biggest contribution to countless children's understanding of print is the last page of the book where the words 'and it was still hot' stand alone. Because it is such an emphatic statement it is easy to enunciate each word clearly and point to each at the same time. However, students need to know that children often bristle and reject pedagogic moves of this nature if they are overdone or at the expense of the enjoyment of the story, the entering of the 'secondary world' that an author has created. We must be guided by the child's interest. Many children pay attention to the print that is within illustrations, reading it off readily in the way they read print in context in the world outside. Jessica notices that Max's private boat has Max printed on the bow. (She also, incidentally, knows the writing must be round the other side, when Max is on his homeward journey. So much for Piaget.) She may soon link that with Max's signature on his monster drawing at the start of the story.

And so we observe Jessica's journey towards becoming a reader. We listen to and read other accounts of slightly older readers demanding countless re-readings and developing favourite books whilst they turn themselves into readers. We listen to tapes of still older children and reflect on their miscues and what those miscues reveal of the children's reading experience and view of the task. The patterning, allusions and cohesive features that make for degrees of difficulty in texts are also usefully revealed through the analysis of miscues. Gradually our intending teachers perceive that what is 'basic' in literacy is not to do with sounds and letters, with cracking a grapho-phonic code. Those skills are acquired in the comfortable pursuit of meaning in significant text and context. That those skills are also acquired in the much slower act of writing also becomes evident as students watch and monitor the steady development of early writing towards standard orthography and control over conventions. When the call goes out for a 'return to basics', students and teachers need, ever more enthusiastically, to devote time to the sharing of books which create and invite co-creation of a secondary world.

Fortunately, despite periodic, reactionary and over-publicised statements, there is plenty of support for this broader understanding of what is basic to reading, not least in HMI reports and National Curriculum documents and the excellent Primary Language Record. As with all learning, however, authoritative statements are only convincing if they interact with students' own observations, reflections, debate and research.

What I would like to give a flavour of, to close this piece, is how we work with students on B.Ed. courses to raise their (and our own) awareness of the act of reading. We are, inevitably and rightly, I believe, some distance from a study of literature which demands great works and a refined sensibility in the reader who approaches them. The legacy of this approach to literature-teaching is a room of silent students waiting to be told what to think. The personal responses students make to what they read are important, not least because we observe how young children invariably bring personal experiences to bear on stories they are told. However, beyond the enjoyable and significant unearthing of the individual links we all make, it is evident that we employ other and more subtle understandings to make the text mean.

We saw Margaret's students doing that with the opening of *The Unvanquished*. Our students are asked to keep journals of books they read, such as Rebecca West's *The Return of the Soldier*. What is exciting in their record of expectations, predictions, responses and reflections is how they indicate their understanding of narrative conventions. One student, with years of reading experience behind her, writes after the first twenty pages: 'All this golden sunlight, beauty, peace and complacency. It's got to be punctured. Rebecca West is setting it up in order to knock it down. And why has it got to be shattered? These insufferable snobs have got to be taken down a peg or two. Things have got to change.' A much less experienced student speaks initially of being wearied by 'so much boring and flowery description'. After discussion, argument and more reading, boring description is revealed as full of telling detail which can be added up and organised so that expectations are aroused. This sort of alert reading gives us the satisfaction of noting that in the flowery description, there are slight references to a bad dream, a dead child, no letter for a fortnight, brittle beautiful things. All sound as minor notes which are held until their time for darkening the text arrives. Students note these, often as mysteries, and read on, tolerating the uncertainty until explanations emerge. The more experienced readers seem also to note such detail as the 'veracious' tortoise-shell brush owned by Kitty ['Be careful. Tortoise snaps so.'] and the 'unveracious' tortoise-shell handle of Mrs Gray's deplorable umbrella and to let these details impinge on their consciousnesses as symbols of the class divide and of the temporary and tenuous hold Kitty has over her privileged happiness. Another student rejects the book initially, saying she is not interested in 'such unbelievable women'. It is almost as if she believes Rebecca West did not have the skill to write about more agreeable people. The two cousins, who would indeed be unpardonable in real life and possibly unbelievable in current life, become fascinating if we can see them as skilful constructions of an author writing in 1918. Rebecca West intends us to think ill of Kitty; she plants enough clues. We add them up and earn ourselves the readerly satisfaction of seeing her mightily discomfited.

From Jessica's active, game-like engagement with the wild things to the confident construction of reality in adult novels is a path of great interest and complexity. It is one of the privileges of working with Initial Training students that we can keep both ends of the continuum in sight, that we can move about on this spectrum, allowing the similarities to illuminate the whole process. Teaching teachers about literacy becomes a question of discovering what we take for granted about our literary competence and acknowledging that the major difference between ourselves and our young pupils is that we have read, and have had read to us, a great many more books. In these difficult, pressured days, when teachers seem to be in a state of 'high perpetual alarm' (Margaret's phrase), the only way that children learn the lessons of reading is still if their teachers make sure they do a lot of it. This was the message of Margaret's retirement speech and, although Margaret has sown many another fruitful seed over the years, I believe it has been her consistent message throughout her years as a teacher and writer.

PHILLIDA SALMON

Old Age and Storytelling

'The art of storytelling,' says Paul Ricoeur[1], 'is not so much a way of reflecting on time as a way of taking it for granted.' In personal remembrance of things past, life and storytelling seem to have a reciprocal relationship. Oral narration is a particular reworking of experience which the listener receives as a tale, beginning and ending in the present. As she looks at the viewpoint of an older teller recalling her life for her younger contemporary, Phillida Salmon is critical of the school-based opportunism of this encounter. She points out its temporal, psychological and social complexity and shows that there are within it more important latent possibilities. As an educational psychologist, Phillida Salmon has the extra insight and pedagogic skill to make teachers' common-place assumptions, their 'taken-for-grantedness', into new roots of personal and social growth. Young listeners and older storytellers, she says, may be able to 'transform both their perspectives'. As this is an apt description of all teaching and learning, this essay is an appropriate place to consider, in the afterglow of its wisdom, the extent to which our freedom as teachers to invent and go forward is embedded in our sense of history and our common shared responsibilities.

'You must have so many memories!' says an 80th birthday card. Its message echoes the approach of a growing movement in our society, a movement which addresses old people as the repositories of human history. One of the by-products of this movement has been a transformation of the connotations of reminiscence. So far from conjuring up the image of Grandad tediously repeating his war story for the *n*th time, reminiscence now carries clear overtones of importance and respect. There is reminiscence therapy, included in the activity programme of many institutional settings for the elderly. This therapy has its own language and resources. It speaks of memories as enhancing self worth, as providing the basis of one-to-one and group relationships, as offering anchors in the confusion of dementia. Reminiscence therapy draws on a variety of props and materials: packs of memory joggers, comics or magazines, items of clothing or domestic objects. There is a series of cards entitled Nostalgia, which represents, for instance, old vehicles, royal personages, or banner headlines from the past. All these aids have as their function the calling up, in old people, of personal memories, to be shared with staff or fellow inmates.

More broadly, old people's memories are now increasingly seen as a rich resource in the construction of recent history. The situation of those who have experienced, first-hand, such major events as the First World War, the 30s Depression or the flight from the Uganda of Idi Amin, make them valuable consultants for anyone engaged in the task of historical reconstruction. In the work of Age Exchange or reminiscence theatre, the dramatic enactment of life in a wartime munitions factory or London during the Blitz, draws, necessarily, upon the personal memories of those who actually lived through these situations and who, through contributing their memories, act as vital partners in such work. The remembered experience of old people also provides the essential material of the growing educational movement known as oral history. Many school projects now involve children in interviews with their elders, whose memories are then reworked into accounts of local or national history or incorporated within displays or exhibitions about life in earlier times.

On the one hand, the attitude which underlies all these developments is surely something to be glad about. Reminiscence therapy and oral history, in their different ways, acknowledge the human worth of old age. They define the heritage of a long life as having its own unique value. They insist that elderly people have something important to offer society, something from which younger people, if they will, can learn.

All this represents a welcome departure from the profound ageism which, in most spheres of life, characterises our society. Yet if the potential of this movement is to be realised, we need, I think, to look very closely at what is actually involved when old people are invited to tell their stories.

In the scenarios I have described, there is typically a dichotomy between elderly people and those who act as audience for their memories. In a simple way, old people are defined as possessing stories, younger people as not possessing them. The stories themselves are seen as being *about the past*, and the narrators as interesting because they have lived in that past, and can therefore tell how things were. This means that the remembered experience of an old person is viewed from a vantage point which takes it as *contrast*, to point up the present. The trouble is that to a life which is seen as fixed in the past – in times and places which are essentially 'other' – its audience can only bring, at best, a patronising kind of admiration. From the safe, secure superiority of the modern present, the listener wonders, condescendingly, how they managed in those days, living so primitively, understanding so little of what we know today. And as the representatives of those far-off times, old people themselves become quaint, oddities, museum exhibits to be marvelled at. Anachronistic, old-fashioned, irrelevant, they can hardly be expected to be taken seriously in the modern world.

Characteristically, being old means being denied a personal stake in contemporary life. It is often said that old people have no tomorrows, only yesterdays. In one sense this is true, but perhaps *only* in one sense. The human meaning of time is surely much more complex. As people sometimes discover, on learning of their own mortal illness, the brevity of a future need not render it futile or invalid. Whether we are old or young, being alive means that we are *present*, as human beings, in the world of today, and, therefore, of tomorrow.

In an interview he gave to Richard Ingrams, the cellist Paul Tortelier rejected the usual ascription of old age and insisted on being called a contemporary.

> He likes to remind the musical public that there are still a
> few people around who can compose melody. In his eyes
> there is no such thing as Modern Music. Clutching my
> hand he says passionately, 'If you touch me you will see that
> I am alive. So I am a contemporary, am I not?'

Tortelier's perspective is, of course, that of an exceptional man. One aspect of this distinctiveness is that, because of his outstanding and continuing musical career, a high premium – in every sense – is set on his personal story. The situation of Tortelier is very different from that of most old men and women, whose lives carry, for the usual audience of their stories, no such special charisma. The narrators of oral history do not as a rule hold positions of prestige or influence in contemporary life. And this fact has some profound implications for the stories they can, and cannot, tell.

So far from being the prerogative of old age, stories do, in fact, constitute the very substance of the whole human enterprise. It is actually through the stories we tell that we engage, with others, in our most intimate and our most far-reaching undertakings. Our personal narratives give us each our own unique place in the human world. They enable and entitle us to adopt particular stances, forms of agency, ways of being. And the moments when we tell our stories are precisely those moments of potential personal opportunity, of possibilities of human enlargement. Making a place for themselves in the world of the infant school, even very young children tell each other stories which will act to establish their rights and status in the group. In older childhood and adolescence, personal narratives become more first-hand, more elaborate, more distinctively shaped for a particular audience. The tale you tell your peer group is rather different from the private story told only to your special friend. Between lovers, two personal stories, uniquely framed, are told conjointly, delicately interweaving their strands into a tapestry which can hardly be disentangled. The shared story is not just a preparation for the relationship between them or a commentary on it: the story actually constitutes their way of relating.

In the course of living, we all tell much more limited stories than this. But here, too, the tale we offer is the way in which we establish our future position in the context of our offering it. As a candidate for employment, as a newly qualified teacher, as a defendant in the dock, we muster what account we can, to convince the audience of our worthiness, our potential, accomplishment, competence or good faith. In these, as in all story-telling contexts, it matters what we say. Consequences for the future hang upon the narrative we present.

For an old person cast in the role of storyteller, all this is likely to be rather different. To the usual sort of audience, the narrative is likely to be of essentially academic interest. It seems to speak of how things were, in a world long gone, and thus to have little import for living now. For a primary school pupil doing a project, or for a staff member at a day centre, the precise details of the story do not really matter. Whether this old woman did marry her first suitor, or another one, whether or not this old man followed his father into ship-building; it really makes no difference. Any story will do. But in fact this listening attitude has major consequences for the kind of narrative that will emerge. The best, the fullest, the most illuminating stories are those whose true details need, genuinely, urgently, both to be told and to be heard. Because the position taken towards old people is typically so dismissive, their human stories, if they can be told at all, can appear only in the most truncated and distorted forms.

It is, of course, the relationship between storyteller and audience which governs what can be said, and heard. In the current movement to validate the experience of elderly people – oral history or reminiscence therapy – this is essentially a relationship between relative strangers. Such a relationship, of its nature, gives pride of place to History with a capital H: a history which is necessarily generalised, simplified and patterned by current interest. The particular, personal, idiosyncratic details of living are of secondary interest only. An elderly woman, trying to describe her early adult life, may notice signs of impatience and boredom in her listener, who is only waiting for her to speak about her experience of the First World War. In this situation, it is not very surprising that old people sometimes magnify or embroider their personal involvement in the macro-events of official history. To have been under fire in the trenches, to have lived on scraps and gone barefoot in the Depression, may be the only way of holding the interest and respect of your audience.

For elderly storytellers and their listeners, one obvious fact glares out: their present predicament. While in the past they may have lived as respected participants of the community, contributing to social life in a whole variety of ways, most old men and women are now more or less disconnected from the social nexus, unable to make much contribution, or help to develop the lives around them. Whether explicitly or not, this fact has its own huge impact on the story. For human stories go on and, from the vantage point of their telling, earlier events are seen as leading up to later ones; and the current end of the story in some sense governs what is to be made of its earlier phases.

There is a study by Daniel Bertaux which illustrates this very vividly. Bertaux collected the life histories of men who had worked in the French bakery trade, interviewing them and their wives, in great detail, about their apprenticeships, their bakery work, their marriages and family life, their leisure, health and retirement. He looked particularly at the accounts given by two groups of men: those who had succeeded, and those who had not succeeded, in becoming self-employed and setting up their own bakeries. The two sets of stories were strikingly different. For instance, both groups of men had experience, as apprentices, of three years of almost intolerably arduous work. In return for their board and lodging, they suffered a daily routine which involved being roughly awoken at three a.m., work in the bakery for nine hours, then, after a four-hour break for rest and sleep, many hours delivering bread and cakes, followed by additional duties in the shop or garden. In this situation, harsh, even brutal, treatment was the rule; falling asleep or slowing up on the job was usually punished with punches and kicks from the baker. Yet, as Bertaux found, the stories which these two groups of men gave of this period in their lives differed markedly. If the storyteller had never succeeded in establishing himself independently, but had remained employed all his working life, his account was likely to emphasise all the tribulations and humiliations he had suffered as an apprentice: the bullying, the exploitation. For those who had become independent, these details were characteristically lacking or glossed over; what their accounts made salient were experiences that were pivotal to their eventual upward social mobility.

How their present disempowerment comes to influence their personal stories may be different for different old people; but it is likely to have a profound effect. The punchline, the 'point' of some stories, whether explicit or not, is that of a dismaying contrast. This may be more or less affirmative. 'You might not think so, to look at me now, but I was really a somebody.' Or, 'If I had known then that it would all come to this...' The here-and-now may give a poignant edge to past glories, or it may simply cancel them out.

All human stories are, obviously, essentially affected by the psychology of their time. In necessarily trying to make sense of their own present predicament, old people are likely to draw, intuitively, implicitly, on the individualistic psychology of our own culture. This, at its most broad, portrays human beings as closely linked in with their destinies. That is, though individuals are not necessarily seen as *responsible* for everything that happens to them, their fate is nevertheless assumed to fit closely with the kind of person that they are. In such a philosophy, the disempowered situation of old age is seen not as the outcome of questionable socioeconomic arrangements, but as the product of ageing itself. It is not surprising, therefore, that many elderly people, in the stories they tell of their lives, make recourse to an ageist psychology, which portrays them as deteriorated people, whose present situation merely reflects their own social non-productiveness. In many such stories, there is a sad, even guilty refrain: this state of things is no more than I deserve.

Another side of the same kind of psychology is the enterpreneurial mentality, which is particularly evident in the present-day political ethos. This sees individuals as essentially free to make their own way in life, as possessing personal autonomy, as determining their own personal destinies. It is, I think, a psychology to fit male, rather than most female lives. Just as the Thatcherite ideology is more easily lived out by men, so, in telling the story of their lives, there are probably more elderly men than women who account for their experience in these terms. This is a view in which agency and intentions hold the central place, in which the events of a life are seen as failures or successes, for which the person is himself ultimately responsible. However inapplicable it may be to the lives of most women – and, of course, ultimately to those of men, too – this philosophy of personal autonomy does, I think, exert a huge influence on the thinking of people of our time. For instance, in the radio programme, *Desert Island Discs*, which invites distinguished individuals to reflect back over their lives, in conjunction with choosing eight records, the most popular record choice of all must be Frank Sinatra's 'I did it my way'.

Yet ultimately, this philosophy cannot encompass, cannot sustain, the living of human life. It is not just that personal destiny involves the unpredictable, that we are all subject to unforeseen, often deeply unwanted, events, to the capriciousness, the haphazardness, the arbitrariness of life. More than this, our living is essentially, inextricably, embedded in a historical, social and cultural world. As individuals, we are interdependent with this world; this means that our actions cannot be separated from their human surroundings. Of many people who have written helpfully about this, I should like to draw on David Plath and to quote from a chapter he wrote called 'Old Age Brinkmanship'[2]:

> We are born alone and we die alone, each an organism
> genetically unique. But we mature or decline together; in
> the company of others we mutually domesticate the wild
> genetic pulse as we go about shaping ourselves into persons
> after the vision of our group's heritage. Perhaps the growth
> and ageing of an organism can be described well enough in
> terms of stages and transitions in the individual as a monad
> entity. But in a social animal the life course changes have to
> be described in terms of a collective fabricating of selves, a
> mutual building of biographies.

In Plath's words, we go about shaping ourselves into persons 'after the vision of our group's heritage'. When we arrive into life, it is as part of an already existing, inter-subjective world, a pre-established symbolic order. It is this world, this order, which must guide our own living, on which we must draw, as individual people, to sustain our own participation in human life. This means that our personal story must fit into the existing, on-going stories of which we find ourselves a part.

But human history means that stories change. What passes for the best, the most credible, the most interesting, the truest human story in one era will not do in another. In changing contexts of inter-subjectivity, there are different vocabularies, different grammars, another discourse for living and accounting for living. Because it is socially constituted, the story of personal life is histori-cally relative and specific to particular social contexts. What is crucially distinc-tive about being old is the situation of spanning, in oneself, the living of qualitatively different human stories.

For old people as storytellers, this has many and sometimes quite compli-cated implications. The most obvious consequence of their situation is that of non-intelligibility. For a story to make sense, the audience and the narrator have to share a vast reservoir of taken-for-granted understandings: assumptions which, like the air we breathe, need not, and *cannot* be put into words. But where, as, for example, in an oral history project, the teller and the audience differ by at least two generations, the cultural gulf is likely to be as wide as the one between an Indian storyteller and his baffled, non-comprehending British listeners.

Still more fundamentally, because of the cultural embeddedness in which we all live, the *value* which was accorded to the projects, activities, involvements of the old person's younger life is no longer present and perhaps not even recognisable in the cultural world of today. The whole standpoint from which life was lived and mean-ing given is altered, perhaps greatly altered. For elderly people living now, this is probably most particularly the case where women are concerned.

When an old woman speaks now of her life, lived from the early part of the century, with her young adulthood falling in the 20s, she is likely to be describing beliefs, practices and undertakings which are not merely alien but even to some extent actually repugnant to her much younger women listeners. Her commitment to monogamy, to family and domestic life, her unquestioning acceptance of her economic, social and sexual dependence on a man, her total blindness to her own 'oppression': all this seems to a modern generation to be almost unbelievably benighted. The goals of such a life: decency, respectability, bringing up a family, standing by your man, may look to today's young woman quite pitifully limited. Measured against feminist standards, this woman's life project shrinks into litt-leness; an unimpressive thing, carrying no inspiration for today.

On her side, the elderly storyteller is likely to be quite as much out of sympathy with her listeners' perspectives. Part of this has to do with privacy and reserve. What is nowadays unquestioningly accepted as public currency, in spheres of personal relations, for instance, or sexual experience, was, in earlier generations, something you very much kept to yourself. The expectation, or demand, that an old woman should tell her audience – perhaps an audience composed of virtual strangers – all about her most intimate relationships, is likely to seem an intrusion of the most blatant sort. Nor, in the culture of fifty years ago, were women's lives perceived as proper material for telling. History itself, as many people have said, is a history of men's doings, men's interests, men's lives. Even beyond this, the consciousness of pre-feminist times, in defining women's spheres as essentially supportive of male activities, viewed female lives as not salient in themselves. As those involved in oral history are apt to discover, elderly women are often very reluctant to speak about their own experience. And their non-comprehension, perhaps even horror, at the lives being led now by young women, is likely to make for difficulty in the fundamentally communicative task of story-telling.

In the picture I have painted, elderly storytellers and their audience face each other across a huge cultural gulf. This makes it almost impossible to achieve the very goal for which reminiscence and oral history are valued: learning from the past. As long as the standpoint from which a story is told and the standpoint from which it is heard remain unintegrated, nothing can really be understood. It is only in the possibility of *recasting*, reconstituting, a human narrative, that new understandings become possible. Where the narrator and the listener stand estranged, there can be no such reworking. The old woman tells her life story to a group of adolescent girls. She is embedded in the value system in terms of which her younger life made sense. They, on their side, listen to her account from a standpoint which counters and dismisses her vital undertakings. Nothing is really learned in this situation, on either side.

As storytellers, the old are valued as the narrators of history. Their audience comes in the hope of learning something more than the events themselves: something which will really *explain* how things came to be like that. How could people do that, let that happen, why didn't they, how could they not have seen? etc. etc. But somehow, in these life stories, this vital material never seems to appear. The events are told as they were experienced at the time, embedded as they were in the very conditions which allowed things to happen as they did. As Leonard Cohen, the song-writer, remarked in a tv programme, about one of his songs:

> That was in the 60s. But we didn't know it was the 60s then.
> We thought it was just ordinary time.

And yet, it is the relation of two different standpoints, two ways of telling a story, which offers, potentially, an escape from cultural constraints and an illumination of ultimate human possibility. As long as we remain embedded, we can never see the channels through which our contemporary cultural script obliges us to run. Old people, embedded in the channels of *their* earlier lives, remain as imprisoned as the younger people trapped in contemporary ones. Only if they can, together, bring their most fundamental assumptions and conventions into relation, may they be able to rework what each has taken for granted, and so transform both their perspectives. In this, the act of story-telling has to become what it should always be: not a one-sided act, but a collaborative creative endeavour.

A rare instance of how this may sometimes be possible is the story of Simone de Beauvoir. Her life was, of course, a very remarkable one, lived at the forefront of the social and political struggles of her day and involving radical and personally courageous activity which she continued late into old age. This life – the life of a woman – has inspired very many other women, across a wide social and cultural span. I think the story of de Beauvoir could not have been so exemplary had it not been that she herself *told* it, throughout the course of her life, in autobiography, fiction and, perhaps most crucially, in her lifelong correspondence with other women. Her continuous engagement in life and her on-going dialogue with others, whose experience and concerns covered a huge range of female situations, meant that the vocabulary she developed, and the terms of reference she used, had meaning within the lives of women of all ages. Her own account proved to have great power. It enabled her to resist the various attempts that were made to assimilate her story into demeaning kinds of narrative: to dismiss her personal situation as the product of social or sexual pathology. She remained, throughout her life, the author of her story.

But finally, de Beauvoir did not compose her story all alone. If a life story is to have import for other lives, to make a difference to ways of living now, it has to be constructed together with others. That means that old people need to remain a part of on-going life. Only in the meeting of different views of human experience, engaged and eager exchanges of storytellers and their listeners, may rest the possibility of moving beyond where we now are, of glimpsing new horizons to human life.

This essay originated in an address to a conference of the British Psychological Society, Psychotherapy Section, on 'Rhetoric, Discourse and Psychotherapy' in Dumfries, May 1989.

[1]Ricoeur, Paul (1988), *Time and Narrative*, University of Chicago Press
[2]Plath, D.W. (ed.) (1983), *Work and Life Course in Japan*, Albany, State University of New York Press

MARGARET MEEK

Literacy: redescribing reading

The study of literacy brings together writers, analysts and researchers in many disciplines. The complexities of learning to read and write are woven into sets of social practices. Yet children come to understand reading very early and to do it well in the first decade of their lives. Some of the recurring issues in earlier essays emerge here in the context of change: the notion is that reading, far from being an accepted set of traditional operations, is always in need of redescription. The central issue lies not in ways of teaching reading but in what children think it is good for.

Although we cannot really separate reading from the other functions of language – talking, listening and writing – we do it all the time. The reasons for this are historical and complicated, but the persistent rationalisation is that, by demonstrating in their early years that they can learn to read, children show that they can learn in the way that counts in school. So reading is often used interchangeably with 'education' and 'literacy', as in 'well-read'. Amongst other things, literacy is the set of social practices for which schools are held responsible in a society which writes to itself. Whenever there is bad news about education generally, standards of reading and writing are held responsible for more generalised failure. There are always six million illiterates: not always the same people. But no one says in the same breath that there is accurate evidence from Book Trust that children spend many millions of pounds of their own money on books.

Those who criticise reading and writing rarely take any responsibility for their improvement. One of the great myths of literacy is that there is never enough of it around, nor enough of it to go round. Divorced from authoritative studies of its roots, untethered to any social context in the lives of real people, unconceptualised for the most part, literacy floats through educational debates as a single independent variable, invoked whenever children or adults learn to read, when writing is examined for marks and where applicants write letters for jobs. More often than not literacy is described and argued about with little reference to its rich history, ingenious technologies, institutional frameworks and the different unpredictable uses that people have made of it. The sixteenth-century miller, Menocchio, whose life in reading is so vibrantly described by Carlo Ginzburg in *The Cheese and the Worms*, is someone whose schooled reading let him acquire the texts and the knowledge of the inquisitors who accused him of heresy. His story also shows that his contact with written culture released for reflexive understanding a wealth of oral tradition: 'the popular roots of a considerable part of high European culture, both medieval and post medieval'.

We can profitably think of 'fruitful exchanges moving in both directions between high and popular cultures' when we look at modern stories for children against the background of the lore and language of the playground which appears most vividly just before children learn to read.

The social processes of literacy have always been related to what is produced by technologies, especially those used in institutions for specific purposes. Michael Clanchy shows how the monasteries acted as scribal co-operatives in medieval England when the cost of quill pens was high, which made them a privilege of the wealthy. Learning to write in school now may happen round a computer. The suggestion is that, two decades hence, the young will have easy access to the new machines for all the purposes now served by pens and pencils. How likely is this, when we know that, historically, access to powerful technologies has always been socially restricted?

More particularly, we should ask what our current understanding of the differences between girls' and boys' uses of writing and reading contributes to our awareness of literacy in general. Understanding 'the novel as a form which women writers have used to question and challenge men's appropriation of women's experiences', as Jane Miller puts it, changes the ways in which literature is now read in classrooms. The discourses that arise from different interpretations of texts are only just beginning to emerge as a matter for serious study.

These are only hints of some of the things that have to be considered in the history of literacy. Comparative studies of cultural differences of the kind embarked on by Brian Street and others are necessary to dispel easy generalisations about what people value in their literacy. The prophetic enthusiasm of Freire has to be compared and contrasted with the apparent inability of traditionally literate societies to urge more people to read and write better than their ancestors.

Teachers helping a child to begin to read or marking pupils' writing face the implications of the fact that, although we have a thousand years of vernacular texts we have had only 120 years of compulsory instruction in reading and *scribing*, and fewer still of any child being helped and encouraged to *compose* in written language right from the start. We can read a scholarly modern study of literacy that doesn't mention literature, or one which speaks of reading as if it were a neutral process apart from what is being read. There are books of literacy criticism which refer to 'the reader' with no sign of curiosity about how readers become, or what counts as being able to read the texts under discussion. Instead of benefiting from academic investigations of its nature and social practices, 'literacy', as part of learning, suffers from the divisions of academic labours and subject exclusivenesses. A PhD in literacy risks accusations of being over-generalised or hybrid if it doesn't seem to be grounded in a recognised scholastic discipline: history, sociology, psychology, rather than in studies of its use, both in and outside school.

These things are said as prologue, for I don't want to go down that broad road. But it seems to me that any educational institution which takes itself seriously must make the conceptualising of literacy or, as I now say, *literacies*, and the critical examination of the concomitant social and cultural practices in addition to school pedagogies, a priority for teaching and research. The reason is clear. Now, as at all other times of fundamental social change and intellectual shift, the functions of written language are also changing. The most clearly visible signs of change (note, they are the consequences and not the cause) are the new exotic and desired technologies, for which computers are the symbol.

We have given some thought, I know, to literacy in other countries with shorter literate histories than ours. I believe we recognise and understand the ideological nature of literacy. In practice, as we tap our word processors and read our preferred texts and say in lectures that literacy is a matter of human rights, have we also asked ourselves about the ways in which reading and writing can be used against people? Differences in literacy are not only the results of social differences. Literacy also helps to perpetuate them. What do we do about that in teaching practice? Literacy isn't the same in North Peckham, North Westminster, North Harrow. Any educational institution which takes itself seriously must take literacy seriously. An initial training course for new teachers cannot treat literacy as an 'optional' subject. If the National Curriculum expects pupils to leave schools able to read, understand and respond to 'all kinds of writing', then we need better research into how this, in more than a small percentage of the population doing A levels, actually comes about.

I suggest, therefore, that the time has come for educators, that is teachers, theorists, parents, curriculum designers, philosophers, economists, psychologists and social thinkers, whatever our disciplinary allegiances, to reconsider reading. The briefest glimpse of the world our children enter is enough to make plain the reason for this. Reading and writing are now, simply, different from what they were when most adults went to school, because the social uses of literacy have changed and are changing. When I came to the Institute of Education, the University of London computer occupied two entire houses in Tavistock Square and looked likely to stay there. Those who could read its print-outs were cabalistic gnomes. Now, even before they can read, four-year-olds can call up files on personal computers, play games and compose poems and tunes on them. Reading, in my view, therefore needs to be *redescribed* so that the teaching and learning of it does not remain a privileged activity for those who have access to texts and technologies.

I snip this idea of redescription from the work of Richard Rorty. By decontextualising it, I offer a different view of the process. Instead of Rorty's notion that we redescribe what we take for granted in order to stay the same, I want to look at what seems to be the same but is, in fact, different.

Because they read with little difficulty, most people believe that reading, as learned in school, is a well practised and confirmed set of traditional exercises which teachers should supervise and administer in lessons. The assumption is that everyone has at some time learned the relationship of sounds to letters and the sooner children learn these by diligent application of 'the rules', a closed system of classification, the better it will be for them throughout their schooling. There is a marked reluctance to accept that what is understood about learning in general – that the learners' view of the task plays a significant part in their mastery of it – applies particularly to learning to read, as children cannot easily determine what reading is by watching skilled readers doing it. Reading needs to be redescribed because the notion that it is an unchanging activity is, clearly, wrong. The continuous debate about how reading should be taught is not about method but about whether or not the kind of reading which has traditionally been the privilege of a limited number of children in school should become the entitlement of all.

Consequently, there is for some publishers and educators an impulse to retain what Rorty calls 'a final vocabulary'.

First, the verb 'to read' has to encompass nowadays not only all print in the public domain: from scholarly manuscripts to junk mail, bills, advertising and T-shirts but also tv screens, bank statements, architectural and engineering plans, the scripts supplied to politicians, weather charts, X-rays and scanners. The growth of a widespread miscellaneous literature from children is a prelude to it all. The economics of designer graphics may seem instances of the ordinary: but they are, in fact, epiphanies of what we only partly explain about current reading practices. The simple fact of television, and the question-begging nature of tv literacy make the redescription of reading not only necessary but inevitable.

Second, look at us. How comfortable we are in our specialised manuscript and print literacies, with our preferred texts and our certainty as we approach them. Reading, did I hear you say? Well, it's just reading. In research, psychologists, sociologists and linguists tend to regard reading as a 'universal constant'. The anthropologist Brian Street confirms this. Learned in the first decade of our lives, our problems and difficulties overcome by proper practice or perhaps diagnosis (in some contexts reading is a medical matter), reading seems to those who do it well a means of advance to the higher skills of cognition, logical thought and self-conscious reflection. Is not that what we expect of our students? In them we see the mirror image of our own reading habits. (We tend to reject them if we don't.) Reading for pleasure or for profit is so ordinary for us, so much part of the taken-for-granted that it rarely becomes the what-do-we-mean? The exception is, of course, reading whatever we call literature, texts where reading is both the means and the end. Literature problematises reading, calls into question the universal constancy of reading in general. No one can have failed to notice that some texts, detective stories, for example, resist our school-established habits of reading. Confident literates are not always the most practised ones. They just have a small repertoire of preferred texts.

Third, definitions of literacy have always been throughout its history in the hands of the literate. We, as privileged literates, are those who define what counts as *schooled* literacy. We are the gatekeepers, the conservatives. We perpetuate the myths that literacy, especially essay writing, is necessary for logical thinking – oral communities manage syllogisms, after all – that written texts contain autonomous meanings (Olson), that literacy separates the economically productive from the others. The myths remain in our education system because we act as if we believe that in children, as in history, orality gives way to writing, despite all we say about the importance of talk in learning.

The most serious myth about reading is that it has to be taught in school, when we know this is only part of what happens. As a result young teachers of young children are subjected to unproductive bickerings about teaching methods instead of being effectively helped to understand why the debates – about phonics, whole words and 'real' books – raise now, as Ian Michael has shown they did in the eighteenth century battles about syllabification, 'battles disproportionate to their importance and as ill-informed as they are passionate'. I don't believe we necessarily make reading *easier* by finding a new method of teaching it. Debates about the teaching of reading perpetuate false orthodoxies about language, that language itself shows to be useless. While it is true that the sounds of words are significant in learning to 'tune a page', children learn language tunes in language play and rhymes. No one recites 'hey diddle diddle, the cat and the fiddle' with the primary purpose of teaching the rules of phonology, but that's what children learn, not because it's important but because it's fun. Our longing for certainty in the teaching of beginning reading shows only too clearly the limits of our intellectual reach on this topic. No matter how well authenticated the method, children do not want to read unless they discover what's in it for them and what could be pleasing to teachers. One thing only is certain; if they never find out what reading is good for, they won't want to do enough of it to learn the real reading lessons: how to read *new* texts with the confidence of being able to make them mean. The inroads into this problem are being made more by teachers than by theorists. Instead of discussions of method on school in-service days, teachers need help, and encouragement to describe and to theorise what they see in lessons where children actually read, from the nursery to the sixth form.

Here are two linked examples of what concerns us. The first is the most traditional school situation I can think of: reading a book in order to learn. For some time now I've been persuaded that the schooled literacy of many children is a single monitored move from the reading scheme to the topic book: the assumption being that one learns to read in order to read to learn, and that learning is about 'retrieving information from print', a phrase much in vogue and retained in the Cox Report. What happens, I ask myself, when we *retrieve* information? How does it become understanding? The current answer is that reading must be taught as 'study skills'. Here's Cox: 'Pupils should be taught how to respond to the way information is structured and presented so that they are able to identify keypoints.' That is, the information will always be presented so that their reading instruction will fit the nature of the text. As the result of investigations I know this doesn't happen. I guess you do, too, but it's worth another minute of our time to consider the privileged position of 'the text book' or the 64-page topic book usually found in series, as these form the bulk of most school library non-fiction stock and the basis of much topic work. Choosing these books for school libraries is a strenuous business, so it is haphazardly done. Even all the care of the *The Times Educational Supplement* judges cannot save a good topic book from being remaindered, while series packs of titles such as 'On the Seashore' sit unopened on the library shelves.

The kind of snooping research I engage in took me to a small comprehensive school for girls where over about two years I watched thirteen-and-fourteen-year-olds retrieving information for projects in a school library which had been reorganised as a centre for resource-based learning. The librarian had taught a good course in study skills. The pupils were at home in the library and confident in their use of it. There wasn't much browsing in the non-fiction, more work-sheet matching. Pupils having a good read were visible near the stories, but not round the encyclopedias. As long as they were 'looking up' references or facts – the date of the battle of Trafalgar – all was well. But for all its privileged position the text book doesn't offer up its contents without a struggle. Information has to be prised out, like molluscs off a rock, if the reader begins from an unprivileged position, i.e. not knowing much. It is good to know how to make books work, but the move from information to understanding – comprehension, remember? – involves a more dialogic engagement than many pupils ever discover. Moreover, the text-book is a strange product. If the researchers' question is, Who is the Pope? the answer is neither straightforward nor clear at first asking.

During my period of library-lurking I had an unprecedented chance to read books on the subjects set for projects. Except in very rare cases and despite publishers' claims to the contrary, information is offered to pupils in a form that suggests that all facts are neutral, agreed, equally processable in different domains of skill and cognition. Paragraphs of prose set between pictures of dubious authenticity and value are the model of reading for the work-sheet. I was persuaded that interest in the lives of the Romans in Britain is more successfully awakened by a novel of

Rosemary Sutcliff than by most of the non-fiction texts about the period in use below the sixth form. History, geography and science inspire passion in their adherents. Why then are school books so organised that children's care for the planet meets with so little response in those who write topic books for them?

When I broke out from my watching and became an unofficial research assistant to those girls, I discovered that, given two different accounts of the slave trade, they could argue coherently and well. The books didn't help them to do this, they could do it already. But the authorised texts conveyed the teacher-preferred version of what they were expected to write, the authorised answers. When they really *wanted* information and responded to what they had read, the girls read colour supplements or watched tv.

'Information,' says Gregory Bateson, 'is the difference that makes a difference.' It has to be embedded in contexts of human meaning, 'brought alive', adds James Britton (in the The Bullock Report) 'in the mind of every knower'. The pupils' preferred form of information texts was of course narrative: they could handle biography, life cycles, Marie Curie. The lives of composers and artists were handleable contexts for science and music and art. In Religious Education, Florence Nightingale emerged as a favourite humanitarian heroine. Here, their problem was to separate the myth of the angel of Scutari from the hard-headed organiser of men in power. Yet nothing that the girls wrote from their reading of more than one source about Florence Nightingale revealed their skilful questioning and debate about the femaleness of nursing, which was the aspect of the topic that really gripped them and kept them reading, this time with less limpness. There is a series of pedagogic problems in this, I know. But I am still convinced that the important one centres on a need to look seriously at the printed material we offer the young in the content areas of the curriculum. If we are going to rely more and more, as it seems we are bound to, on packaged material for classroom use, then we must have a more critical awareness and judgement of the texts, the information they contain, and the ways by which these are approached as reading and writing. There is ample evidence that the *elective* reading that the young do after school, the reading that powers their interests and makes their personal lives richer, is awakened in their younger encounters with subject matter. Ecologists have personal histories to prove it. So we should know more about reading in learning; for we have been blocked in this area by our conviction that there is little more to be learned about reading in the content areas, only more content. I doubt this very much.

In the lives of most children in school, the traditional forms of reading-to-learn from books (memorising) has been added to, and in some cases replaced by, watching tv. This is the modern children's encyclopedia, which provides information direct, in moving pictures, sequenced, completed. Looking feels like learning. The transformation of a caterpillar into a butterfly is a classic example. The viewer sees it happen; the voice-over guides the looking. Tv seems to open up subject matter while text books close it down..But neither in tv watching nor in reading texts is there a direct move from information-getting to understanding. We know something about the role of group discussion in this matter, but we still privilege individual reading and writing. The difference tv makes is that it creates readers.

In what sense, then, is watching television a literacy? How do we read – if that is what we do – moving pictures on a screen? Media studies have shown how television productions are linked to the structures of culture and power, as are edited and printed texts. But as yet we are only at the beginning of our knowing about how different audiences understand and interpret what they see. (We know a great deal about what they *watch*.) Children seem to acquire and cope with the rhetorics of screening enough at least to adapt them for their own purposes, without direct instructions and the need for tests. Classroom discussions now have the conventions of chat shows: ('Let's just bring John in on that one...'). From television, children seem to be acquiring competences of sustained *oral* performance, the production of spoken text, not least in the cultural groups where oral traditions are at least as strong as literate ones.

The new television text, characterised by news bulletins, film reviews, weather forecasts and other informational monologues gives the illusion of speech; but such text is, in fact, reading. This spoken prose that rolls before the eyes as written text is what the French call *écrit sonore*, 'sounded writing'. Modern lectures are just that: you could have read this. I'm putting the voice in. Carol Fox shows that, without any instruction, children can create oral texts like those delivered by announcers. Jean Dunning has some remarkable examples of secondary school pupils who refuse to write but can sustain long oral productions, where the language forms are those of writing. Utterances of this kind bring written and spoken language closer together. The face and voice of the newscasters, while never conveying approval or disapproval of what they are reading, humanise the written-to-be read texts. There are no embedded clauses; punctuation pauses conform to breathing needs rather than stylistic rules. When the pupils narrate or report at length, their texts are more formal than their conversations. These are new socio-linguistic practices, where those who listen in a group: a class, an assembly, a television lesson for children, a network of viewers for television, are called into being by the speaker. The utterers actualise audiences who are part of the new rhetorics of the culture. The way of calling into being, and the reasons for it, are as significant as what the audience actually hears.

In the sounded writing of news bulletins we can hear what also becomes obvious in the oral performances of the young: the generality of narrative, or what I still want to call *storying*. As narrative has moved to the front of literacy theorising since its early appearance in structuralist writings, the exploration of its nature and kinds, its forms and functions has proceeded apace, and storytellers have reappeared to redescribe the primacy of orality. There was less of this about in 1977, the year of the publication of *The Cool Web*, but new text books about reading suggest that stories are special at all levels in school. Here's how Wayne Booth, in a lecture given in honour of Harold Rosen, interpreted what teachers were doing in 1984.

> You have gone beyond recognising that we are to an
> astonishing degree a product of the stories we have taken in.
> What I hear you doing – and I think it has never been done
> before in the history of criticism or education – is turning
> the coin around in order to say something like this:
>
> 'Who I am now is best shown by the stories *I can now tell*
> and who I am to become is best determined by the stories I
> can learn to tell.'

In the last ten years we have learned to tell all stories differently. We know that the forms of our language use betray our prejudices about race, sex and class. Any redescription of reading must have this conscious sensitiveness about it and a determination that we shall not ignore those things at any cost in the case of children learning to read. They must learn to read and to tell different stories of differences. We have also discovered that it is no longer possible to say that literature is an agreed list of great books – the must-be-reads of the well-read – and we know the traps of simplification and stereotype in the mass media. Reading and telling will simply be different if we are intent on being fully conscious of their inequalities.

Reading and literacy, and learning in relation to development, are all in danger of disappearing into what Rorty calls 'a final vocabulary'. A vocabulary, he says, 'is final if it is as far as its possessor can go with language to describe what matters most to them'. That means in this context that for some people the base line of 'development', 'decoding', 'correctness', 'skill' is never called into question. Reading and literacy are crammed with the final vocabulary of military metaphors: 'strategies', 'word attack skills' and the like. A new description of reading could change what reading *is*; it should certainly change the way we look at it. But first, we have to escape from those endless arguments about method: the final vocabulary that includes 'real books' as well as 'phonics'. We have to keep our understanding of reading open. My colleagues and I tried to see what went wrong with reading in secondary schools and we decided then that our characterising of the pupils as 'poor', 'backward', reluctant, 'retarded' became part of their problem. To consider them *inexperienced* didn't teach them to read, but it made all the difference to how we went about it. Suppose we now began to speak of reading in terms of *dialogue* and *desire*; would that not be a better beginning?

If we are to redescribe reading, we have to begin with how people do it, and what they do it for. A description of literacy always has to include its uses, so we make lists of social texts. But the poems in the Underground sit next to the advertisements. They aren't read in the same way. So we need to know more about how, in our multilingual, multicultural society, people read for dialogue and desire, before they go to school, while they're there and afterwards. Schooled literacy is only part of the picture.

Then, we must be more open about children learning to read. In the last few years the scene has completely changed. Good ethnographic studies show the entry of children into written language in all kinds of cultural diversities. Children and adults sharing texts is not just a good thing, it's an important series of understandings about how reading and writing are transformed into personal knowledge.

What stands out for me from recent studies is the network of connections that children employ to link their particular oral traditions, not just stories but sayings, proverbs, jokes, the dramatic interactions of arguments, and a range of vernacular texts, with the formularies (not formalities) or what for them are important ways of saying. Where instruction in learning to read does not threaten children with the power of the standard language, they come to know reading and writing as different kinds of language acts. They read something, they write something, before they try to put the connecting bits of the process together. In tackling a whole story, a complete poem, however short, children manifest the surplus of feeling, the urgency of discovery, the pleasure of curiosity, which we have all seen on good days but can never quite describe. Where in a book about teaching reading do you find a sentence which goes, 'It is quite usual for young readers to lick enticing pictures of oranges and ice-cream.'

In our contemporary environment pictures are special. Not only on television but in all art, craft, design and technology. Without any direct instruction children read pictures before they are a year old. As the Chevalier report on the teaching of French in France says: *La sémiologie a donné à la lecture de l'image ses lettres de noblesse* (semiology gives the reading of pictures its letters patent). Because we lack philosophers like Bachelard, who found in the study of images a way of linking his passion for science and poetry, we do not know how to help children to read Anno's *The Earth is a Sundial*. Children's books are, essentially, picture books. That said, I hasten to add that adults have to give themselves lessons in order to read picture books.

Just how experimental, investigative, joyous and surprising is the early reading of contemporary children's literature is something that has to be experienced to be understood. When they say they 'love' books, children confuse us by recalling our lost wholeperson-ness about reading. But when we look at the books themselves, we are apt to divide them into plain-realist and fantasy-fantasist. The present situation in picture books make nonsense of our miniaturising of children's literacy and literature. Alison Lurie's claims for its subversive nature are well put. But even more remarkable, in terms of both composition and production, is the way the books themselves match the over-coding propensities of young readers. David Lewis shows that the main features of picture books are those of boundary breaking, excess and indeterminacy. That is, far from simply repeating the structural genres of realistic narrative or the fairytale, artist-authors now encourage new readers, those who are not yet seduced by the rule system of realism, to resist the notion that a picture is a simple illustration, in favour of a generation of meaning in the counterpoint of the images and the texts. That's what children learn to do in *The Jolly Postman*. You can't tell the story of the book, nor describe the pictures, nor make clear what the letters do. There are too many voices. But the readers know exactly what to do. They tell other stories in the same parodic vein. They write other, more, letters. When a boy sends a letter to the Ahlbergs allegedly from a soldier in the army of the Grand Old Duke of York and complains that his feet hurt and his boots are worn out he knows exactly what the nature of the metafictive is.

Children's literature, as displayed in the picture books of today's artist-writers, are, says David Lewis, 'open, playful, parodic...' I also believe that they handle dangerous topics better than we adults sometimes understand. The Wild Things don't threaten children, but Sendak's understanding of childhood guilt threatens adults.

It is in the arena of children's books that we find the most striking evidence for the need to redescribe reading. My conviction was confirmed by a more systematic enquiry into the ways in which children of different ages encountered Ted Hughes' *The Iron Man*. One of the many outcomes of that experience was an understanding that we have to listen much more to what children actually tell us about reading and how they do it, not just in answer to our questions, but in relation to texts and how they read them and what they want to know about reading in the world. When reading is still newish for young people, the ways in which they talk about it do not include our more final vocabularies.

That is why I am enthusiastic about the Primary Language Record and dubious about Standard Attainment Tasks. Tests are the ultimate in final vocabularies. (Think of 'reading age'.) So are teachers' assessments, unless they let the children's words come through. Listen to this child in the Primary Language Record. 'I'll never be able to follow that, it was so brilliant and it's still in my head.' What does she mean by 'still in my head'? A redescription begins there.

I may seem to have assumed that reading means reading words, texts, literatures, pictures and print; the usual fix, the daily hunger, as Bachelard calls it, of the privileged literate. But, I have a suggestion based on my failures, an understanding I learned from my children and one I now make on behalf of my grandchildren. We must extend our notions of literacy, the uses and functions by which it is described, to include the images and *notations* which are common, current and important in our world beyond language in print. Representations of the world can be read in other places than in books. Other symbolic systems map our world as metaphoric recognitions of space and time, form and colour. Musicians, mathematicians and artists have more in common with poets than any of us make plain, so rooted are we in the final vocabularies of our specialisms. Yet, within these specialisms, we are constantly engaged in redescriptions which only other specialists understand. Surely, it could be possible to redescribe reading to encompass these other notational processes. I want to believe that, not least because I know that the young will quickly become sophisticated users of all new technologies more quickly than their elders and that they need *alternative* ways of describing and framing both what they know and what they imagine could be the case.

Some of my most important dialogues about reading have been with children. The firstness of reading encounters are visible in early classrooms at any age. For a certain space, and in spots of time, young people are untrammelled by the need to make the right response, the one their elders expect. As they try out new texts, the ones they are growing into, we see them doing things that our final expectations – an idea that there's nothing more to know about reading – have almost blinded us to. They open our eyes again.

This essay originated in a valedictory lecture to the Department of English, Media and Drama of the Institute of Education, University of London, 1990.

Anno, Mitsumasa (1985), *The Earth is a Sundial*, The Bodley Head
Bachelard, Gaston (1947), *L'Air et Les Songes*, Librairie José Corti
Barrs, Myra *et al.* (1988), *The Primary Language Record: handbook for teachers*, The Centre for Language in Primary Education
Bateson, Gregory (1978), *Steps to an Ecology of Mind*, Paladin
Chevalier, Jean-Claude, *Textes produits par la Commission de Réflexion sur l'Enseignement du Français 1983–1985*, Centre Départemental de Documentation Pédagogique
Clanchy, Michael (1979), *From Memory to Written Record: England 1066–1307*, Edward Arnold
Dunning, Jean (1985), 'Reluctant and willing story tellers in the classroom' in *English in Education*, vol. 19, no. 1
Freire, Paulo and Macedo, Donaldo (1987), *Reading the Word and the World*, Routledge

Fox, Carol (1990), 'The genesis of argument in narrative discourse' in *English in Education*, vol. 24, no. 1

Ginzburg, Carlo (1980), *The Cheese and the Worms*, Routledge

Graff, J. Harvey (1987), *The Labyrinths of Literacy*, The Falmer Press

Hughes, Ted (1968), *The Iron Man*, Faber & Faber

Lewis, David (1990), 'The constructedness of texts: picture books and the metafictive' in *Signal*, 92

Lurie, Alison (1990), *Don't Tell the Grown Ups*, Bloomsbury

Meek, Margaret, Warlow, Aidan and Barton, Griselda (1977), *The Cool Web: the pattern of children's reading*, The Bodley Head

Meek, Margaret *et al.* (1984), *Achieving Literacy*, Routledge

Michael, Ian (1987), *The Teaching of English, from the Sixteenth Century to 1870*, Cambridge University Press

Miller, Jane (1986), *Women Writing about Men*, Virago

Ong, Walter J. (1982), *Orality and Literacy*, Methuen

Rorty, Richard (1989), *Contingency, Irony, and Solidarity*, Cambridge University Press

Scribner, Sylvia and Cole, Michael (1981), *The Psychology of Literacy*, Harvard University Press

Street, Brian (1987), *Literacy in Theory and Practice*, Cambridge University Press

Notes on Contributors

MYRA BARRS is the Director of the Centre for Language in Primary Education. She has worked as a teacher, an educational publisher, and a Local Education Authority adviser. She is co- author of *The Primary Language Record Handbook* and of *Patterns of Learning* (CLPE). Her other publications include articles on dramatic play, writing development and narrative, and *Words Not Numbers*, a pamphlet on assessment written for the National Association of Advisers in English.

JAMES BRITTON is Emeritus Professor of Education London University: formerly head of the Department of English, University of London Institute of Education where he was Director of the Schools Council Writing Project which led to *The Development of Writing Abilities 11-18* (Macmillan 1975). He is the author of *Language and Learning* (Penguin 1972), *Prospect and Retrospect* (ed. Gordon Pradl) (Boynton Cook, 1982), joint author, *Language, the Learner and the School*, 4th edn (Boynton Cook, 1990).

TONY BURGESS is a Reader in the Department of English, Media and Drama, University of London Institute of Education. He is co-author of books on writing and language and diversity. His current interests include philosophical and historical issues in English teaching.

AIDAN CHAMBERS is an author, publisher and teacher. His most recent novel is *The Toll Bridge* (Bodley Head).

HENRIETTA DOMBEY has worked for nearly twenty years in the Department of Primary Education, Brighton Polytechnic. Before moving into teacher education she worked in Inner London primary schools, where she started to learn about teaching children to read. Her own children then showed her something of the power of pre-school literacy learning, prompting her to investigate this further.

CAROL FOX taught English in Inner London Education Authority secondary schools in the 1960s and 70s. In 1980 she began her research on children's invented oral stories at Newcastle Polytechnic. She is now Senior Lecturer in the Department of Primary Education, Brighton Polytechnic.

ANNE-MARIE GOGUEL is Maître de Conférences in the Faculté des Sciences de l'Education, University of Burgundy, Dijon. As agrégée in philosophy she taught in lycées in Dijon and Paris. A fellowship from the Commonwealth Fund Foundation took her to Columbia University, New York, where she studied sociology with Robert Linton and Margaret Mead. A formative decade of her teaching life was spent in Madagascar where she worked in a lycée in Antananarivo, the capital. She is a member of the Association Francophone d'Education Comparée and vice president of the Association d'Education Comparée en Europe (CESE).

JUDITH GRAHAM is a Reader in Language and Literacy at Avery Hill College, Thames Polytechnic. She has been both a student and a colleague of Margaret's at the University of London Institute of Education and worked with her on *Achieving Literacy*. She has recently written *Pictures on the Page* (NATE) on the role of illustrations in children's literacy development.

EVE GREGORY is Lecturer in Education at Goldsmiths' College, University of London, where she teaches primarily on language and literacy courses. Her particular interests are the development of bilingualism in young children and the social and cultural aspects of learning to read.

JOHN HARDCASTLE taught for fourteen years in a boys' comprehensive school in Hackney, East London and was subsequently an advisory teacher in the Inner London Education Authority. He is now Lecturer in the Department of English, Media and Drama at the University of London Institute of Education. He is the author of 'Piece of the past: classrooms as sites of cultural making', 'Different possibilities' and, with Tony Burgess, 'A tale of three learners'.

KEITH KIMBERLEY taught for fifteen years in Inner London Education Authority schools before coming to the Department of English, Media and Drama, University of London Institute of Education in 1979. He also worked in the Institute's Centre for Multicultural Education and was a founder member of the editorial team of *Teaching London Kids*. He was co-editor, with Jagdish Gundara and Crispin Jones of *Racism, Diversity and Education* and author, with John Hickman, of *Teachers, Language and Learning*. His research interests, which were well advanced when he died in January 1991, were concerned with assessment arrangements for English.

JOSIE LEVINE is Senior Lecturer in Education, University of London Institute of Education and an Educational Consultant. She is closely associated with the innovation and development of interactive pedagogy for multilingual, multicultural classes, and with the teaching and learning of English as an additional language through mainstream education. She is editor of *Bilingual Learners and the Mainstream Curriculum*, Falmer Press (1990), which was written in conjunction with experienced teachers collaborating in an action-research project.

DAVID LEWIS teaches at the School of Education, University of Exeter. He has taught in both secondary and primary schools and as a lecturer in primary language at Goldsmiths' College, University of London. His interest in children's books dates back to the time when, as a classroom teacher, he read to other people's children during the day and his own at bed-time.

ALEX McLEOD taught English in New Zealand and in London before joining James Britton on the Schools Council Writing Project at the University of London Institute of Education, where he became Senior Lecturer in English. After retiring in 1988, he spent half a year as visiting professor in the Language and Literacy Division of the School of Education, University of California, Berkeley. His current interests include critical literacy in urban schools, especially writing.

MARGARET MALLETT, after teaching in primary schools in Northumberland and Kent, gained an MA degree at the University of Sussex. She worked on the Schools Council 'English 8–13' Project and wrote Schools Council Working Paper 59, 'Talking, Writing and Learning 8–13' with Bernard Newsome. She now teaches at Goldsmiths' College, University of London, on B.Ed and MA courses, and is researching into the way children use non-fiction in the primary years.

MARGARET MEEK SPENCER joined the Department of English, University of London Institute of Education in 1968. During her time in teaching there was significant growth in the understanding of children's language and thought, of professional associations, such as the London Association for the Teaching of English (and of the National Association), of research in classrooms and extended professional studies and of children's learning to read and write. All this let her enjoy and profit from extensive contact with teachers and children, as well as her distinguished colleagues in multicultural London, in France, Canada, Australia and South Africa. On her retirement in 1990 she became Emeritus Reader in Education.

JANE MILLER has taught in Inner London Education Authority schools and, since 1976, in the Department of English, Media and Drama in the University of London Institute of Education, where she is a Reader. She is the author of *Many Voices. Bilingualism, Culture and Education*, *Women Writing about Men* and *Seductions. Studies in Reading and Culture*. She is also the editor of The Virago Education Series and of *Eccentric Propositions. Essays on literature and the curriculum*.

GEMMA MOSS taught English in secondary schools for seven years. More recently she has been tutor for the English and Media Post-graduate Certificate in Education at the University of London Institute of Education and has worked for the Open University. She is author of *Un/Popular Fictions*, a book about girls' romance writing. She is currently researching the informal literacies children develop outside the school classroom.

PHILIPPA PEARCE has worked for children both in radio (as scriptwriter/producer in BBC Schools Broadcasting) and in publishing (as Children's Books Editor at André Deutsch). Finally she became a freelance writer: *Tom's Midnight Garden* (1958) is perhaps her best-known book. She now lives and writes in the Cambridgeshire village where she was born.

HAROLD ROSEN is Emeritus Professor in the Department of English, Media and Drama at the University of London Institute of Education. He was formerly the Head of that Department. Before that he taught in secondary schools. Currently he runs the London Narrative Group and is Chair of the Multilingual Initiative in the Centre for Multicultural Education of the University of London Institute of Education.

PHILLIDA SALMON was for eleven years a clinical psychologist in the National Health Service. In subsequent academic work she has striven to make room in developmental and educational psychology both for feeling and for social aspects. Recent books are: *Living in Time* (Dent, 1985) and *Psychology for Teachers* (Hutchinson Education, 1988).

PETER TRAVES was brought up and educated at schools in Birmingham, at the University of Wales, Swansea, from 1968 to 1973, and at the University of London Institute of Education from 1973 to 1974. He worked as a teacher of English and Humanities and later as an advisory teacher in the Inner London Education Authority. He became English adviser for the London Borough of Waltham Forest in 1985 and for Shropshire in 1989.